Transitional Puzzles

I receive many books nearly every day. When I glimpsed at yours I was impressed right away by the independence of your thought and the terse style reminding me of Caesar's 'De Bello Gallico'...

Albert Einstein, 28 July 1953, after reading the author's first book *For Democracy.*

Transitional Puzzles

*Reflections on Social,
Economic and Political Issues*

AMLAN DATTA

SSAGE Los Angeles • London • New Delhi • Singapore
www.sagepublications.com

First published in 2009 by

 SAGE Publications India Pvt Ltd
B 1/I-1, Mohan Cooperative Industrial Area
Mathura Road, New Delhi 110044, India
www.sagepub.in

SAGE Publications Inc
2455 Teller Road
Thousand Oaks, California 91320, USA

SAGE Publications Ltd
1 Oliver's Yard, 55 City Road
London EC1Y 1SP, United Kingdom

SAGE Publications Asia-Pacific Pte Ltd
33 Pekin Street
#02-01 Far East Square
Singapore 048763

Published by Vivek Mehra for SAGE Publications India Pvt Ltd, typeset in 11/13 pt Book Antiqua by Star Compugraphics Private Limited, Delhi and printed at Chaman Enterprises, New Delhi.

Library of Congress Cataloging-in-Publication Data Available

ISBN: 978-81-7829-883-2 (PB)

The SAGE Team: Elina Majumdar, P.K. Jayanthan, Amrita Saha and Trinankur Banerjee

To
Dear Kitty
My Gentle Wife

Contents

Introduction

A simple idea needs no introduction, it just introduces itself. What about ideas which are not that simple? The relation of parts to the whole provides a key to the deeper meaning of a complex intellectual or imaginative construct. Deconstruction in its simplest sense is the art of separating the parts and putting them together again meaningfully. However, there are alternative ways of performing this exercise, yielding significantly different results. The ambiguity inherent in a complex theme or text makes livelier the alternative interpretations it invites. The given theme itself does not lack variety. It may stand for any one of a number of kinds of things, such as a literary piece, a life notably lived, a period of history, a social philosophy.

He who sets out to expound a significant theme is initially faced with a choice. Should he take up the constituent parts separately, dwelling on the intrinsic importance of each part as a thing of interest in itself, or must he attempt to focus on the unity of the whole? It stands to reason that he should do both, for nature does not present unity and diversity as alternatives; they are two faces of the same reality. A glimpse of an evolving unity helps one to understand better the nature and significance of a struggling diversity. This is how we understand best the world around us.

Man, it has been said, makes his own history. He does it through a struggle for overcoming contradictions. There are conflicts and contradictions of different kinds. Every epoch in history tends to be dominated by a particular kind of conflict and people belonging to that epoch become strongly inclined to interpret all history in the light of their fragmentary experi-ence. It often happens that when a new age arrives, people are handicapped by a kind of impaired vision as they live in the twilight of a past epoch. Thus, a shadow falls between consciousness and existence, for consciousness is not solely determined by the experience of time present; it is strongly influenced by inherited prejudices, memories of old enmities and the enchantment of an imaginary past. Enlightenment never ceases to be a struggle of escape from old and strongly entrenched habits of thought and feeling. This provides a background for the role of reason in the making of history.

Our own epoch is dominated by a major contradiction which is quite special. In its range and implications for the future, it is unprecedented. Let us pause and consider the matter. Since the 1970s, an increasing number of people all over the world have become conscious as never before of the spectre of an ecological imbalance carrying with it the threat of a global disaster. The scale of this impending catastrophe makes it truly unprecedented. The problem can also be viewed in terms of the possible consequences of a big war in future. If a third World War does happen, it will demonstrate once for all and rather too late the ultimate unity of interest of all mankind by plunging the whole world in a common ruin. The idea of the human family has been preached by saints memorably since ancient times. In our own time, it has received material confirmation of a new kind.

Interactions, both positive and negative, among different parts of the world have existed for a very long time. Despite this interrelatedness all past history has been the history of local civilisations: Mercifully, the devastation caused by the fiercest of wars in earlier times was local devastation. Notwithstanding the talk of 'globalisation', so common today, civilisations continue to be local in spirit. 'Clash of civilisations' continues unabated and provides at this hour a leading theme for animated discussion. On the one hand, the threat to human survival is a global threat; on the other hand, humanity stays stubbornly divided and fragmented in spirit. This is the great contradiction that afflicts human society today.

When we look for an explanation of this curious situation, we risk getting confused by a multiplicity of proximate causes. What we need is an enquiry at a deeper level. The search at that level leads on to a broader perception of the human predicament. This is a totality in which pieces of knowledge acquired from different fields combine and each piece receives an enhanced significance by virtue of that combination. For a true understanding, it is best to look at the human condition in an evolutionary perspective.

Among the factors which interact among themselves and chart the course of history, human nature is often thought to be a comparatively stable and changeless element. There is some truth in that thought, but it needs to be qualified in at least two ways. Changing forms of social organisation influence human nature by promoting some psychological tendencies and discouraging others, supporting certain aspirations and producing unforeseen discontents. There is also something else worth taking into account. Human consciousness itself has stages of development. This makes any simple concept of a fixed human nature untenable. It will be just as well to elaborate on this theme.

Human beings, to begin with, are ego-centric. This accords with nature's scheme. A person has to protect his body as a primary condition of survival. Since no two persons share the same body, attention to one's body makes one self-centred as a matter of physical compulsion. However, it is also part of nature's design to motivate human beings to reproduce themselves. Certain basic emotions of sympathy and mutual attraction, such as the attraction between the sexes and parental affection towards the offspring, are, so to speak, decreed by nature. The family comes to be included thus in an expanded image of the self. To a great extent, all kinship bonds, including the feeling of tribal solidarity, can be similarly explained. Such feelings belong to a primitive level of consciousness where active rationality does not play a major role. That is where 'primitive communism' belonged. However, that was not the end of history.

Trade played a vital role in guiding society towards new forms of human relationship beyond kinship. This equally marked a new stage in the evolution of human consciousness. Along with trade a calculating reason gained ascendancy and became influential, although 'infra-rational' psychic forces did not cease to play a role in human affairs. As our way of life changes, so does our way of thought. The 'calculus of pleasure and pain' induced a change in the concept of welfare. A normal family has a certain idea of collective welfare and a gain to one member of the family is felt as a gain for the whole family. Trading parties compete as well as cooperate, but each party has an idea of its separate interest, and cooperation itself is based on calculated self-interest.

In the hedonistic ethics of a commercial civilisation, happiness is measured separately for each individual. Also an idea gains ground that commodities, sold and purchased, provide the principal means of procuring happiness. To a large extent, this makes happiness indistinguishable from sensuous pleasure. The basis is laid for a materialistic ethics.

These ideas have played a positive role in liberating human mind from the stranglehold of 'supernatural fears'. But they have their own shortcomings and so they cannot provide a lasting basis for a sound philosophy of life. Some of these shortcomings are simple, others more subtle. It is well known that the additional pleasure that a consumer derives from any particular commodity starts diminishing beyond a point as more and more of it is consumed. It is possible to seek an escape from this situation by courting a variety of luxury goods. But this route of escape creates at least two kinds of problems. Only an affluent class can choose this route. The 'conspicuous consumption' of this affluent class sharpens discontent among a much larger class of people who cannot afford that style of life. An unequal competition for wealth undermines the basis of happy social relationship and beyond a point, luxury cannot compensate for the loss of genuine companionship. There is an additional complication that tends to go unnoticed. The rich are envied, but it is doubtful if they are enviably happy. Bondage to luxury cripples even the capacity to distinguish between purchasable excitement and the joy that proceeds from true union. Jesus Christ made an insightful statement about this disability of the rich.

There is a state of union which ought to be valued not for the sake of any material gain, but for its own sake. This is not as uncommon or mysterious an experience as it is often supposed to be. One can detect it in the laughter of a child, although people made skeptical by the disappointments of life often fail to recognise it even when they come by it. Nature itself has planted in the human mind the capacity to feel an incomparable sense of freedom in motiveless union of what is within and what is without overstepping the boundaries of a senselessly isolated self. A conscious recognition of the value of this freedom marks the beginning of that stage of consciousness which can be called the spiritual stage. The spiritual goes beyond the rational, but does not contradict reason.

Two contrary tendencies of the human mind are ever at work side by side. On the one hand, there is inertia which makes one generalise from the present state as the only natural state and a reasonable basis for deriving rules for all time. On the other, there is an evolutionary force, *élan vital*, which does not allow the human consciousness to stay permanently at rest, but urges it on to move from one stage to another. For expository purposes, it is useful to mark out three such stages. Again, there are forms of social organisation which link up with states of consciousness. It is evident that the dominant form of social organisation today has been determined largely by the requirements of commerce and the market economy. Economic and political powers have got intimately intertwined. Power, economic and political, is what leaders of this society aim at and accept as the purpose of their life with that devotion which religious people reserve for God. Other considerations exist but peripherally. Thus, for instance, when one has amassed enough wealth, it is considered proper and decent to use a small portion for charity, an act which still leaves one's central purpose in life unaltered. This is a view of life which is difficult to reject effectively because power belongs to those who conform to it. Nonetheless, a rebellion against the status quo is unavoidable with unforeseeable consequences.

There was a time when Marxism promised to provide a major plank for an ideological and political assault on the bourgeois civilisation. It now appears that communists in India and elsewhere professing the Marxian ideology have virtually adopted the essential features of the order which they once wanted to overthrow. The spirit of rebellion against the dominant order of the day must now seek an alternative route and a new philosophy of life. In fact, there are several alternatives and some of these are unsafe, even regressive. What has been called 'religious fundamentalism' provides such a regressive ideology, leading back to a lower level of consciousness, marked by collective hatred and organised intolerance.

The fascination of totalitarianism in one form or the other has misled successive generations in recent history. History counsels abundant caution. One may seek an exit from the existing situation, but there is the risk of landing in a worse situation unless one has the right sense of direction. One has to take reasonable precautions against losing one's sense of direction.

Reasonable precaution quite often takes the form of hedging or combining opposites. It is a good idea to combine a movement of protest and resistance against injustice with a programme of constructive work and a visible commitment to peace. It is better still to link this up with a careful analysis of the nature of the contemporary global crisis. Let us present the problem in a material context. Spread of industrialisation across the globe is a major feature of the history of our time. Industrialisation has been justified on the ground that it is necessary for alleviation of poverty. But there are alternative patterns of industrialisation. The really important question relates to choice among these alternatives. The history of state-sponsored industrialisation from the time of Peter the Great to modern China, not excluding market-based economies, suggests the presence of a special tendency at work. Industrialisation has proved attractive to nation states because it is necessary for military power. A widely adopted pattern of industrialisation leans distinctly towards heavy industry geared to the production of military hardware. Along with that come as a matter of necessity a centralised political system, growth of a powerful managerial stratum of society, a new middle class which lauds and leads this pattern of development, a consumerist culture and supporting so- cial norms. An unavoidable outcome of this situation is a crisis wrapped in a dilemma. Competitive programmes for strengthening national security lead to a frightful accumu- lation of weapons of mass destruction. What looks prudent for individual states considered separately takes the character of an increasing threat to the collective security of the world as a whole. It is not easy for any single nation to opt out of this march towards a collective doom. This makes a concerted peace movement an essential requirement for overcoming the contemporary crisis.

Success along this line cannot be achieved overnight. There is no alternative to a gradual process of restoring sanity in human affairs. The spirit of the peace movement must percolate to all the constituent parts of society. It must also set in motion fresh ideas on the political and economic reorganisation of human society with an accent on decentral- isation of power and the readjustment of education to the requirements of peaceful and sustainable development.

The question of the correct pattern of industrialisation and appropriate technology should be settled in this larger context. Most of our thought is done in parts, thus leaving a special space cut out for philosophy. It is the task of philosophy to provide a vision of the whole to illumine and hold together the otherwise undirected parts through gentle persuasion.

Institutions are materialised ideas. It is not enough to have new ideas; we need a change in the material outfit of life. But all institutions are corruptible; therefore, it is not enough to have just a new set of institutions, however ingeniously designed. We need new institutions and energising ideas in close embrace and a wakeful social conscience keeping vigil. We have to have a sense of history and, at the same time, be watchful of what is happening right now. Man, like other animate beings, lives from day to day. But, unlike other animals, he has the sense of an ancient inheritance and a moral commitment to a future beyond his own generation.

This small collection of essays talks of both ideas and institutions. It does not talk in the manner of expounding an erudite and all-embracing view of the world, but treats the subject in small bits and pieces. Each piece can be read separately. Yet there is an interconnection among the different parts, something to which this introduction attempts to draw attention.

Some of these essays were written at a time when the Soviet Union was still intact though under severe strain. I have not tried to update these articles. Nothing has happened to warrant a revision of the basic argument running through these pages.

1

Our Ever-Increasing Family

How large is the human family? In AD 1700 world population stood at around 600 million; in AD 2000 it exceeded 6,000 million. If we divide this period of 300 years into two equal halves, we make an interesting discovery: the numbers doubled between AD 1700 and 1850, but increased at least five-fold in the next 150 years. This shows a marked acceleration of growth of population in recent history. What is the explanation for this phenomenon?

Slow growth of population in earlier times resulted from a high birth rate combined with an almost equally high death rate. In more recent times, the death rate has declined, thanks to such factors as progress of medical science and improved public hygiene. The birth rate also declined but not as fast as mortality. The more rapid growth of population observed in contemporary history has been the outcome of this widening gap between birth and death rates.

In industrially advanced countries, growth of population has been effectively halted by a significant reduction of birth rate. Thus we get three different scenarios corresponding to three stages of economic development. At one end, both fertility and mortality rates are high, and economic conditions are backward and stagnant. At the other end, both these rates are low and, with some exceptions, there is a resulting approach to a stationary population. Most countries of the so-called Third World belong to an intermediate stage where the birth rate is significantly higher than the death rate. It is these countries that we have in mind when people talk of the threat of 'population explosion'. This, therefore, is a regional phenomenon, but its consequences are global as well as local and worth illustrating.

An inevitable consequence of growth of population is that in many parts of the world, forests are cut down to make room for new and expanding human settlements. This trend is difficult to resist although the harm done by continued deforestation is now widely understood. Ecological imbalance and environmental pollution are not confined to any one country. Industrially advanced countries contribute powerfully in their own way to worsen the global problem. But population explosion in the developing countries is one of the factors which deepen the crisis.

In different kinds of economy, the problem of unemployment has different roots. In the less developed economies, rapid growth of population is an important aggravating factor giving rise to chronic underemployment. Handicapped by poverty and lack of education, rural areas generate surplus labour faster than the organised sector of the economy can usefully absorb. Jobseekers moving from villages to cities make the distressing discovery that there are much fewer jobs around than seekers. In the process, we are faced with a social problem with complex ramifications. The increasing incidence of unemployment sharpens social conflicts and pollutes culture and politics.

In India, where the larger society is a collection of diverse communities, the more disadvantaged tribes and castes seek relief through a system of reservation of jobs. But this creates additional bitterness on account of mounting unemployment all around which makes the task of achieving social integration particularly difficult.

This again is a problem which does not stop at national boundaries. Just as jobseekers move from rural areas to cities within a country, they also cross national frontiers and migrate to comparatively prosperous countries. The host countries accept the skilled and professionally qualified immigrants more readily, while attempts at entry by others are resented and resisted. As immigrants come from a different social background, the problem of social integration presents itself in a difficult form all too clearly. It is very unfortunate but not strange that such ethnic encounters result in a new upsurge of racist sentiments.

It is interesting to contrast what is happening today and what happened in the formative stage of industrialisation of the West. In that earlier epoch, the pressure of population in the West was appreciably relieved by large groups of people crossing the seas and colonising elsewhere, particularly in the so-called New World. The original inhabitants of those new lands were harshly subjugated and pushed down. Since then the historical context has been totally transformed. When the surplus population of the newly industrialising countries sets out to cross the seas, what happens is a 'brain drain' rather than a reduction in the pressure of population at home.

If rapid growth of population has aggravated economic and social problems both in the Third World and in the international community, it is obviously a matter of urgent importance to control the size of the population in the major developing countries. This was recognised in India's official policy as early as in the days of Prime Minister Jawaharlal Nehru. Yet India's performance in this area has been unimpressive. What makes it so difficult to control the growth of population? It may be useful to put the same question in a different form. We noticed earlier that in the developing economies the decline in birth rate has a tendency to lag behind that in the death rate. Obviously, there are some factors, including certain deeply entrenched habits and ideas, which resist attempts to lower the birth rate. It will be helpful to promote a public debate on the relevant issues. Experience shows that an official policy cannot succeed without an enlightened public opinion and a corresponding organisation to support it.

There is an impressive variety of mistaken views on the question of control of population which deserves to be banished. Marxists once believed that the idea of overpopulation was a fraud invented by apologists for capitalism to hide its inherent shortcomings and that poverty and unemployment would disappear with the advent of socialism. This Marxian misconception lived a sheltered life for a number of decades, thanks to the historic accident of the first 'socialist fatherland' being established in the Soviet Union, a country where the extent of the territory was unusually large compared to the size of its population. However, the more pragmatic Chinese communists adopted a policy which recognised the reality of the demographic problem.

At the other end of the spectrum, there is a large section of pious people who believe that every baby is a gift from God and has been equipped with a pair of hands which, if properly used, can take care of the problem of adequate livelihood. This is a simplistic view which ought to be treated with caution if there is any truth in the preceding short survey of grave and complicated problems arising from the rapid growth of population in the developing economies.

There are still others, conservative moralists, who would accept the reasonableness of limiting numbers but would not approve of any method for achieving that limitation other than strict abstinence. This is an unrealistic prescription for a major part of the people for whom sex is the least expensive source of pleasure and relaxation after days of hard labour.

In India overpopulation manifests itself first and foremost through underemployment in rural areas. Education among women, though to be desired greatly, does not directly help reduce the incidence of unemployment and underemployment or augment available opportunities for productive work. What can we do about that? This is a vital question.

Tagore spoke of *Palli Sangathan* or rural reconstruction. He thought of reorienting education for rural areas and other

4

rural institutions to make them effective instruments of that high objective. If we want to share that vision, our gram panchayats must not function as battlegrounds for rival castes and political parties hungry for power.

They have to make it their principal mission to work patiently and imaginatively towards the reconstruction of rural society and its productive activities on the basis of the widest possible neighbourly cooperation and self-help, supported by an appropriate culture to make progress in that direction as smooth as possible.

Family planning basically represents the idea of man consciously and rationally choosing and moulding his future rather than helplessly surrendering to fatalism. As such it can be integrally related to the spirit and programme of a comprehensive and enlightened movement for the betterment of social life at the grass-roots level. It is at that level that the success of family planning is most required. It has to be achieved with as little delay as possible.

Prejudice against the female child acts as a very serious hurdle to rational family planning. Preference for a male child upsets family planning and social development in a number of ways. The firm advice not to have more than two children per mother is interpreted in practice to justify having two sons for every woman. But if this is how the goal is set, the number of children for a mother, on an average, would approach four. Not less deserving of notice are some other consequences of a preference for the male child. For instance, in many families, education of the female child suffers comparative neglect. This adversely affects the quality of the population and distorts the social mechanism for controlling the frequency and spacing of childbirth. Let us consider these two points.

It is well known that the neglect of the female child is related to the fact that in a traditional and patriarchal society a daughter leaves her father's family after marriage and normally joins her husband's family and takes care of her parents-in-law. However, we should remember that she still remains

5

part of the same larger society. If every family takes insufficient care in bringing up its daughters out of a narrow concern for its exclusive interests, the general welfare of the larger society is bound to suffer. The widely prevalent discrimination against the female is socially harmful and, therefore, morally wrong.

Women are more genuinely interested in family planning for obvious reasons. It is, therefore, important to create conditions in which they have the power to play an effective role in matters concerning birth control and family planning. Education and the opportunity as well as competence for outdoor work help women to secure that position where they can be active agents of change in social mores. It is not accidental that in Kerala, where education among women is more widespread than elsewhere, the rate of growth of population is appreciably lower than the all-India average.

One last thought is that economists have talked of an optimum size of population. The idea is that the society would be economically better off with that size of population than with a larger or smaller size. With changes in basic conditions, the optimum might also change. Now, is it possible in a similar way to think of an optimum average life expectancy for a given community? It is not easy to consider this question dispassionately because people tend to assume that a longer life expectancy is always better limitlessly. But is this assumption rational or is it simply dictated by a blind and obstinate fear for death? It may be good to think over the matter calmly and let the gentle breeze of reason lead us wherever it may.

Let us assume that we have reached a size of population, an optimum size, where it would be best to stabilise it. So beyond this point, the number of new entrants into the stock of population should not exceed the number that exits over any given period. The longer the average life expectancy, the fewer the number of deaths within that period. As mortality moves towards zero, the number of permissible births

6

will also move in the same direction. The population will come to have an increasing number of old people and a diminishing proportion of the young, if this trend continues indefinitely.

It is hardly necessary to carry this argument any further to show that this leads to an undesirable situation. It is good to have a fair proportion of young and fresh minds in the population. It is true that some old people still remain fresh and productive. But it is only fair to assume that the proportion of fresh minds is comparatively higher among those who are young.

It will be unkind, inhuman and unrealistic to have a compulsory exit policy for people above a certain age. But it will be only humane to have a culture and a climate of public opinion in which aged people feel free voluntarily and gracefully to withdraw themselves. The opposition to euthanasia prevalent in many countries is simply not rational, although its misuse by interested parties should be guarded against. Reverence for life, which deserves to be applauded, must ultimately mean reverence for that continuous stream of life which flows on beyond all incidents of individual death.

With more than 6,000 million people around, one should guess that our planet has already a sufficiently large population for healthy and creative interaction. Conditions do differ in different parts of the world. But, on the whole, we the people of the world are an aging and perhaps overgrown family. In the years ahead, the aim of public policy ought to be not so much to add to the existing numbers as to maintain a healthy proportion among the young and the old while facilitating a smooth transition from one generation to the next. More important than stretching the lives of aged people at great expense is to keep the waters clean and sparkling in the ever-refreshing stream of life.

2
Unity Today*

Why is it important to discuss human unity today?

I suggest that a few things did happen in recent history to make this theme of human unity a specially important one for our time. Specially important today as such things were unknown in earlier centuries, during the times when the Christ or the Buddha lived and preached. Let me illustrate. August 2005 was the 60th anniversary of an important event in human history. What was it? It was the bombing of Hiroshima and Nagasaki in August 1945. There is no parallel for that in the whole of human history. It stressed something special, it stressed one simple fact that at last mankind had at its disposal sufficient destructive powers to destroy the whole of mankind. There have been wars in the past. The history is full of wars. But the earlier wars had local significance. Now at last, we have arrived at a special juncture in history, when the whole of mankind may perish on account of something done by mankind itself in a mad moment of fury. When the Buddha spoke of '*Ahimsa*', it was neither in the power of mankind to do this nor in the power of any great king or emperor to destroy the whole world by using the kind of bombs that were used in August 1945. So, this is something

---

*This is the transcript of a recorded speech at the Ramakrishna Mission Institute of Culture.

special, stressing the importance of human unity in a very negative way — and yet in a powerful way — stressing the unity or the common interest of mankind for survival. If mankind must survive, it must either do so unitedly or get destroyed in a global disaster.

Now, something else has also happened. Something else which is less dramatic than the bombing of Hiroshima and Nagasaki, but which also stressed the importance of human unity, again in a negative way. In course of the last three decades, particularly since the 1970s, there has been a great sharpening in the consciousness of thinking people about a possible ecological crisis coupled with pollution of the environment. Again, the contrast with earlier times is worth stressing. Since the beginning of the Industrial Revolution, we could speak of environmental pollution on account of some special developments connected with industrialisation. Some of you may remember the words used by Blake about the 'Satanic wheels' — the factories with their smoking chimneys. These factories caused environmental pollution but again, just as the earlier wars were local wars, so also the factories with their smoking chimneys could only lead to local environmental pollution.

But now we hear of something different. I think it is a language quite unknown to earlier generations, for example, the term global warming. Global warming, many of us now are familiar with the phrase. I do not think, even half a century earlier, people were familiar with the phrase — global warming. This is happening on a global scale, not simply locally. We are told that something has happened to the ozone layer. The consequences are global. We are told that snow in the Antarctic is melting. It might lead to a rise in the level of the oceans and eventually to submerging of low-lying lands across the world. It may be land as close as the south of Bengal, as far as Florida in the United States of America, or elsewhere — but this is something global. It makes us think of human unity in a very different setting. There is no parallel to this in the past. So, whether it is war or ecological disaster, we have now a special background — a special historical background for contemplating the question of human unity with a different kind of urgency, unknown in the past. When great men spoke of human unity in the past, they were talking of a very high ideal, sometimes in an idiom of prophetic vision. But now, there has to be human unity just for the sake of survival of mankind. Not a question of somehow creating a paradise on earth, but something much more terrestrial. So, I do think that we have today a historical background for discussing question of human unity with a special sense of urgency unknown in the past. I am astonished to find that some of my friends even today do not seem to perceive this simple truth. For instance, about a month back, I wrote an essay in Bengali and I said that war today is something very special; a global crisis today is something more special than whatever we had before. Then a letter was published, protesting against the article and questioning why I said wars were special. Wars have taken place throughout history and so why were wars so special? I am astounded that we did not realise that to say that there have been wars throughout history is one thing, and to look at the possibility of global destruction through the use of nuclear weapons today is something quite different. We would be foolish to minimise the consequences of wars today by simply saying that there have been wars all through history, so why are we so upset? We are upset because there are some special circumstances that make us upset. So, that at least partly answers the question with which I began — why is it important to discuss the question of human unity today. I have given a partial answer to the question saying that it is important because today mankind as a whole is confronted with the question of survival in a very special way, which makes it necessary to think about this whole question of human unity today as something quite unique, something quite different from whatever existed in the past. So, human unity today is important in a very special way.

Now, suppose you find this argument persuasive and so, let me hopefully assume, you agree that the goal of human unity today is of great importance — great practical importance — more so than anything in the past. Now, it sometimes happens that a particular goal or object is important, yet we simply do not have the instruments at our disposal to serve that objective or to move towards that goal. What I have said so far only shows that human unity is an important goal or objective; but do we have the instruments necessary for achieving that objective or moving towards that goal? At one level, the answer to that question would again be *yes*; we have the desired instruments at our disposal for achieving that objective; we have at our disposal such instruments to a far greater extent than what existed in the past. We all know that as a result of the electronic revolution, the technological revolution that has been underway in the course of the last few decades, it has been materially possible to bring different parts of the world closer together, materially possible to do that to a far greater extent than was ever possible in the past. It is so easy today for somebody in this part of the world to communicate with the farthest part of the world. Today we can visually observe whatever happens in a distant part of the world. Visually observe it sitting here, thousands of miles away. Even ordinary citizens can do that, thanks to the television and such other technical devices. It is so easy for people from one part of the world to fly and reach another part of the world, almost in a way which was unimaginable in the past. I had read a book *Around the World in Eighty Days*, but now how many days do we need to go around the world? Earlier it was thought to be something spectacular, but now that seems to be very slow. Today we need a fraction of that time to go round the world. So, if it is a question of material instruments for achieving human unity, then we have at our disposal such instruments to a far greater extent than existed in the past. On the one hand, we have this objective of human unity, and on the other hand, we have the material instruments, which at least at first sight seem to make it possible, to make it practicable, to achieve that unity, if we really want it. What then is the problem if human unity is so very important—so important that human survival depends on it? Science and technology have already put at our disposal instruments which should be very helpful as aids for promoting human unity—then what is the problem? There must be some special obstacles on the way to human unity and these obstacles are not in the nature of presence or absence of material instruments for achieving unity. There must be obstacles of a different kind.

What are these obstacles to human unity? Now, we can think of these obstacles from different points of view: psychological, political, economic and so on. If we are seriously concerned with the objective of promoting human unity, then we have to pay attention to these obstacles. Let me tell you something about psychological obstacles, political obstacles and things like that.

It seems that there is in human nature an amount of aggressiveness and violence that is specially dangerous at a time when we have at our disposal such weapons of mass destruction. It is not very difficult to understand why humans have such a beastly nature. Man had to survive in a brutish environment in an age of savagery when human beings were surrounded by other ferocious animals. That occupied a long period of history. And at that time, this natural endowment of cunning, aggressiveness and violence helped human beings to survive in that savage environment. So, the amount of aggressiveness and violence that we find in human nature is explained not by the needs of the world today but by the needs of what mankind required for survival thousands of years back. Human nature today has not been formed simply by the circumstances of today. It has been formed by circumstances over a very very long past. So, the amount of violence that we find in human nature today is understandable when we think of human beings placed in, let us say, that environment.

After that, what has happened is that human nature has changed comparatively slowly and man's physical power has changed much more rapidly, thanks to the development of science and technology. So, we have today human beings with incomparably greater power derived from science and technology combined with their human nature which was suited to the environment many thousands of years ago but not necessarily suited to the environment of our time. There is a cruel discrepancy between our psychological legacy and our technological attainment at this moment. This is one thing to remember. Now, what is the benefit of remembering such things? The benefit of remembering such things is simply that it adds to our self-knowledge, to our awareness of the limitations of human nature. And knowledge itself does have a role. It not only has a role in the field of engineering, but also has, or should have, a role in the remoulding of man himself, not simply in the remoulding of environment, but in the remoulding of the inner nature of man. A certain amount of self-knowledge has to precede the remoulding of human nature from within.

Now, I take you to something closer to the social sciences, because I want to pass on gradually to politics and economics. Consider one very basic question—the question of the identity of the individual. Psychologists are specially interested, among other things, in what is sometimes called a 'Crisis of identity'. Now, consider this question of identity of the individual. How do we identify an individual? We identify an individual by relating him to a group. You may say that he belongs to such and such family—that is part of his identity. Some might say he belongs to such and such language group—he is an Englishman, a Russian, a Bengali or a Tamil, Chinese, Japanese or whatever—so we can identify him by relating him to a linguistic group. Or, we may identify him by saying that he belongs to such and such sect or religious community—may be he is a Christian or a Buddhist or a Mohammedan or a Jew or whatever else he may be. These are ways of identifying an individual. Or how else do we identify? We identify an individual with reference to various groups like belonging to a family, a linguistic group, a religious group, some cultural group and so on. That is the way to identify an individual. As a matter of fact, an individual does not belong to one group but simultaneously to a number of groups. For example, maybe by profession you are a doctor, so you belong to a group of doctors. Let us say that by religion you are a Christian, so you belong to the group of Christians. Let us say that by race you are a Mongol, so you belong to the group of Mongols. So, you are a doctor, a Mongol and a Christian and by convergence of all these identities you become specially what you are. Simply saying you are a doctor will be too wide, similarly to say you are a Christian will be too wide. But if we put all these together, you will be more specifically identified. Now a problem arises there. What is the problem? The problem of reconciling different identities. That we are human beings—well, that is of course the fundamental identity of a human being. But when you want to identify more specifically, you have to add so many other things and these group identities become essential. Now what happens if we put these things together? A little while ago, I have said that there is this aggressiveness in human nature, much more than we need today, and now I am saying that an individual is identified by his belonging to a particular group. What happens when you put these two things together? Just as an individual has an ego, a group has a collective ego. When you think of yourself as belonging, let us say, to a particular religious community, that particular religious community has its own collective ego and this collective ego can be very aggressive—very aggressive under special circumstances. Under some special circumstances in the history of United States, the Blacks and the Whites began to coexist. But the Blacks have their own collective ego and the Whites have their own collective ego, and these two collective egos clashed. The problem was aggravated by social dominance. Or let us take a more simple example. The world is divided into nations. A nation has its own collective ego, and as I said, thanks to the special degree of aggressiveness in human nature, this collective ego also developed a special degree of aggressiveness — collective aggressiveness. So, mankind is divided into different groups, and individuals are impelled by their power impulse to act through these collective bodies. Nations go to war. The British may go to war with the Germans. The Britons as well as the Germans have their collective egos and there is the inheritance of human aggressiveness taken over from the past and there are the weapons of mass destruction, not taken over from the past, but more recently invented. You put these things together — the weapons of mass destruction and the collective egos and aggressiveness and then you have some understanding of the basic causes of conflict. Human unity is an objective of great urgency, but now we are confronted with this human situation: on the one hand, human unity — objective of great urgency — and on the other hand, a humanity fragmented into conflicting collective egos. So that is where we stand and we have to think of ways and means of overcoming the problem. Humanity fragmented into innumerable groups and these groups are often at war with one another. War is an extreme form of conflict. But there are other forms of conflict too. So, humanity is caught in a chaotic situation of groups in conflict with one another.

An attempt must be made to arrive at some kind of an order amidst this disorder of clashing groups. Now, let us think of historical experiments. The leading historical experiment of arriving at some kind of order out of this discord is an imperialist power — an imperialist power that can impose a certain kind of order among groups which are in conflict with one another — that is what the Roman Empire tried to do 2,000 years ago; that is what the British Empire tried to do in more recent history, even the Soviet Union

15

built up its own kind of empire extending from Siberia to Czechoslovakia. So, this is the imperialistic solution to the problem of disorder. Imperialism, which means that among these many groups which are in conflict with one another, some group, for one reason or another, becomes more powerful than the other groups. It is not necessarily the largest group that becomes the most powerful, but some groups become more powerful than other groups and this group that becomes more powerful than other groups tries to create its own zone of dominion or empire, and there it tries to bring some kind of order that it thinks best. As I said, it is not always the biggest group that does this, but the group rendered most powerful by some historical circumstances. Surely England was not the biggest group in the world, but for some reason or the other, it became a very powerful imperial power. Or, if we think of the Far East, in the earlier part of the 20th century, Japan was not the biggest country but somehow it became the most powerful. And just as little England came and tried to create order in India, a country so much larger than Britain, so also little Japan invaded a much larger country called China and tried to establish some kind of — well, Imperialists sometimes give beautiful names to what they achieve — 'Sphere of Common Prosperity', and came to establish imperialist dominion in the Far East. These are only examples of what was attempted historically. But as soon as you think of these examples you can also see that these do not really provide a durable solution to the basic problem of human unity. The order created by an Imperial power does not last. It is something temporary. The Roman Empire did not last. Even British Empire, which boasted that the *sun never set* in the empire, did not last, and of course, the Soviet Empire did not last. Empires do not last. Therefore, we are driven again to the basic question — what do we do to secure a more durable solution to the basic problem of achieving human unity?

When you put a question like that, you can at least conceptually think of an answer, from the way I have presented it. I talked of the collective ego of groups. Now, why does an individual feel such a strong allegiance to a group? That individuals feel strong allegiance to groups is a fact. Nationalism is an example of the strength of the feeling of allegiance of an individual to a nation. What in India we call 'communalism' — whether it is Muslim communalism or Hindu communalism or whatever it may be — is another terrible example of the feeling of allegiance of an individual to a group. Even tribalism is a good example. The individual member of a tribe does have a strong feeling of allegiance to the tribe. As a matter of fact, tribalism is the basic model of such a feeling of allegiance of the individual to the group. But why does the individual have such a feeling of strong allegiance? I guess that there are several reasons for that. One is that the individual apart from the group feels rather helpless. As part of the group, he feels more secure. Allegiance to the group, to a great extent, is a matter of a feeling of security. As something apart from the group, the individual is weak, but as part of the group, he feels strong. So, his allegiance to the group is partly a question of feeling of security by virtue of his membership of the group. There are also other reasons. A group has its own culture — whether it is based on language or religion or culture or whatever it is, a group has its own culture. So, the individual belonging to that group gets used to expressing himself through the symbols used by that culture, for example, he gets used to expressing himself through his own language, also the forms of festivals and celebrations recommended by the religion to which he belongs. So, his allegiance to the group arises from the fact that it provides him with a very basic support of self-expression. The cultural group to which he belongs provides him with what is essential for his self-expression. So, partly because of the feeling of security that he needs, and much more positively on account of the urge for self-expression, which is so basic for a human being to flourish, he feels strong attachment to the group of which he is a part. But this still leaves unsolved the problem of securing human unity and lasting peace.

What can be a more durable solution? Now, I suggest that a durable solution must be of the form of a federation of all these cultural groups—a kind of a loose union of all these groups. What are the requirements of that federation or union? It must permit a certain amount of cultural autonomy because culture is the essential medium for the self-expression of the individual. Also, these groups must have a certain possibility of self-government. There should be liberal space for cultural autonomy to actualise itself in political terms. One of the merits of this arrangement is that it will prevent excessive concentration of political power, unless this is offset by an adverse authoritarian tradition. If we look at contemporary history with these ideas in mind, we will find that mankind is indeed grouping its way towards some such solution. What is the European Union trying to achieve? There are two groups called Frenchmen and Germans and other European countries who fought against one another terrible wars, the First World War and the Second World War, and now these countries are trying to build up a kind of loose union of these groups — these cultural entities. I guess that, in our Indian subcontinent, if a solution is at all found in future to our problem, then here also, ultimately, there will have to be a kind of loose union for the whole sub-continent. Here the federating units, each retaining a great deal of autonomy, will endow themselves with an arrangement for common defence, thus ensuring collective security at substantially reduced cost and a zone of peace favourable to all. The problem that mankind has in general is also the problem of the Indian subcontinent, viewed separately. Just as the world as a whole can be destroyed by a nuclear war, so also the Indian subcontinent can be destroyed by a nuclear war, if such a war at all happens. India has nuclear bombs, and Pakistan too has nuclear bombs. Either we produce these bombs at great expense, never to be used, signifying an awful waste of resources, or we produce them to be actually used and that will mean total destruction of the whole subcontinent. The question of how to build unity in the Indian subcontinent is at par with the larger question of how to build unity for the world as a whole. The nature of the problem is basically the same, and the nature of the solution will also be basically the same. The nature of the solution is that we will have to move towards a loose union of autonomous units. I think this is a great task for the age in which we live today. I think there is no greater task than striving to move towards that kind of a peaceful union. That is the only way for people to survive.

I should end with just one other thought, and that is, when we talk of a purely political order, whether it is imperialism or a fraternal union of consenting autonomous units, we talk about that whole thing at the level of organisation. Now organisation is important, but I would add just this — there is no organisation which alone can solve the problem. There is no organisation which cannot be corrupted. It is impossible to think of an organisation which cannot be distorted and corrupted unless it is sustained by a kindred spirit directed towards the approved goal. The 20th century has taught us many things. Over the whole century people talked of capitalism and socialism, and that both, thought of just as organisations, are capable of being totally corrupted and distorted and converted into a machinery of oppression. Capitalism can be that. Socialism can be that. It is impossible to define an organisation by its outward features and say that if you have these outward features then the problems will be solved. Organisation is indeed important. I am not trying to say that it is unimportant. If I thought so then I would not

19

have spoken about it at such length. But I do want to add that no organisation, simply as an organisation, can finally solve our problem. No organisation is beyond the reach of corruption.

Along with the material outfit, there has to be an inward change in men. The problem can be solved only if we can combine what is outward with what is inward. It is only by such a combination that we can reach a practicable and durable solution to the problem.

3
Transitional Puzzles

The major features of the present age, including its forms of government, arts and technology, morals and styles of life, are meaningfully yet loosely related to a central drama, a story which takes its character from an intricate combination of wars—local and global—and the transition from an agrarian to a predominantly industrial economy. This transition to an industrial society does not take place at the same time in all parts of the globe. Its design has not been the same everywhere. Nor has the process been completed yet. History reveals alternative paths of growth. In what way and how far to carry this process forward is an important question for the future of human society. On the answer to that question will depend the vital changes in the physical environment of our planet during the coming decades as also prospects of sustainable development and a safe future for mankind. To argue that man can have no control over the process of this great transition is to offer a counsel of total despair and loss of faith in the power of reason. We have to look at the past, try to understand the nature of the problem and chart out our course for the future.

Let us take a quick look at past history, hoping to gain some understanding of roadblocks and guideposts for the future.

England was among the first countries to make regular and substantial transfer of land from production of crops to other productive uses. Plots of land scattered in open fields had to be 'enclosed' to facilitate this process. This was done quite early to facilitate sheep farming. The Enclosure Acts of the 18th century came closer to what can be properly called the Industrial Revolution. There are a few special points to bear in mind for an understanding of the English experience. It was common among families of English landlords to send out younger brothers for non-agricultural occupations, such as long-distance commerce, leaving the management of land to the care of the eldest brother. Thus the English family system could be more easily adjusted to the requirements of an industrial transition. Add to this the fact that, thanks to geographical discoveries, a 'New World' had already opened up where people could migrate to seek fortunes abroad.

Despite these favourable circumstances, the English experience of the transition to industrial society was by no means happy. In fact, this was a particularly unhappy period in the life of the English people. This is a view which is clearly reflected in the literature of that period. It finds eloquent confirmation in the laws enacted at that time to enforce order. The blessings of democracy were enjoyed by a small upper class in society. The Poor Laws bear unmistakable testimony to the misery of the common people, which imperialist plunder in colonies did little to alleviate. There was a great increase in the number of uprooted 'vagabonds' thrown up in the turmoil of the industrial transition in England and extremely harsh methods were prescribed to deal with these restless and helpless people. The moral feature in Marx's denunciation of capitalism is easy to understand and easier to sympathise with against this social background. There is enough evidence of man's inhumanity in the social history of England in the 19th century to make any knowledgeable person with a modicum of conscience sit up and think of an alternative path of development.

Unfortunately, the Soviet Union failed to show the desired alternative. In some ways, the problem of transition to an industrial society in Stalin's Russia was very different from that in England in an earlier century. One basic difference can be very simply stated. England is a comparatively smaller country with a high density of population. The Soviet Union, by contrast, is a huge land mass with more sparsely populated areas. In the drive towards industrialisation, it is not the acquisition of land for setting up industry which presented the main problem in the USSR. Rather it was the procurement of surplus food stock from the farmers to feed the towns which appeared as a crucial bottleneck.

In the late 1920s, the Stalinist leadership (opposed by the Bukharin faction) resolved to launch an all-out collectivisation campaign in the agricultural sector. It was argued that collective farms would provide an organisational base for higher productivity. However, there was also a more compelling consideration. It was guessed rightly that collectivisation would strengthen the control of the party over the agricultural sector and so make it easier to achieve higher targets of centralised procurement of grain to meet the needs of the industrial sector. The campaign for rapid collectivisation started in 1929 and some writers have designated the next five years the period of 'the Soviet Great Leap Forward'. Statistics relating to progress of collectivisation and changes in agricultural production and procurement over these years are available from Moscow and these tell a grim story. The percentage of crop area collectivised rose from 33.6 in 1930 to 87.4 in 1934; grain harvest is estimated to have declined from 83.5 million tons in 1930 to 67.6 million tons in 1934; and, despite this decrease in production, state grain procurement rose from 10.8 million tons in 1928 to 22.1 million tons in 1930 and stood at approximately the same height thereafter (22.6 million tons in 1933). It remains only to add a brief note on the methods by which this extraordinary operation was carried out.

Stalin's speech at the 15th Party Congress (December 1927) on the subject of transition from agriculture to industrialisation sounded moderate and reasonable. Referring to the economic situation prevailing in Russia at that juncture, he asked, 'What is the way out? ... The way out is to unite the small and dwarf peasant farms gradually but surely, not by pressure but by example and persuasion, into large farms based on...collective cultivation of the land' (Nove 1969). The Soviet 'great leap forward' was actually executed not by 'persuasion' but by a massive and ruthless use of force. A very large number of people who refused to cooperate were exiled forcibly to Siberia and a very large number perished. Demographic studies put the number of unnatural deaths in these disturbed times at several millions and the horror of it all is unforgettably depicted in Russian literature by great writers, such as Solzhenitsyn and Pasternak. Among the leaders of the Communist Party of the Soviet Union (CPSU) in the 1920s, there was no disaccord on the need for industrialisation. But Bukharin proposed a strategy of economic development that would have been more peaceful. It did not fit in with Stalin's power game and was rejected. Yet it helped inscribe on the agenda of history the need for a peaceful transition from agriculture to industry.

In some ways, Japan provided a model of transition which contrasted sharply with the Russian experiment. Nobody can miss the striking difference between the natural endowments of these two countries. Japan has to manage with much less land relatively to the size of her population. She is also deficient in essential mineral resources for industrial development. This gave rise to the need for supplementing her internal resources with supplies from outside to carry through any big programme of industrialisation. By the very logic of these restrictive conditions, Japan could not be as self-sufficient as Russia or the U.S.A. in her pattern of economic development. This partly explains, although it does not excuse, Japan's imperialistic aggression in the early stage of her industrialisation. This remains a blot in the history of her economic development in the early part of the 20th century. For the rest, the path of development which she chose was marked by some commendable features.

For instance, Japan wisely gave high priority to education for the people. It is worth nothing that she came to have a largely literate rural population already before the Russian revolution. This made it possible to raise agricultural productivity substantially without any drastic change in the size of land holdings. Side by side with large-scale and monopolistic enterprises, a good deal of attention was given to small-scale and light industry which blended with agriculture and provided employment to rural people. Also, methods of business management were devised which aimed at and drew strength from a reconciliation of tradition with modernity. In the economic transition of paper, agriculture and industry played admirably complementary roles. At the same time, there was a strongly authoritarian element in Japanese society which cannot be safely recommended today.

Does this brief report have any message for us?

India is in transition. This has to be accepted as a historical necessity. But history also teaches that there are alternative paths of development. We have to choose our path cautiously if we want to avoid grave problems for the future. We cannot avoid industrialisation. But a simple affirmation of the need for industrialisation does not take us far in the actual formulation of a correct policy. Some recent incidents at Singur and elsewhere have started a public debate on this subject. It is to be hoped that this debate will be so conducted that it produces not just a lot of heat but also some light.

We are apt to be deceived by some ideas which look simple and convincing at first sight. Taken this for an example, industry marks a higher level of productivity and higher earnings; therefore, transfer of labour from farm to factory should be recommended. The trouble with this line of reasoning is that it oversimplifies a complex situation and can be dangerous if pushed hard. We should bear in mind that in a number of countries, including India, 'jobless growth', as a UN Report notes, has become a matter of grave concern threatening social stability in recent years. The Tatas have offered to invest money at Singur to produce small cars on a vast tract of land taken over from farmers. It should be noted that it is not simply the owners of land who will be displaced by this operation, but a much larger number of marginal cultivators who work on that land without owning it. It has been vaguely suggested that these people will get employed in the new industrial establishment and they will be better off in consequence of this change. This surely is grossly misleading. Our poor cultivators, six decades after independence, are still mostly illiterate and the only productive skill they possess is tilling land. Industrial employment calls for a very different set of skills and habits. Transition from agriculture to industry carried out in this fashion may only lead to a net increase in unemployment. It will create a large number of uprooted 'vagabonds' joining the ranks of beggars and criminals.

The projected enterprises will throw out agricultural labour and at the same time create employment and some special positions available mostly to people from a different stratum of society. The leadership of this country is recruited in large part from the upper strata. Our policy decisions are coloured by the class composition of this leadership. It is not displaced tillers of land but children of middle and upper class families who will get preferential treatment in the special economic zones which are in the process of coming up. This does not mean that we have to totally abandon this policy. But we have to move with circumspection. We cannot do any permanent good even to our cities without paying attention to our countryside in a constructive way. A sick countryside makes cities sick and vice versa. Our industrial policy should be concerned with this total perspective. Our preferred pattern of industrialisation should reflect that concern.

Adam Smith made a perceptive distinction between two kinds of industry. There are those that are the offspring of long-distance commerce, which get increasingly bound with the world market. But there is also a different kind of industry which can be called the offspring of agriculture. These come to life by a process of organic growth from within agriculture itself. A healthy rural economy does not live on agriculture alone. It needs the support of other complementary activities, including rural industry. In the absence of this support in adequate measure, the rural economy falls sick. The remedy for that sickness does not lie in the setting up of industry typified by production of small cars.

Beyond rural industry, our national economy will surely find room for other kinds of manufacturing and service-related activities. In the choice of location of such activities, the state should be guided by wider considerations than what private enterprise left alone would take into account. For instance, the government should be interested in the development of backward regions. It has a special responsibility to provide infrastructural facilities and offer suitable incentives to attract private enterprise and reduce regional disparities. Simultaneously, there should be a broad-based two-way campaign of education to teach the people as well as learn from them and so make them willing partners in programmes of development. This is a condition precedent for a smooth transition from agriculture to industry in a democratic society.

There are ample examples of forced transitions in other countries and other epochs. For India, these are wrong precedents. Our society and polity are so constituted that an assault on the democratic tradition will have costly material consequences apart from being morally wrong. Recent incidents in West Bengal illustrate that the ruling party has a strong temptation to enforce its will by relying on force. The organised violence of the state has provoked counter-violence by the people. If this process is carried far, the country will move inexorably towards a condition of civil war. In contemporary conditions, there is a risk of this getting mixed up with an already prevailing trend towards terrorism and counter-terrorism. It provides a fertile ground for separatist forces and fundamentalist reaction to grow in strength.

How a totalitarian state would handle such a situation is a different question. India's path of development has to be consistent with democratic norms. Non-evidence may suggest to some people too high an ideal. But we in India have to strive and maintain certain standards of mutual tolerance and peace within our civil society and with our neighbouring countries if we want to achieve a moderately crisis-free transition to a tolerable future. The past is an imperfect guide. However frequent wars might have been in the past, the battle really worth fighting today is the battle for peace.

Reference

Nove, Alec. 1969. *An Economic History of the USSR*. The Penguin Press.

4

Economics of Urban Agglomerations

A Pioneer

Some rather neat models of the distribution of economic activity over space can be evolved on the basis of considerations concerning transport cost. The pioneer theoretician in this field was Johann Heinrich von Thünen, a North German farmer, who theorised on the basis of practical experience at the beginning of the 19th century. His book, usually referred to by its abbreviated title, *Der isolierte Staat*, appeared way back in 1826. The problem of *location* discussed by von Thünen can be set forth in this way.

Let us imagine a self-contained domain, a plane of uniform fertility and equal ease of transport in all directions, with a town at its centre. This central town provides a market for the products of the surrounding country. Now, what would be the most rational pattern of cultivation under these conditions? Fruits and vegetables, cereals, meat and cheese and other things can be offered in the market. How would the plane surrounding the central market be divided up for the production of these several commodities? The answer to this question can be found by considering the cost of transport per unit of a commodity relative to its value. Some commodities like fruits and vegetables are perishable and, therefore, these would be grown nearest the central town. Among other commodities, those that are bulky or heavy in relation to their value and, therefore, have a higher cost of transport per unit of distance, would be grown closer to the centre than other commodities. Thus, for instance, cereals would be produced nearer the market than wool, meat or cheese.

Reasoning in this way, von Thünen mapped out concentric belts around the central town as a rational pattern of cultivation, with gardens offering fruits and vegetables occupying the nearest belt, animal farming on the farthest side and cereal cultivation somewhere in between.

In this connection, he made one of the earliest and most striking uses of *marginal analysis* in economics. How far would the cultivation of, say, a particular kind of cereal extend? The greater the distance over which a particular commodity has to be transported to reach the central market, the greater its cost. Beyond a certain range, the additional cost would not be justified by the price this commodity fetched on the market, and it would be better to utilise the land for producing an alternative commodity with less transport cost per kilometre in relation to its value.

Thus, von Thünen's analysis laid the foundations of a *central place theory* of utilisation of space. It inspired others like Walter Christaller to develop this kind of analysis further.

In the actual world there are townships, towns and cities or, more generally, *central places* of different orders of economic importance. The central town in von Thünen's model had certain essential ties with the surrounding country from which it bought various products and to which it supplied certain other products. A number of such towns may have a common need of some commodities and services that they can all obtain more economically from a central place of a higher order of importance.

In the same way as we have villages or agricultural settlements encircling a nuclear township, so there can be a number of such townships distributed around a city, which itself would thus be a superior central site in relation to the surrounding urban agglomerations; and so on till we come to the *metropolis*, the apex of this hierarchy of central places. Just as towns and villages mutually support each other, so do the higher and the lower orders of urban agglomerations.

Centres of Activities

Corresponding to the gradation of central places, there is a gradation of central goods and services. For instance, central places of a lower order are often best suited for goods connected with lower stages of the processing of agricultural produce, while these depend on a central place of a higher order for certain superior goods and services.

Thus, all these places are *settlements* from the metropolis down to villages, and these tend to fall into a *symbiotic pattern* of graded interdependence or, at least, these should in a rational economic order.

In industrially developed countries reality quite often approximates this model, while in underdeveloped countries the model could provide guidelines for planning industrial location.

There are many reasons why the economic landscape in underdeveloped countries often diverges sharply from the pattern described above. In some of these countries there is a striking lack of intermediate 'central places'. A metropolis tends to dominate over a vast backward countryside. Or, a few large and overgrown cities stand in striking contrast to a very large number of villages with some very weakly functioning towns to mediate between the two extremes.

An Indian example based on a study made by E.A.J. Johnson will serve to illustrate the point. Kanpur[1] with approximately a million inhabitants (at that time) is a major city of Uttar Pradesh, the most populous Indian state. Its relation to the surrounding region is described by Johnson in the following words:

It serves as a metropolitan centre for a region that covers approximately 17,000 square miles inhabited by about 10 million people. If one follows the official census definition of a town, thè urban hierarchy of the region would consist of one *central city* (Kanpur), 24 towns, and 11,239 villages; which means that there would be but one town for every 468 villages. The 24 towns vary in size from around 5,000 people to 95,000, with the median population in 1960 about 16,000.... The glaring weakness in this regional urban hierarchy is the utter inadequacy of the number of towns, since none of them could possibly service 468 villages, even if one were to assume a complete network of good roads, which would be completely unwarranted.[2]

Data collected by the Uttar Pradesh Traffic Survey way back in 1966 indicate that virtually no agricultural produce in the Kanpur region is carried further than 25 km. 'Marketing', as Johnson points out, 'is seriously limited by the insufficiency, poor quality, and seasonable impassability of roads, and this infrastructural deficiency means that villages can be isolated even though they are not very far from towns'.

We have here not only a description of a glaring defect in the pattern of urban development in some underdeveloped countries, but also the beginning of an explanation for this state of things. The first impact of *modernisation* in these countries came in the form of the opening of an export trade. The transport network in the dependent country came to be so constructed as to facilitate the movement of raw materials from the primary producing regions to the port and thence to the foreign market. Little attention was given to connecting towns and villages or overcoming barriers to interregional trade within the country.

Before World War I, Brazilian cotton could be purchased more cheaply in Liverpool than in Rio de Janeiro, although Liverpool lies at a distance of over 4,000 miles from the Brazilian cotton-growing provinces of Bahia, Pernambuco and other districts in the north, while Rio de Janeiro is situated about 1,100 miles away.

In north India, only one principal line of transport running from east to west was developed at that time. For rural settlements which did not lie close to this main line, intercommunication offered great difficulty. This is a deficiency which could have been overcome by road development, but comparatively little was done. Johnson (1970) points out in his study that Uttar Pradesh is 'so lacking in surfaced roads that it has only 1/32 the mileage per 100 square miles of area that Japan has'. Other factors have also contributed to regional economic disparity and the poor development of trade between *town* and *country*. Credit, for instance, came to be more easily available for mercantile activities in the foreign trade sector than for other productive activities. Moreover, a tremendous disparity appeared in educational facilities between the *metropolis* or the *principal cities* and the *rest of the country*.

All these explain the dominant position occupied by a few big cities in the economically backward countries, the weakness of towns of the intermediate order and the stark poverty and ignorance in the countryside. This is the background of the Gandhian reaction against big cities.

Marx, studying the early stage of industrialisation in west Europe, was impressed above all by the exploitation of the proletariat by capitalists. Gandhi, looking at the economic landscape of India under British Rule, was horrified at the exploitation of the country by the cities. Both generalised from their experience.

There can be little doubt that the pattern of urban development in many colonial countries was a major cause of economic illness. It unbalanced the rural economy as well as the national economy. It produced unemployment and underemployment by weakening the traditional subsidiary industries in *villages* and by attracting people to the *cities* in much larger numbers than could be gainfully employed there. It broke up communities faster than it could reunite people by new ties of productive work.

All these seemed to Gandhi to be the inevitable consequences of industrialisation as he viewed it. Instead he
pleaded for village-based industry. 'Industrialisation on a
mass scale', he explained in reply to a question by Maurice
Frydman, 'will necessarily lead to passive or active exploitation
of the villages.... Therefore, we have to concentrate on the
village being self-contained, manufacturing mainly for use.'[3]
He would, to be sure, permit a few large-scale industries,
but it is village industry which would typify the economy
he stood for.

But the best way to vitalise the villages is to allow them to
interact with towns. The problem of rural poverty cannot be
solved by the villages withdrawing into themselves. *Market
towns* and other *medium-sized towns* have an essential contribution to make to rural development. The villages cannot
produce from within themselves all the ideas and all the
goods that they need for their economic uplift. A town
within easy reach of the villagers can provide these essential
ingredients of growth. If such towns do not exist in sufficient
number, it should be made a conscious aim of economic policy to create these. There are many potential 'central places',
which can be activised by proper facilities being provided
for this purpose.

The importance of road development has already been
stressed. There are serious gaps in the system of supply of
credit which can be filled up. The government can take up
projects of 'industrial estates' to initiate development in areas
that lack the necessary infrastructure for manufacturing and
trading activities. Even in economically backward regions
entrepreneurial abilities *potentially* exist. Industrial estates
can serve as seed-beds for such latent abilities to fructify by
making available to prospective entrepreneurs a prepared
tract of land improved with roads, factory buildings, power
supply and a variety of services, so that a community of enterprises is able to function there in close proximity and so succeed where each of them might have failed had it tried to
develop separately.

A few words may be added here on the size of the firm. There is a belief that industrial development leads inexorably towards large-scale enterprise. How far is this true? And how far is large-scale production made necessary by considerations of economic efficiency? There are cases in which technical factors make large units of production more economic. But the success of large firms is not always due to technical factors. Such firms also have other advantages, for instance, in bulk sale and purchase or the provision of credit.

Surveying the Japanese experience between the two wars, E.P. Reubens wrote:

> In the technological operation alone, the Japanese have shown themselves very ingenious at adapting their system of small-scale production to the lines in which they have special advantages... many a small shop found that the operation of a single machine-unit could be at least as efficient as the operation of a long line of such units, if there was no *concatenation* between the same. (Reubens 1947)

Thus, small firms show good results in many cases when they work for bigger firms which help them with credit, supply of raw materials and marketing of products. If these same facilities are offered by government agencies or cooperatives and provided these are efficient, an alternative institutional framework will be available within which small units of production can function successfully.

But this statement also needs to be qualified—where the demand for standardisation is high, large units of production have often a special advantage. It is not without some significance that in Japan already in the interwar period large spinning and weaving mills manufacturing standardised piece-goods mainly for export existed side by side with small weaving sheds catering for the home market.

Since the supply of trained and efficient managerial personnel is limited, large units of production or a large number of smaller units brought together may be conducive to fuller utilisation of the managerial factor. This already suggests the next point. Though the purely technological advantages of large-scale industry have sometimes been exaggerated, there is a strong argument for a certain crowding of firms in the same locality. The case for dispersion of economic activities makes sense when it is advocated in reaction against overconcentration of industry and commerce in a metropolitan area.

But it should not be pushed too far. The efficiency of a firm does not depend only on investment made within that firm. There is also such a thing as social capital of which the benefits are not confined to any individual firm. A fuller utilisation of common services is made possible by the localisation of industry at a central place. The case is not so much for setting up factories in innumerable villages as for a kind of bunched dispersal of industry all over the country.

A large and unified internal market gives an undoubted advantage to some industries which can function most effectively only on that basis. Yet there are other industries for which a local base is advantageous. In the same way as a nation requires a policy of protection for 'infant industry' in the early stage of its growth, so also regions within the national territory need special assistance for some of their promising industries. This does not mean that all regional demands of this kind are justified. On what basis should the choice of industry be made then? To a great extent, the criteria for location of industry are much the same whether they apply at the national or regional level.

Those industries should be protected which at the end of a period of special assistance would be able to dispense with such props and hold their own in free and fair competition on the basis of such advantages as local availability of raw materials or proximity to the final consumer resulting in lower transport cost. Some industries may be unable to grow in the backward regions because other factors are not equal, so these may need to be sheltered while measures are taken to provide the same with some essential facilities which these lack now.

But an industry which will have to be 'nursed' permanently will be a permanent liability. It will not, therefore, qualify for protection. There is only one major point where the symmetry of the argument breaks down in its application at the national and sub-national levels. Defence against other states is deemed to constitute a sufficient reason for protecting some industries within the national territory irrespective of considerations of comparative advantage. Such considerations cannot be a determining factor in regional economic policy except in so far as national security itself requires it. The division of Europe into multiple states in the 19th century was not, from an economic point of view, an unmitigated evil. Perhaps it made possible a more variegated and widely dispersed economic development than would have been achieved otherwise. The major economic cost of this division was its outcome in war.

These are some of the most important issues or considerations that have propelled urbanisation in the past. These are also concepts equally relevant in today's context of the emergence, development and proliferation of urban agglomerations vis-à-vis the prosperity or otherwise of the rural outbacks and countrysides. These, then, are also considerations which are valid for the formulation of a national policy on rural and urban development.

Notes

1. The erstwhile concepts about towns or cities like Kanpur developed here by the author are valid even today in terms of social and economic principles.
2. As a basis for comparison, we may note that 'in developed countries such as Britain, the United States, Germany, France and Japan, the ratio seldom exceeds 15 villages per market town': it is at least 200: 1 for

India. Any change that has since taken place is only a matter of ratio and proportion.
3. Harijan, 29 August 1936.

References

Johnson, E.A.J. 1970. *The Organization of Space in Developing Countries.* Cambridge: Harvard University Press.
Reubens, E.P., 1947. 'Small-scale industry in Japan', *Quarterly Journal of Economics*, August.

5

Sustainable Growth

In a global perspective, the second half of the 20th century was a period of remarkable economic growth, riding the waves of a new technological and industrial revolution. With its innovative base in electronics and bio-engineering, this revolution continues to dominate the scene today. Unsurprisingly, the process of economic growth has not been smooth all along. Signs of instability were more marked at certain times, particularly towards the end of the century, for diverse reasons. There was the 'oil crisis' and, more recently, several countries have been hit by acute financial crisis.

However, financial crises are usually symptoms of deeper disorder, so we have to look behind what the classical economists called the monetary veil. This deeper probe brings us face to face with a reality which is radically different from anything that received serious attention in earlier epochs of economic history. The beginning of the 21st century is a suitable time for development economists to look before and after and try to arrive at an understanding of the nature of sustainable growth for the future.

The present epoch is in many ways significantly different from earlier ones. Let us take note of some of these differences and consider their consequences. The first half of the 20th century saw two world wars. There was an interval of 21 years between the end of World War I and the outbreak of World War II. More than half a century has passed since the end of the last world war. During this period, there have been many local military encounters, but there has been no hot war between the superpowers. In a manner of speaking, this has been a period of comparative peace. But the level of military preparedness has remained extraordinarily high.

Defence expenditure has never been so high in earlier times. Now, add to this an additional fact. High military preparedness, as measured by the level of defence expenditure, has gone hand in hand with a high tide of consumerism. This is an extraordinary combination. During a hot military encounter, it is normal to take measures to restrain civilian consumption. Rations are a normal feature of a war economy. Nearly four decades of cold war has left behind this strong legacy of a combination of militarism and consumerism. Conspicuous consumption among a small elite was by no means unknown before. But in its broad sweep, the current consumerist tide has no parallel in the past.

There are many examples in the distant past of great empires breaking up and ruling aristocracies coming to grief when a policy of military adventurism was joined with an unbridled indulgence in ostentatious living. This does not simply tell us something about the evolution of ancient society: it also has a message for modern policy makers. An inordinately large defence expenditure represents in effect a high level of unproductive investment. When this goes with a high propensity to consume, the national economy can only be expected to get unbalanced. This imbalance produces inflation, budgetary deficit and adverse balance of payments even when the nation concerned is as rich as the USA. For poorer countries in a similar situation, the resulting distress can only be more acute.

It is arguable that these same circumstances also provide an impetus to growth. The industrial revolution of our time has been propelled by major technological innovations derived in very large part from defence-oriented research. Growth and instability can very well go together and have a common causation. There is nothing wrong with this argument except that it leans towards short-sightedness. For an adequate consideration of the theme of sustainable development, the horizons of our inquiry have to be widened. It is necessary to include within our purview matters pertaining to a number of allied disciplines along with and beyond economics. A line of development can be unsustainable for a variety of reasons. To take a simple case, it may be critically dependent on a natural resource which is limited in supply, non-renewable and without any suitable substitute. The 'oil crisis' of the 1970s brought into view such a situation. This highlighted a question of 'limits to growth'. The trouble with fossil fuel is not simply that it is limited in supply. It has other disadvantages too. It is amenable to monopolistic control by a small number of states. Moreover, it is 'unclean'.

Imagine a situation where petroleum is readily available all over the world. Even then it will be hazardous to burn it in unlimited quantities. Obviously, economic growth based on conventional use of fossil fuel is not sustainable beyond a limit. So people are looking for methods of more economical use of fossil fuel and, what is more important, alternative sources of energy. Atomic energy is one such alternative. It promises to make available a virtually unlimited supply of energy. But, it is not 'clean'. The fact that its production cannot be easily limited to a small number of states counts as a grave disadvantage. It carries with it an enormous risk of polluting the physical as well as the political environment.

When we look at the problems of economic development in this wide perspective, we begin to realise that humanity has arrived at a stage of evolution, technological and political, when defence-oriented research can no longer provide a reliable roadmap for the way ahead.

Some economists of late have significantly drawn attention to the importance of improving the quality of life of the common people and pleaded for restoring to the word 'wealth' its original meaning of well-being. However, development planning in the Third World continues to be dominated by

41

a nearly single-minded concern for a high rate of growth of national income. There are some simple arguments in support of this line of thought.

With a high rate of growth, it should be easier for the government to collect a large revenue. This will make it possible to sanction larger public outlays on education, health and, more generally, the infrastructure for economic and social development. Moreover, a high rate of growth will generate more jobs and so reduce unemployment and poverty. This line of reasoning deserves a hearing.

However, this is still a flawed and incomplete reasoning. A system of political economy rooted in the Bismarckian tradition is positively disposed towards a state-sponsored programme of social security supported by a high level of public expenditure on health and education. This is seen to help a nation achieve both power and a prominent rank in what is now called human resource development. Market-driven 'socialism' cheerfully accepts this new orientation of economies. Yet this falls seriously short of the full requirements of a new concept of development adequately designed to achieve a breakthrough from the evolutionary impasse which the world economic order has reached today.

A closely related point is also worth noting here. There are certain patterns of community relationship which play a protective role in society. When an indefinite extension of the commercial spirit tears apart this protective cover, a bruised human psyche takes fearful revenge.

6

Industrialisation and Social Reconstruction

At the time of independence, an enlightened section of Indian nationalists had put their faith in industrialisation as the path of modernisation and economic emancipation of the people. Gandhi's warnings were dismissed with a polite nod. It was believed that with the progress of industrialisation the excess population in agriculture would be steadily absorbed in industry and the burden of unemployment gradually removed. This has, in fact, not happened. It is time to consider seriously what the basis of our more optimistic anticipations was and why they went wrong.

The basis of our anticipations was provided by a model drawn from the Western experience of industrialisation. There the growing industrial sector did help remove the surplus labour force from land and, except for pockets of poverty, it did help to raise the standard of living all around. Why was our experience after independence so different? There can be no doubt that the demographic factor accounts for much of the difference.

In the 40 years between 1951 and 1991, the population of India grew at a rate of nearly 2.5 per cent a year, while in some other countries of the Third World the rate was even higher. At a comparable stage of industrial development of Britain or France, the growth of population was never as fast as that. For

Britain in the middle of the 19th century, for instance, the average annual rate of growth of population was below 1.5 per cent. Moreover, Europe at the early stage of development was able to get rid of its surplus population which migrated in large numbers to the New World. In the U.S.A. and elsewhere, with vast sparsely populated land, large numbers of immigrants could be absorbed with ease. For India today, there is no such outlet for surplus population. Some of our best brains migrate, but that is a different matter.

There is one more important difference. The advanced technology of today is much more labour-saving than was the advanced technology of the 19th century when the West completed its period of industrial take-off. We have to make use of modern technology in the organised sector of the Indian economy. But, however fast the modern sector may be made to grow, it cannot, under these conditions, absorb all or most of our large surplus labour force. If providing full employment is a major task, this cannot be accomplished by sole reliance on the market economy geared to industrialisation along conventional lines. This should set us thinking that we are, in fact, in the presence of a problem the like of which classical political economy was never called upon to face.

The Indian economy has a modern sector and a traditional sector. There are those who say that this duality should go. But should it? And how? The modern sector has come to stay until and unless we are prepared to give up many things on which we depend today. Are we as a nation ready to disband our army and entrust our safety to non-violence? India is a democracy and the people evidently are not in favour of unilateral disarmament. Therefore, we have to support the production and supply of arms and defence equipment which in turn presuppose advanced technology and a large cluster of high-tech industries. There is, to be sure, no good reason why South Asia should not move towards phased disarmament through mutual agreement. But that takes time.

Meanwhile, we will remain busy keeping continuously abreast of new technology, because it does not really make sense to maintain an army and then keep it insufficiently trained and poorly equipped. Beyond defence there are other material interests too. We have a rapidly increasing number of managers, engineers, university teachers, bureaucrats, politicians, businessmen and professional people of all sorts. How far are we prepared to deprive this new middle class of the comforts and incentives offered by modern consumer goods? Against the pressing imports of consumer and capital goods, we have to arrange a sufficient volume of exports. But we cannot effectively compete in the world market unless we attain certain standards of quality and efficiency in our export sector activities. All these things add up to a modern sector of some size. This is the sector for which a policy of liberalisation and free flow of capital and technology and openness to the world market appears to be required, although adaptation to local conditions must go hand in hand with modernisation.

It is an error to minimise the importance of this sector for orderly development in the immediate future. Yet, a policy of exclusive dependence on this sector will equally be a mistake.

In view of the size of our population and the capital intensity of modern technology, the organised sector of the Indian economy cannot provide employment for a sufficient number of people. Supplementing that sector must be, therefore, another area of economic activities, equally important, but based on quite different principles. These activities have to rely chiefly on local resources and produce for the domestic market, mainly for local consumption. They need sheltered markets, perhaps reserved areas of production. Such competition as they face will have to come from within their own category. They have to depend on appropriate technology designed to meet their special conditions. They will need to be sustained by a culture and a life-style hospitable to them

45

and other institutions of local self-help and self-government, inspired by the same culture.

It is not quite clear what name one should give to this sector. The word 'traditional' does not exactly fit, for in some ways, the underlying conception is quite radical. Appropriate technology is not the same as traditional technology; in many ways, it will have to be enriched by new science, knowledge and experiments. One may call it the small neighbourhood sector, because it will have a strong preference for small units of production and a decided orientation towards the local community or neighbourhood, without, however, ceasing to be hospitable to others in a true neighbourly spirit. While the modern market economy has historically led to the disintegration of traditional community ties, the small neighbourhood sector will help reintegration.

There are those who are pleased to call this new 'communitarian' idea romantic. They consider the complete victory of the modern sector to be inevitable. But can the so-called modern sector of our economy really take care of growing unemployment and disintegration of social ties? Is it not equally 'inevitable' that these same conditions, if allowed to grow unchecked, will breed violence and terrorism and lead eventually to a complete breakdown of society? We have to think constructively about how to prevent such a breakdown.

7

Beyond the Short Run

In the long run we are all dead, so said a famous economist. Here is a proposition which most people receive with an immediate nod of assent. Yet it is open to serious objection. Granted that there is something substantial to be said in favour of that proposition, there is also something to be stated against. Is it right to fix the boundaries of the word 'we' so very narrowly? Our children and grandchildren live on, so we should hope and act in that hope. Tomorrow is another day as important and as real as today and, under certain circumstances, it is even more important. It is only a degraded 'practical' reason which fails to recognise this. Let me illustrate, starting with comparatively trivial yet relevant examples before I pass on to ideas at a higher level.

Suppose one gets a feeling of discomfort, say, an ache in some part of the body. Even when it is not something very serious, one is often in a hurry to get rid of it. There are two courses open to us. One can take a 'pain killer' which will bring quick relief. But such medicine has 'side effects' which, in the long run, are not negligible.

There is an alternative course. One may rely on the natural powers of recuperation of the normal human body to combat and remove the ailment, though this might take rather more time to work. Combined with some natural precaution, this is in many cases the wiser course in the long run.

In some special cases, external assistance is advisable. But, as far as possible, one should let one's inner powers play to keep oneself fit. Neither the one nor the other course is wrong under all circumstances. The point is to strike a right balance. This is not always easy as our commercial civilisation has a vested interest in advertising the supposed benefits of depending on purchasable external assistance. But this is to take a short-term view of what is advantageous in the final analysis. It is wrong, both for the individual and for the larger society, to belittle the benefits of self-reliance, allowing the pressures of the present moment to override a wider view of the good.

Let us restate the basic issue to give it a more general form. Short-term problems cannot be ignored; sometimes they are pretty pressing. But it is possible to respond to them in alternative ways: usually problems in practical life have alternative 'solutions'. The 'commonsense' solution, which may look 'self-evident' to the uncritical mind, derives its power from the fact that it is guided by what is immediately evident and fails to take into account the wider consequences or the long-term effects of present action. An alternative approach tends to be less popular because it involves a certain amount of abstract thinking and 'idealism' with which many people have little patience. Yet the future of the society depends even materially on that other approach.

A series of short-term 'solutions' to recurring problems can pave the way to an ultimate disaster. It is easy to illustrate this with examples of families and nations sunk into terrible indebtedness because of a habit of improvidence or devastated by self-fulfilling suspiciousness and its aftermath of mounting violence.

An 'idealistic' approach, which is in fact more truly and deeply practical, starts from the other end. It forms a vision of a decent future worth striving for and then tries to build up support for such reforms and remedies for current problems as to help the movement towards that future, with enough flexibility to take inexperience on the way, but never losing sight of the ultimate end.

48

Underlying this divergence of approach, there are other differences, such as differing interpretations of history and beliefs regarding possibilities of improving human nature. The practical idealist does not mind being branded a 'visionary' or 'utopian'. He is a man of faith in the sense that he does not accept the inevitability of an irreversible defeat. A constructive debate should relate to ways and stages of approaching the ideal. At that level the distinction between pragmatism and idealism progressively loses its sharpness.

Having distinguished between different levels of pragmatism, it is time to illustrate these differences with more concrete examples even at the risk of provoking a fresh debate. The climate of ideas in the 20th century has been strongly influenced by a variety of strongly held views of basic conflicts among classes and nations, races and religious sects and communities. Some of these theories are partly correct, but only partly so, which makes a dogmatic adherence to them easier to that extent, yet harmful.

Consider, for instance, that very influential theory, the ideology of class conflict or a basic antagonism of interests between capitalists and the working class. Those who have unquestionable faith in that theory strongly believe that it is in the interest of the capitalist order to keep the workers ignorant and poor as that makes it easier to exploit them. But this is not the whole truth. Standards of labour productivity can be raised by education and improved health of workers. This is not beyond the comprehension of enlightened capitalists and the state bent on industrial development, as economic history amply demonstrates. Between the two classes, there is both a conflict and a complementarity of interests. Nothing less than that corresponds to the whole truth. A party or a state which is handicapped by short-sighted ideas on this subject cannot serve effectively the long-term interests of either the capitalist or the working class.

8

The Great Transition

Modern history is very largely the story of a great transition, the transition from a predominantly rural society to an expanding industrial order. This industrial transition has breathtaking achievements to its credit, which make it look very attractive. But it has also created serious problems which threaten to imperil the future of human society. Over the last few decades, the ecological aspect of this threat to the future, which prompted some very knowledgeable observers to call it a 'global crisis', has been extensively studied and reported. In fact, this inquiry has been so extensively done that intelligent citizens today can easily get hold of the relevant literature and gain familiarity with the fast developing ecological problem, if indeed they are not already familiar with it. There are other basic elements of the great transition, which still require to be presented in a historical perspective. To be sure, these too are widely known; but somehow their significance remains inadequately understood. Side by side with the ecological crisis, there is a social crisis, no less real, which needs attention.

'The industrial revolution caused unspeakable misery in England. I do not think any student of economic history can doubt that average of happiness in England in the 19th century was lower than it had been a hundred years earlier.' These are strong words. Yet these were written not by a romantic admirer of ruralism, but by as rational an observer of modern times as Bertrand Russell in his long essay on *The Impact of Science on Society*. Obviously, it was not his intention to create prejudice against science as such — in fact, he was an ardent advocate of the scientific outlook — but he simply wanted to report faithfully the misery that visited the common people as distinct from the privileged classes in England during the industrial transition. This happened in England despite colonial exploitation abroad. We have to try and understand this phenomenon.

Quite often the misery of the common people in the early phase of industrialisation is explained by capitalist exploitation of labour. However, the employed labour force, which was directly controlled by capital, was arguably not any worse off than the rural poor. The 'unspeakable misery' that Russell noted can be more significantly related to the painful increase in the number of people involuntarily unemployed during the industrial transition. In the long run, industry created new jobs which absorbed a good part of the labour force that it displaced. But, as Keynes memorably remarked, in the long run we are all dead. What critically matters is the experience of the process of transition. In theory, there is a movement from a low-level equilibrium position to a possible higher-level equilibrium. In fact, a stable equilibrium is never finally established as new disturbances occur ever so often. The spectre of involuntary unemployment continued to haunt Britain beyond the end of the century. However, we are concerned here with the early phase of industrialisation and what happened to the society during that phase. Let us look at the matter a little more closely.

The rural economy, as it existed before the rise of capitalism, was quite often poor, but it was free from mass unemployment in normal times. At this point, let me quote a few supporting words from Joseph Schumpeter, unquestionably one of the greatest economists of the 20th century. In his *History of Economic Analysis*, Schumpeter (1996) observed, 'Mass unemployment...was unknown to the Middle Ages except as a consequence of social catastrophes such as devastation by wars and plagues.' He went onto add:

> The rising capitalist industry in the long run absorbed un-employment ... when the pace of industrial development quickened in the second half of the 18th century, technological unemployment put in an appearance as a mass phenomenon and frequently overshadowed that long-run effect. This ex-plains why the rising factory system was associated with so much misery. For a time, though not everywhere to the same extent, all barriers to the deterioration of the worker's lot were giving way.

This, in its own way, confirms the truth about the increasing misery suffered by the working people in the West in the process of the industrial transition. The careful reservation expressed by Schumpeter in the words 'though not every-where to the same extent' deserves attention along with his more general statement. In fact, it has far-reaching implications worth exploring.

There is an idea of wide currency that industrialisation is bound to arrive at sooner or later and it is unwise to delay its arrival. The trouble with this kind of advocacy is that it is too simplistic. The point at issue is not about delaying or has-tening the course of industrialisation. It is about choosing the right path of development. Development is not one inevit-able, choice-less track. There are alternative paths to growth and patterns of industrialisation and man has the capacity to choose one or the other course after due consideration of possible consequences.

There are important differences in the circumstances at-tending the process of industrialisation in different parts of the world. We in India must take note of our distinctive cir-cumstances and choose a strategy of industrialisation best suited to our case. It will surely be a mistake to take the West for a model and try to imitate it ignoring differences in histor-ical situations. Between the present situation in India and that obtained in the West in the formative phase of industrialisation, there are many points of contrast. We will specially note two, where the contrast is highly significant.

Before we proceed further, it will be useful to recall some basic facts relating to social and political transformation in the modern period. It is well known that the Industrial Revolution was preceded and accompanied by a commercial revolution arising from rapid growth of long-distance trade. Equally important was the emergence of the modern state which played a crucial role in the unification of the domestic market in the countries concerned. These changes were propelled by a city-based new middle class with a vision and an economic agenda largely unknown in traditional society. The emergence of a new ruling class in a position of power is not a phenomenon confined to capitalist development. In one form or another, it has happened in so-called socialist societies too. Entrepreneurs, bureaucrats and professionals including political leaders combine in varying proportions and constitute typically the new middle class, which is the ruling class in multiform societies with programmes of economic modernisation.

We turn now to some tough problems. These are complex problems of diverse provenance, but let us try to form a reasonably clear idea about them. An industrial society depends for its efficiency on certain habits, such as punctuality, and certain secular values, of which sanctity of contract is a leading example, which do not have strong roots in rural life. Also, the impact of industrialisation in a predominantly traditional society tends to weaken certain social bonds and customary obligations and this creates an atmosphere of psychological insecurity and a sense of creeping anarchy all around. Added to these, there are certain material tasks which require urgently to be accomplished during an industrial transition. Accumulation of capital is a leading example of these basic material tasks. In the early phase of industrialisation, extraction of surplus from the agricultural sector acts as a major support for accumulation of capital. To undertake or assist in undertaking such activities comes then to be perceived as an essential function of the state. But going beyond these, there is something that presents itself as even more basic. Holding the society together through the strains and stresses of a protracted period of industrial transition appears to the ruling class, rightly or wrongly, as its historically prescribed role. Idealism and hunger for power get easily combined in that role.

How has the state actually performed this historic role? The Industrial Revolution did not put in an appearance at the same time in all countries. It came sooner in some parts of the world, later in others, and there are countries where it is yet to come. The circumstances in which the experiment of industrial development has been made are dissimilar from one case to another. However, one fact stands out despite this diversity of circumstances. In notable cases, programmes of industrialisation have been carried through by harshly authoritarian methods. This does not necessarily mean that despotism provides a more favourable climate for industrial development. There are many cases in which authoritarianism coexists with economic backwardness. But the fact remains that in most countries of large size, the early phase of rapid industrialisation unfolded when democracy, as we understand it now, had not yet struck roots.

Examples lie scattered over a fairly long stretch of time. China today is openly a single-party dictatorship. Stalin's Russia was ruthlessly despotic. In England at the time of the first Industrial Revolution, the right to vote was still restricted to the propertied classes and women of all classes were excluded from that right. In all such cases, the very harsh methods adopted for protecting social solidarity and promoting industrialisation are clearly incompatible with democracy.

This makes the Indian experiment a historic exception. No country of India's size and importance ever attempted industrialisation within the political framework of a democratic constitution. India needs democracy. The tradition of this country and its incomparable cultural diversity make democracy mandatory, a practical necessity. There is no other way of holding this country and its people together for any reasonable length of time. We need democracy to avert civil war and prevent further fragmentation of this land. We can amend the form of our democracy, but we cannot afford to discard its kernel, the basic rights which constitute its inner identity. Amartya Sen's great idea of *Development as Freedom* may be easier to protect in industrially more advanced countries. But it remains valid and valuable for India. We have to seek out patterns and methods of development which make it compatible with democracy along with its key concept which is freedom. Will the ambitions and ideology of our ruling class permit this?

There are reasons to believe that India's preferred path of growth and, indeed, its pattern of industrialisation should be different from the model provided by the West. Quite apart from idealistic grounds, there are differences in material and historical circumstances which point towards this conclusion. Let us start with a wrong line of reasoning and try to understand why it is wrong. India has to get rid of poverty.

The West has, it is thought, banished poverty, thanks to high industrialisation. India has to learn from this demonstrated experiment for removal of poverty. The West did inflict a great amount of 'misery' on itself and its colonies to climb the height it has reached. But we should not feel deterred. If need be, we have to be ready to pay the same price. This is how the Westerniser's argument virtually runs. To a good part of the new middle class in India, this line of reasoning sounds persuasive and it has some merits. Yet it is deeply deceptive.

More painful than steady poverty, more destructive of self-respect and more disruptive of social relations is involuntary unemployment, which robs a person of the right to claim something from society in return of something he has contributed to it. India is already burdened with a great deal of unemployment, urban and rural. The West too was deeply troubled by 'mass unemployment' with the onset of industrialisation. At a later stage of development, it introduced a system of social security to take care of the unemployed. The Indian government promises to do something similar here. There are reasons to believe that this cannot be done effectively, given the quality of our administrative machinery and the present stage of economic development of the country. In some respects, the situation in India today is more desperate than what the West experienced at any stage.

There are special non-repeatable circumstances which made it possible for the West to negotiate its industrial transition without a total social breakdown. When the disruptive potential of industrialisation was at its worst, England could dump its socially unadjusted 'vagabonds' in large numbers in Australia, while many religious dissenters escaped persecution and found a spacious home in North America. The pressure of population on land in this part of the world is incomparably more adverse than in America. And India has no substantial outlets for its surplus population; what it has are routes for 'brain drain', which does not exactly solve the basic problem. Even if there are some escape routes for children of the new middle class, the situation is grim for those lower down. The service sector does mitigate the problem somewhat, but by no means sufficiently. New large-scale industry will expectedly come up and there should be some space for it. But to the extent that such industry makes use of labour-saving technology, it can go only a limited way in reducing unemployment in India. This should make us pause and ponder. Pressure of unemployment creates acute social problems and fuels political extremism. Already 'fundamentalism' of the Right and the Left has appeared as a destabilising factor. The future of democracy is unsafe in India unless something can be done to effectively contain mounting unemployment. A policy of control of population is to be recommended strongly.

But its effects can be perceived only after a somewhat long time interval, since those who will enter the labour force after 15 years from now have already born. That still leaves largely unaddressed important issues centring on the vital subject of education for a safe future. It will take a separate essay to do justice to that theme.

Let me do a rapid recapitulation and conclude. The industrial transition was a painful experience in the West, made tolerable by special circumstances. Unlike the West in its period of take-off, India cannot find an open outlet for its surplus population in colonies beyond its shores. As modern technology at this hour is much more capital-intensive than what the West had to do with in its critical period of industrial transition, India cannot solve its problem of unemployment by one-sided dependence on large-scale industry. We have reasons to depend substantially on village industries and dispersed growth centres to arrive at a tolerable solution of our pressing problem of unemployment. Our ideas on rural development should get adjusted to this altered vision. To be sure, our cities too need care. But unemployment and unrest in our cities cannot be restrained so long as the countryside stays in disarray. If the tide of globalisation overflows, it will spell doom all around. This sets the new perspectives for the future development of India and large parts of the Third World. A section of the ruling class instinctively recoils from these ideas, but it has nothing better to offer. We need a balanced development of the city and the countryside. Away from an impending global crisis, these alternative perspectives indicate the way to a hopeful future. It is time for India and the rest of the world to rethink.

Reference

Schumpeter, J.A. 1996. *History of Economic Analysis*. USA: Oxford University Press.

9

Towards an Alternative Economic Order*

When the historian in the 21st century looks back on the 20th century, he will notice two significant revolutions, one which dominated the first part of the century and another which gradually started gaining momentum towards the end of the century. The two revolutions are very different in character. They are a study in contrast. In order to present the second revolution that is silently taking shape, so silently that many of us are unaware of its taking shape at all, in order to explain to you the special character of this revolution, I might just as well contrast it with the first.

I will begin with the first revolution and then talk about the second.

The first revolution was of course the October Revolution which was based on a criticism of capitalism. It wanted to overthrow capitalism and to set up a new social order which could be called socialism or, as some Marxists would prefer to say, socialism that was the first step towards the development of communism, the higher stage. Capitalism achieved a great deal. Even Marx recognised that it was a powerful engine of industrialism, at least in some parts of the West. But it also had certain features which the critics found very disturbing. One can describe and explain some of these features in the

---

*Talks transcribed from tapes.

language of economics or try to express it in more abstract language, the language of philosophy. Although capitalism achieved much by way of industrialisation, it came to be marked by a high degree of inequality in distribution of wealth and income, by economic instability, by trade cycles, by unemployment and, in general, by a great deal of social injustice and exploitation. If we wanted to put this in more abstract, philosophical language, then we could say that capitalism was marked by alienation.

The workers, the producers, the great majority did not own the means of production which really means that they worked not according to their own will but in accordance to a will alien to them. And therefore the system of production, which went by the name of capitalism, meant in effect an absence of freedom on the part of the great majority of the people, because if you work in accordance with somebody else's will, not your own will, you cannot be said to be really free. So, in a way, that was the essence of the criticism. But a revolutionary theory needed something more. This something more, which was provided partly by Marx and partly by Lenin, can be presented like this: that the state in a capitalist society was an instrument of coercion, an instrument of oppression of the have-nots by the haves, an instrument of oppression by the property owners, against those who did not own property. What the revolutionaries wanted to achieve was to seize state power on behalf of the working class, then proceed to build up socialism and eventually communism. In order to achieve that, the revolutionaries led by Lenin felt that a revolutionary party had to function in the name of and on behalf of the working class and help effect the revolution that will transfer power from the capitalist to the proletariat.

Once the revolution took place in 1917, its echoes reverberated all over the world. There were many who felt exhilarated and looked forward to the dawn of a new age, the beginnings, the foundation of a new society. This mood of hopefulness, this dream of a new society resulting from the revolution continued for a fairly long time with a fairly large number of people. It was certainly an experience not confined to any one particular country but an experience which dominated a good part of the world. We know that those hopes were not realised, that the dream was shattered, but it is good to remember that the hopes, the dream did continue for quite a long time. Why is it that the revolution failed to produce the new society that it promised? After the revolution, a powerful state did come into existence as a result of the efforts of the revolutionary leaders. The new state did represent a very high degree of centralisation of power. As the party became co-terminus with the state, the party bureaucracy and the state bureaucracy became virtually one and the new bureaucracy produced, in effect, a privileged class. And in the course of time, the new bureaucracy was no longer seen by the people as representing the people, whatever the revolutionary theorists might say. That it was not seen by the people as representing the people is today obvious. Remember that if the Soviet Union finally collapsed, it was not on account of a defeat in a war. When the Czarist power collapsed that was to an important extent connected with defeat in a war, but when the Soviet Union collapsed it was because the system was rightly or wrongly rejected by people. Some may say the people did wrong to reject it and some may say that they did right. I will say just this, let us for a moment put aside the debate about right or wrong, but why did the people reject it? Why did a whole generation born in the Soviet Union, brought up under the system, knowing the system from within, not care to preserve it but wanted to get rid of it? That happened. The fact is that after experiencing the Soviet system for a full 70 years the people of the Soviet Union did not stand up to defend the system but rejected it. It will be wrong to dismiss this as one of no significance. It must be a fact of great historic significance.

Marx saw a certain contradiction within capitalist society. Obviously a certain contradiction also developed

61

within Soviet society. This contradiction was based on the relationship between a ruling bureaucracy and a people who felt alienated from that bureaucracy. Also there was a singular lack of freedom in Soviet society. Consider a simple fact: in a capitalist society if a worker quarrels with his employer and is thrown out, he is indeed in great difficulty, but he is likely to get a job elsewhere. But in Soviet society there was only one employer, the party, controlling the state and if somebody quarrelled with that one employer he had no other employer to go to. That indicates the nature of the crisis of freedom in Soviet society. Once people got alienated from the bureaucracy, they lived in this very difficult position where they could not afford to express their dissent. They did not get out of the October Revolution the kind of regime of freedom that revolutionaries dreamed of.

So much about the first revolution, which captured the imagination of so many, but which failed to bring in a social order acceptable to the people.

Now I am going to talk to you about the second revolution which is gradually taking shape, which is of a very different kind. I will go on to briefly indicate what are the forces and circumstances that have contributed to the shaping of the consciousness of this second revolution.

It is a revolution of an entirely different character. In the first place, there was the dreadful experience which came at the end of the Second World War. After Hiroshima and Nagasaki, for the first time it became perfectly clear that man had at his disposal sufficient power to destroy the whole of civilisation. Wars there had been in the past, but no war of this kind, no war had ever ended with a warning of the possibility of total destruction. The new situation that developed forced people to think and rethink what to do in future to save human society.

Then there are other things, less dramatic in kind, but none-theless very important. These other things began to impinge on human consciousness with increasing force and effect from the early 1970s. One of these other things related to a consciousness which came to be called the 'limits to growth'. In 1972 the Club of Rome got published a report bearing the title *The Limits to Growth*. It is roughly at this time that Schumacher's book *Small Is Beautiful* also became influential. People became more acutely conscious than before of the fact that there are non-renewable resources which could get exhausted. And once these were exhausted there would be no possibility of sustainable growth which must inevitably mean an unprecedented crisis. To a certain extent, events contributed to the growth of this consciousness, events relating particularly to the supply of oil. But there was also an intellectual movement, a ferment of ideas. Then something else happened. In 1982 a group of British scientists who had gone to Antarctica discovered that the ozone layer in that region had got dangerously depleted, particularly in the month of September. There was a big hole in the ozone layer and that was something fearful. The ozone layer is a kind of shield that protects human life. Had there been no ozone layer, the infrared rays from the Sun would make human life on earth impossible. It was also discovered that the depletion of the ozone layer was not an accidental development but that it was closely connected with certain processes that were a part of what we call modern industrialism.

Now these events and facts taken together have set thinking people all over the world to ponder and consider as never before the necessity of having to either create a new social order or get reconciled to the idea of the eventual extinction of human civilisation.

The new social order which such people are thinking of today can only be ushered in a way very different from what revolutionaries had thought earlier. And some may object to calling it a revolution at all. If you have got used to the idea that revolution must mean a violent seizure of power, then this new development may not look like a revolution. I am not inventing the word revolution. The Club of Rome has brought out another report at the beginning of the decade of the 1990s, entitled *The Global Revolution*. They use the words Global Revolution to describe the kind of development which I am trying to describe. So when I use the word revolution I do not claim any originality. Second, it is indeed a revolution, since after all violence cannot be an essential feature of a revolution. The extent and character of change envisaged in human society is so great and so radical that if you use the word revolution for it, I do not think you will be doing injustice to the word. It is true that this change will take place only gradually, maybe over the next half a century. But half a century is nothing in the scale of human history.

Now I shall draw your attention to certain other basic differences between the philosophy underlying this second revolution, the new revolution, and the philosophy under-lying the earlier revolution.

The earlier revolution put stress on the conflict of interests of two opposing classes. The second revolution puts stress on the indivisibility of the interest of the whole of mankind. This does not mean that those who consider this second revolution to be of great importance do not recognise the fact that there are indeed conflicts of interests within society. There are indeed conflicts of interest within human society between different castes, classes, nations. But there is also an overarching indivisibility of interest. If there is an atomic war, the whole of the world will be destroyed. The atom bomb will not discriminatingly kill off the proletariat and protect the capitalists. It will destroy the whole of civilisation.

If environmental pollution increases to the point where human habitation on the globe is threatened, that will be a common threat to the whole of mankind. Any revolution in future, any worthwhile attempt to restructure the society in the future, must take this indivisibility of the interest of mankind as an important idea. There is also a second point to note. The new revolution attaches great value to decentralisation of power. We noticed how the earlier revolution was miscarried because it produced a new society and a new state representing totalitarian power. So the new revolution, learning its lesson from the earlier one, recognises that a free society has to and can only base itself on a system of decentralised power. These two are very important facts: recognition of the ultimate indivisibility of human interest and a recognition of the fact that a free society must also be one where there is a decentralisation of power.

Third, the new revolution is more conscious of the dangers of violence than any past ones. This is a lesson learnt not only from war but also from earlier revolutions. The October Revolution produced a society and a state where the bureaucracy and the people were set against one another. But the fact that power was seized by a violent revolution had special consequences. Once power is seized by violent revolution, those who come in power cannot get rid of the fear that others would try similarly to take away their power by violent means. The new state has this fear built into it. It looks around for possible counter-revolutions and for hidden enemies who might be conspiring to seize power. This suspicion breeds a kind of mania, a degree of irrationality and makes the system all the more oppressive. So the old idea that violence breeds violence now came to find support in new historical circumstances. These are some of the essential features of the ideas that underlie the new revolution that has started taking shape.

What does this mean in terms of the economic structure and the political structure of society? What does it mean in terms of culture? Let me tell you a few things about the economic structure of the new society and other related matters.

The economic structure of society as formed by modern industrialisation is a very centralised structure. It represents a system with a high degree of centralisation of power. We cannot get rid of this economic structure overnight. Remember that it is bound to continue for some time to come. We cannot set it aside abruptly. It would be wrong to ignore some of its compulsions. But we cannot wait for the demolition of the old structure before we start working for the new. Side by side with the existing system, the foundations will have to be laid for the alternative economic structure.

In the industrial structure we have today, there is mass production of goods for distant markets. The entire orientation of research is towards mass production. Once we decide that we want an alternative structure, it is within the capacity of human intelligence and reasoning to conduct research in that direction—for the utilisation of local resources and local labour for the satisfaction of local needs. Once human ingenuity is directed to the task of building up a decentralised economy, a good deal can be achieved in that direction. It will take time, the new social order will not come suddenly out of the dream of a revolutionary. It will have to work itself out in time. That is the only way, the only feasible way.

Redirection of research is necessary in view of the environmental problems facing us today. I talked to you about the gradual exhaustion of non-renewable resources, the threat of environmental pollution, depletion of the ozone layer and the consequences that follow from the kind of industrialism that we have become used to. Now, technology at any given time has indeed a great controlling power over human society, but it is man who creates technology and, instead of becoming a slave to technology, it must be possible for man to create a new technology so that he can move towards the ends that he rationally and freely sets for himself. This also means a reconsideration of the relationship between man and nature, a reconsideration which has both technological implications and a deeper philosophical implication.

A restructured rural economy can take care of a variety of constructive work along with greater employment much better than what is done now under the supervision of a comparatively more centralised administration. It is easy to illustrate this. A more efficient and equitable system of water management provides good example. This should lay the basis of change in the nature of agriculture, with a systematic development of organic farming, planned afforestation of relatively barren land, agro-based small-scale industrial activities supported by micro-credit facilities controlled by voluntary associations of villagers themselves and better management of public hygiene, health and population control, with an enlightened understanding of how these things are interrelated. It should be stressed that such change requires a basic transformation of our social and political structure breaking down the barriers which obstruct wide cooperation among the entire rural community.

Just as research has to be reoriented in order to achieve the new economic order, so also our system of education has to be reoriented. The system of education that we have today cannot be dismantled all of a sudden, but we can lay the foundations of a new kind of education side by side. What happens today is that we have a system of education such that the educated people in the villages are in a hurry to leave the villages and come to the city, and the educated people in the cities and their children are in a hurry to leave their country and move to the West. Now, surely, a system of education which has these consequences, bringing about this kind of brain-drain, call it whatever you like, of the educated of the villages leaving their villages for the cities and the educated of the cities leaving the less-developed countries in order to find places in the more-developed countries, is not suited to the purpose we have envisaged above. If this is what happens, what does it mean? It means that the educated voluntarily abdicate their role of leadership for building a new society. If you want education to build up a new leadership for a new society, surely there has to be a different kind of education. So when we talk of a new economic order we should simultaneously think about a re-orientation of education and research, consistent with our aims and objectives for the future.

I spoke about two revolutions—one that dominated the imagination of a large part of the world in the earlier decades of the 20th century, and the other that is gradually unfolding itself in the minds of forward-looking people today. Our vision of this new society for the future is based on a recognition of the supreme importance of peace, of decentralisation of power, of the indivisibility of the interests of the whole humanity despite local conflicts.

Based on these principles, the new society will take somewhat different forms in different parts of the world, variations suited to local circumstances. But whatever these variations, they are nonetheless part of a total vision. And those who subscribe to the movement for establishing that new society belong, so to speak, to a worldwide fraternity, loosely organised, not controlled from any centre, yet increasingly in touch with one another, increasingly conscious of the fact that they belong to the same globe and that their understanding of the nature of the global crisis, their understanding of the hopes and aspirations of mankind is basically, if not exactly, the same, yet very similar.

About the form and spirit of that new society, I spoke in terms of its economic structure. I said that there is more to be said about its political structure, its moral and cultural requirements and these are some of the things that I will try to explain in my final lecture.

I talked of some basic principles of peace, of decentralisation of power, of the indivisibility of interest of the whole of humanity—these are all interrelated. When you present a matter a little analytically, you break it up, you display the various parts. But these various parts are still parts of one whole. And it is important for us to understand how they are interrelated and how they are also connected with our diagnosis of, our understanding of the crisis of our time. Let me show this interrelatedness in political terms and how it is all connected with our understanding of the nature of our political crisis which is not simply a political crisis but a social, moral and spiritual crisis too.

Let me start with the Indian subcontinent, but again what I say will have relevance to the world as a whole. I shall come to that later. But it is better to begin at home.

Take a slightly detached yet loving view of this subcontinent. This is one of the poorest parts of the world, and in this poorest part of the world, India and Pakistan live in a state of cold war. Pakistan is ready to produce nuclear weapons as a means of defence against India. India too is ready to produce nuclear weapons in a similar way. Their armies aim to be equipped with arms of the latest technology, purchasing arms from all over the globe and also trying as best as they can to produce them at home. The condition is not much better in other parts of the subcontinent. An emergency has been declared in Sri Lanka. Bangladesh is all the time in turmoil, limping out of military dictatorship into a fragile democracy which threatens to collapse at any time.

Is it not a pity that this part of the world, with such a large population and suffering from such deep poverty, goes on spending huge sums of money for importing arms, for pro-ducing arms, for maintaining modern armies on a competi-tive basis? This is what more or less the Soviet Union and the U.S.A. were doing on the world stage till recently. But America was a much richer country and even the Soviet Union was not quite as poor as the Indian subcontinent. But that was still too heavy a burden on the Soviet Union and even in a way on the U.S.A. If that was so for U.S.S.R. and U.S.A., this must be much more so, much more tragically so for the countries of this subcontinent. And what is all this for? The production of destructive weapons! Are they for use? If they are really used then the subcontinent will be destroyed and humanity on the subcontinent will be perished. But the arms race continues.

Let us also make the optimistic assumption that the governments of India and Pakistan have some control over the use of these destructive weapons. But some of these destructive weapons are falling into the hands of groups of terrorists all over the subcontinent from Kashmir to Sri Lanka and we cannot really control them completely.

Now to try to look ahead, can this situation go on indefinitely without producing an awful tragedy for this subcontinent? That is how the question of peace presents itself on the subcontinent. I talked of the three principles, peace, indivisibility of the interests of mankind and decentralisation of power. I suggest that all these are very relevant for whoever wants to think of the future with good intentions. What can we do?

I do not think that either the government of India or the government of Pakistan can be persuaded to undertake unilateral disarmament.

I do not see the possibility of unilateral disarmament, although to some that would represent a very appealing position. It is not a position which is within the area of political feasibility. So what can be done is to move gradually towards a real accord, a peace agreement, mobilising public opinion towards pressurising the governments of these countries to move towards such an agreement and to make arrangements for the honest and fair implementation of such an agreement. This is the first step in the new direction.

But now I am going to suggest something more that may appear to some of you to be even more unrealistic, but which to me seems to be patently required and should be accepted as possible in future. What we actually have to achieve on this subcontinent is a kind of confederation under which different countries, different regions or areas will enjoy maximum possible autonomy, but the subcontinent as a whole will have one defence. Instead of there being rival armies there will be one defence for the subcontinent as a whole. This is a very rational arrangement. You may say that this rational arrangement will not be accepted because people are not rational. But you have to argue, go on arguing that in a matter like this the price of irrationality in the long run is far too heavy to contemplate with equanimity. What I am saying is not very original. From time to time others greater than me have put forward similar ideas.

I will give you an example. Soon after Pakistan was born — Pakistan in those days had two wings, the Western and the Eastern — no less a person than Khan Abdul Ghafar Khan, the Frontier Gandhi, put forward an idea that was remarkable for its spirit of love and sanity. I stress the word sanity that it represented. He put forward the idea for Pakistan. He said that in Pakistan, there were a number of cultural groups: the Pathans, the Sindhis, the Baluch people, the Punjabis and of course the Bengalis. He said that there should be a confederation for Pakistan. These different people should all enjoy a great degree of autonomy. He knew that in the natural tendency of politics, the Punjabis would dominate Pakistan, and this could only harm Pakistan. Hence he put forward the idea of a loose confederation for Pakistan. And this idea lends itself to be extended to the whole of the subcontinent. It is a feasible idea. What stands in the way are prejudices, narrow sentiments. We could indulge in prejudices and narrow sentiments in the past but as circumstances are developing today we cannot indulge in them without endangering the future of the whole of the subcontinent. So a confederation would be a political order which is in tune with the spirit of the new movement that I am talking about.

I will give you some more examples to show that it is of immense value to the world as a whole. There was the Soviet Union that has now disintegrated. What is a more rational arrangement for the future? I guess that a more rational arrangement will be not to build up the kind of Soviet Union that existed under Stalin, a Soviet Union held together by the

71

power of a monolithic party. What needs to be reconstructed, what needs to be achieved, is a confederation — of the different parts of the Soviet Union. The rest of Europe is haltingly moving towards a similar development, the idea of the European Union. What can we do in West Asia? Iraq and Iran have fought each other for generations, and the Arabs and the Israelites have been fighting. Then there are also other states in West Asia that are not at peace with one another. If you come to think of it, you can see that some kind of confederation is the best arrangement.

What can be done in Yugoslavia that is passing through a blood bath? Some people whose ideas cannot free themselves of the past try to recreate a centralised authority. But that will not work. Again, what we need would be a kind of decentralised political structure.

I have given you simply a few instances, a few cases as illustrations. There was a time when big empires grew up and different parts of the empire were held together by the might of armies. In the new age, there can be no place for big empires held together by the might of armies. In different parts of the world, in tune with the circumstances of each part it would be necessary to have a different political structure, of a much more decentralised kind.

I have said this to show how the questions of peace and decentralisation of power are interconnected. In all these cases, if you have a sense of the indivisibility of the interests of the whole region concerned then you can see that a rational solution to the crisis can only be achieved by some kind of a decentralised order, dedicated to the principle of peace, basically for the interests of the survival of the people if not for any higher ideals.

Now confederation is of course a step in the direction of decentralisation of power. But it is also evident that, politically, we have to move much further in the decentralisation of power. You can have a confederation and yet in each part of the confederation, there can be a high degree of centralised authority. We have to go beyond that. We have now started thinking of rural self-government, of democracy at the root and of power to be decentralised at the village level. So this will be a further step, a necessary step.

I talked to you of the kind of economic structure that we need. There is the economic structure that we have inherited from the past, which, as I said, will continue for quite some time to come in the future. But we have to lay the foundations for and build up a decentralised economic structure and decentralised political power down to the village level as a necessary complement. If we are to build our economy in such a way that a good deal of productive activities are organised at the base with local resources for satisfying local needs, then planning will also have to start from the base. You cannot have that kind of economic order with a plan that is handed down from above. This is a point which is self-evident, that the kind of economic decentralisation that I am talking about requires, as a necessary complement, a kind of matching political decentralisation. Whoever wants the one should want the other.

We talk of panchayats today, of *Panchayat Raj*. It is a good idea but there are still many hurdles. The hurdles are of different kinds in different areas. I come from West Bengal, where these panchayats are to a very great extent controlled by political parties. That is a hurdle.

In other parts of India, the hurdles are sometimes of a somewhat different kind. This is what we have to understand and we have to work on the basis of that understanding, that if we want village *swaraj* or democracy at the base, then it should be something genuine. If the panchayats are controlled by political parties, it is not genuine decentralisation because these political parties are in the final analysis interested in power at the centre, power as higher up as possible, and panchayats under their control are used to achieve this end. That is a political game.

73

What we need to build at the base is something quite different and yet in a way guided by the same principles that I spelt out earlier. Within a village or a block, there has again to be a realisation that despite conflict of sectional and caste interests there is also something like an indivisibility of interest for the village or block as a whole. It is not that these caste and communal conflicts are not rooted in reality. We cannot be blind to that reality; we must take account of this reality and, to the extent that they express the protest against real injustice, we have to organise movements to remove that injustice.

But as in the world as a whole, so also in the village, and even for that matter even in a family, there is such a thing as the indivisibility of the interest of the world, of the village and of the family and if we lose sight of that totally then we cannot really achieve our goal. We have to try to achieve something which in principle Gandhiji never tired of enunciating very clearly. He put forward the method of *satyagraha* which is a method of struggle against injustice. *Satyagraha* believes both in peace and in struggle, not in capitulating to injustice. It tries to suggest a method of struggle against injustice which is consistent with the need for peace and an appreciation of the indivisibility of the interests of men and women all over the country. So when we talk of the political structure, as in the case of the economic structure, these same ideas must guide us — peace, decentralisation of power and an appreciation of the fundamental unity, the indivisibility of the interests of all concerned.

Along with this will also come about a fundamental change in the relationship between man and nature. If we once accept the idea that the pursuit of power, of one nation over another, of one caste over another, of one class over another, is not the right pursuit, we begin to see that it is indeed linked up with a wrong philosophy of life. And even in the relationship between man and nature, you will see that the same idea holds. It is not a question of man demonstrating his dominion over nature, his power over nature, but man demonstrating his feeling of organic unity with nature and the whole of the universe. We cannot in philosophy adopt an attitude of a preference for dominion, and in actual life achieve peace. That cannot happen. If we want peace, that must be a principle that will inform both our social organisations and our philosophy of life.

That takes me on to my next point. Between the two revolutions mentioned earlier, there is a very interesting difference in our perception of human nature. Most of those who put their faith in the earlier revolution believed that if only we can reorganise social institutions, human nature will be cured of all its ills; that whatever is bad in human nature is due to defective institutions; that the chief task is to build up new institutions. That was too simplistic a view to take. It was believed that after the revolution, after the socialist society is built up, a new man will be created; human nature will be recreated. Nothing of the kind has truly happened within our experience. The hypothesis that there is a set of institutions that can finally and fundamentally uplift the whole of human nature remains an uncorroborated hypothesis. I do not mean that institutions are unimportant. Institutions are very important indeed. Had I not attached importance to institutions, I would not have talked at such length about economic and political structures because these are all institutional questions. But let us get rid of the notion that institutions are primary and human nature secondary, that there is a possible set of institutions that will solve the problem of all that is wicked in human nature.

To achieve and uplift human nature is a task in itself. Just as it is an important task to achieve the structure, economic and political, of a new society, side by side there must also be this attempt to create a new man who accepts genuinely the higher values of life. The perception and acceptance of these higher values of life is not something that can be left to come about automatically once a revolution has taken place and once forms of ownership have been changed or new institutions have been built up. That is a wrong idea. We have to pay attention to the whole question of a moral and philosophical revolution as part of the attempt to uplift human nature. The cynic will again observe that this cannot be achieved. There is nothing to be gained by that kind of cynicism. In the face of a crisis, we have to try as best as we can, and even if we cannot achieve as much as we want, we should be able to say that we did try. So this is something which should be seriously considered and attempted.

Connected with this is another fundamental question, namely what constitutes true human happiness? Our in-dustrial civilisation has helped propagate some wrong ideas about that. It is true that poverty is a curse and every attempt should be made to remove poverty and to satisfy the basic needs of man. But beyond the satisfaction of basic needs, it is not true that happiness depends on the ever-increasing satisfaction of ever-increasing wants. The fashionable idea today is that happiness depends on the ever-increasing satis-faction of ever-increasing wants by articles newly produced and then rejected for still other newer articles. This idea did seem very defensible and this was in fact the motive force behind the material progress of society. It is possible that this idea did play a certain role in a particular phase of history. It is possible that it has to play a limited role in certain spheres even today. But by and large, this is an idea that needs to be re-examined and I suggest it is an idea that needs to be rejected.

Beyond the satisfaction of basic needs, happiness depends not on the gratification of sensual desires, but on a liberating feeling of union with something larger than the self. And that feeling of something larger than yourself should itself be such that it helps you again to take in something even larger and wider. This is the idea which tells you that a feeling of union with nature and the universe is good in itself. It is a requirement for a sane humanity, not simply for a model man, but even for a reasonably happy man. For, what is the alternative? The alternative is that you get addicted to certain material devices for gaining pleasure, and it is in the nature of such addiction that after a point those material devices do not yield real pleasure. But any attempt to move away from those devices produces pain. That is the law of addiction.

A philosophy teaches us that it is realistic, rational and materialistic to believe that sensual pleasures are the stuff of reality and that the more you satisfy the senses with material things the more happy you are. Such a philosophy finally produces one kind of bondage or another, in the form of addiction and violence. And this is what is happening all over the world. You cannot simply remove this by restructuring institutions, you can remove it only by an inner realisation of the whole question of what constitutes inner freedom and human happiness.

These are some of the things that we need in order to move towards a new society. I have told you something about an economic structure, a political structure, and the new culture, the new philosophy of life that we require. All these things are interrelated. They have to go together.

A movement in that direction has already started both in rich countries and in poor countries. Even in rich countries, an increasing number of young people are disenchanted and unhappy. When Mother Teresa visited the U.S.A., there were young women who started weeping going close to her, weeping their hearts out, and what is done publicly is done a thousand times privately. So, in a sense, a new movement of the spirit and of social reconstruction has already started. There are hurdles, obstacles in the way and no doubt progress will be halting. Nonetheless, there is no alternative but to press on.

The influence of the first revolution was to a great extent a negative influence. As I tried to show you, the fundamental principles and axioms of, the new revolution are very different from, in fact are the opposite of, the principles of the first revolution. The first emphasised the irreducible conflict of interests. The first revolution was materialistic in a crude sense. It achieved a highly centralised society, militaristic, with a militarism that took pride in announcing that it represented the army of the proletariat. But armies create their own vested interests and it is the proletariat who suffers. The second revolution is of a different kind. It starts with a different orientation. In some ways, it is perhaps less dramatic and yet in its vision, in its implications for the future of man, it is so extensive, I might say, so profound, that it is a revolution of great value.

I come from West Bengal where the influence of the spirit and philosophy of the first revolution has been very strong among people for a long time. I do not expect the people of West Bengal to show the way in the second revolution. When Gokhale said 'what Bengal thinks today the rest of India thinks tomorrow', he was talking from his experience of another age. I guess that for the second revolution, really significant leaders are being produced more in Maharashtra than in West Bengal. Nor do we have to look to India alone. We can look out towards other countries, other seminal thinkers and other significant activists. I know that there is no guarantee that the new revolution will succeed. I also know that you have to hope for success, because unless you hope you cannot try.

10

New Perspectives of
Economic Development

The first half of the 20th century saw two world wars. After the wars, the defence expenditure has become higher than before and has gone hand in hand with a high tide of consumerism. Examples from distant past convey this message to modern policy makers: a large defence expenditure represents a high level of unproductive investment. Together with a high propensity to consume, it creates an imbalance in national economy that results in inflation, budgetary deficit and adverse balance of payments even for richer countries. For poorer countries the distress can be more acute.

It is arguable that the same circumstances also provide an impetus to growth. The second half of the 20th century saw a remarkable growth in world economy. This was due to a technological revolution derived largely from defence-oriented research, and it continues to dominate even today. But that economic growth was marked with signs of instability due to various reasons. And now is a suitable time for development economists to look before and after and arrive at an understanding of the nature of sustainable growth for the future. They should include matters pertaining to a number of allied disciplines along with and beyond economics.

Humanity has now arrived at a stage when improving the quality of life of common people, and not defence-oriented research, will provide a reliable roadmap for the way ahead.

However, development planning in the Third World is controlled by a concern for a high rate of growth of national income. This will enable the government to collect a large revenue, thus making it possible to sanction larger public outlays on the infrastructure for economic and social development. Moreover, a high rate of growth will generate more jobs and so reduce unemployment and poverty. This reasoning has much appeal, but is slow and incomplete. A system of political economy rooted in the Bismarckian tradition helps a nation achieve both power and prominence in human resource development. Market-driven 'socialism' accepts this new orientation of economics but is incapable of achieving a breakthrough from the evolutionary impasse, which the world economic order has reached today. A closely related point should also be noted here. Some patterns of neighbourhood community relationship play a protective role in society. When an indefinite extension of the commercial spirit tears apart this protective cover, a trained human psyche takes fearful revenge.

Neither the market system nor the methods of economic analysis that have evolved along with it is fated to disappear suddenly. Nor do they deserve such a fate. But as surely as these will endure, efforts will be equally in place to lay the foundations of an alternative economic order. There was never a dearth of people, notably non-economists, pleading for an environment-friendly economy. Now we have professional economists, led mortally by Schumacher, who express themselves in a similar vein. Moreover, organised efforts to project this alternative vision of the future are increasingly in evidence. Reference may be made to The Other Economic Summit (TOES) and, closely related to that summit, James Robertson's book, *Future Wealth, A New Economics for the Twentyfirst Century*.

As yet the alternative economic order has managed to get no more than a slender toehold, and its exponents do not command a wide hearing in academic circles. But they deserve wider attention which, it is to be hoped, they will receive.

In the work just cited, James Robertson writes, 'This book is about creating an economy for the sane, humane, ecological (SHE) future, as opposed to the hyper-expansionist (HE) future.' He pleads for 'a multilevel one-world economy'. The qualifying word, 'multilevel', deserves special attention as it discards the idea of a ruthless globalisation reducing the whole world to the flatness of a single market. Describing a key feature of the model 21st century economy, Robertson (1990: 13) explains, 'Instead of systematically creating and extending dependency, it must systematically foster self-reliance and the capacity for self-development... self-development includes the capacity for cooperative self-reliance.'

More emphatically, he observes, 'conventional macro-economic thinking and conventional national economic policy-making are now the biggest obstacles to the emergence of an enabling and conserving multilevel one world economy' (Robertson 1990: 53). What we need is not a uniform global economy, but a multiform world order, with local autonomous associations at the base, regional unions at an intermediate level and a qualified globalisation consistent with this multiformity.

This runs counter to much of what is happening in own time. A process of centralisation of power has been persistently at work in contemporary history. In the world of economics, the centralising tendency is manifested through the growth of monopolies. In the political domain, one observes a notable increase in the power of the state. It is believed that this is necessary for national power which in turn is required for political survival. Is it safe to let this line of reasoning go unchallenged? Are not nation states, competing for military power in the name of self-defence, leading the world tragically towards collective suicide? Even if this extreme outcome is avoided, the consequences of an unrelenting competition for power are appalling enough to require of us to pause and ponder. Centralisation of power creates and continually strengthens a 'new class' seperated from the common people. Ascendancy of this class coincides with a process of devitalisation of culture at the base. People do live longer, a loveless life made endurable by purchasable stimuli and the excitement of negative feelings. Circulation is threatened by organised fanaticism. Struck by terrorist attacks, those who hold power know nothing better than to seek comfort in watching an indiscriminate butchery of presumed enemies by all the more organised and scientifically executed terror. Where do we go from here? It will be unrealistic to expect the new class to disappear or the existing order to be dismantled all of a sudden. But it will be equally unreasonable to expect from this order of things an assurance of ultimate safety for the world. The only realistic course is to start building the foundations of a new order even today without waiting for the existing order to collapse totally. In the Indian context, *Sarvodaya* and a broad humanism provide the cardinal principles of the return-of-the-mill alternative social order.

It is possible to approach the same conclusion by other routes closer to economic reasoning. Let us elucidate. Some of the developed countries of the modern world passed through their phase of industrial transition in the 19th century. Now, there are important differences between that earlier phase of transition and the situation in which the developing economies find themselves today. The West in that earlier phase did not have to face the same kind of pressure of population on land for some simple reasons. The surplus population of the West could migrate to the so-called New World in the Americas, Australia and elsewhere, where there was plenty of empty land. Also the demographic situations then and now are quite dissimilar. The West in that crucial phase of industrial transition was not struck by anything equivalent to the 'population explosion' that we find in the

Third World in contemporary times. Add the fact that the state-of-the art techniques of production today are more labour-saving than those that prevailed in the earlier period. In the poorer, larger and more populous countries of the world today, even though the 'formal' sector is expanding fairly rapidly, it will be unsafe to take it for granted on the analogy of the West that the urban centres can accommodate and productively absorb the excess labour of the countryside. There is not much time to lose. The political implications of the large and persistent semi-literate underemployment in our times are very different from poverty and unemployment in the 19th century, thanks to the spread of democratic ideas in the intervening period, the heightened consciousness of human rights and the information revolution, which fuels the explosion of defeated expectations while weapons of terror and destruction pass increasingly into the hands of the aggrieved and the dispossessed. The simple version of globalisation, which looks appealing and logical to developed countries seeking a vent for surplus capital, is grievously inadequate to meet the needs of this complex situation. Outsourcing can hopefully create some jobs for a literate section of the below force in the Third World. But where is the hope for the rural poor and the unemployed whom the cities both attract and spurn?

Advocates of grassroots democracy at the village level, cooperative and self-reliant, have often been dismissed as ineffectual romantics. Yet such rural communities possess certain features which strongly qualify them as a major con-stituent of an alternative and sustainable economic order. For one thing, they provide a model of rural development in which labour can be productively employed nearer home and so reduce the pressure on the cities. For another, they hold up a way of life hopefully free of that self-alienation which lies at the root of the gravest ills of modern civilisation. Quietly, the stream of industrial development is fending its course in a new direction. There are signs that we are approaching a turning point in economic history. The time has come when we can look forward to an increasing adoption of an alternative source of energy, safe and clean, as the basis of a new technology tragically different from the forces of production which dominated the past. A new technology of such great consequences will demand new social relations. Without a reorientation of habits of thought, such a change in social relations cannot take effect and a crisis becomes inevitable. The perspectives of economic development in the 21st century should be set by the nature of the deepening global crisis in the present age. Political economy must learn to pay attention to these inescapable secular compulsions and frame its message accordingly. A peace movement is a *sine qua non* of this new orientation. Economists can help by explaining the costs of war. The gap between the Third and the First Worlds must get narrower. But this should happen not by the developing countries imitating the richer nations, but by the whole world moving towards an alternative economic order and a new concept of development.

Reference

Robertson, J. 1990. *Future Wealth: A New Economics for the Twentyfirst Century.* London: Cassell.

11

Democracy, Rural Reconstruction and Humanism

We live in uncertain times and look towards the future with mixed feelings of hope and fear. When we try to figure out the possible shape of things in the years ahead, a few special areas of concern and urgent questions, sometimes with ancient roots yet with deep contemporary relevance, claim our earnest attention. Each of them deserves separate treatment, but they are so intimately interrelated that there is something to be gained by taking them up together for a rapid review.

The functioning of India's democracy provides at this moment a major area of concern. It is not always fully understood that our experiment with the parliamentary form of government is truly extraordinary in some ways. No other country with as large and diverse a population, as economically handicapped and educationally limited as ours, ever entrusted its future to representative government based on adult suffrage. At the dawn of Independence, with the subcontinent bleeding from a cruel and devastating partition, our leaders put their faith in the people of India to hold the country together and carry out programmes of economic and social development. That was extraordinary and yet it was a wise decision. We have to try and understand the grounds of its rationality.

A distinctive feature of the society and culture of India is its incomparable diversity. There are a number of other countries which are physically much larger in size. Our great neighbour, China, has an even bigger population spread over a more extensive territory. But in terms of language and religion, not to mention other cultural divisions, India has an unquestionably more pluralistic society. Maoism gave rise to a totalitarian political system which China's more homogeneous society was ready to experiment with. Aided by a talent for orderliness and executive efficiency, qualities with which China has an advantage over us in the same way as Germany has had over Italy, it is now close to attaining the status of an acclaimed superpower, a dubious distinction that her leaders have long craved for. This is not a route that India could have taken even if she wanted to. Those of our leaders who are drawn in that direction are likely to do more harm than good.

The straitjacket of totalitarianism would be too cramping for India's invincible diversity. A dictator from the north would not be long tolerated by Tamils in the south, while southern hegemony over the north is unthinkable. Any serious attempt to impose a totalitarian political system in India would lead to an endless civil war, inflicting a tragic setback to all decent hopes for the future. Leaders like Jawaharlal Nehru had, therefore, good reasons for adopting a democratic constitution when the British left. For one thing, it appeared to offer the best way of avoiding Balkanisation, in other words, further fragmentation of an already partitioned subcontinent. There were other considerations too. Peace and development were high up on the agenda of independent India. It is a cardinal virtue of democracy that it aims to provide peaceful methods of social change and development. Moreover, certain liberal values are an essential part of the idea of freedom as understood by the finest minds among our leaders and these values require the support of a democratic form of government. Political democracy is not all that one wants, but it provides a framework within which both constructive activities and movements of protest against the established order can hope to find their rightful place for a brighter and more secure future under conditions of freedom.

We have recounted briefly the benefits of democracy as a precaution against complacency as well as misconceived criticism. Our society suffers from many maladies and shortcomings. These have to be removed through the organised initiative of the people. Democracy provides a system of rights and duties under which people's initiative can be effectively organised. This, of course, has its risks, so we have to be wakeful. It is not uncommon for the democratic system itself to come under attack and for people not to take sufficient notice until it is very late. There are cases of this happening with tragic consequences. A wise maxim has been extracted from that recurrent experience. Eternal vigilance, it has been said, is the price of liberty. It is time for India to take notice.

We are not talking of distant possibilities. Representative government is already under attack in the world's largest democracy. The assault comes in diverse ways. Intolerance based on religious faith presents a specially acute problem which will be discussed later. There are other less advertised threats to democracy with serious consequences which should not be ignored. Let us consider, for example, the half concealed threat to democracy in a state which has stood out in recent years as an example of political stability. Appearances though can be misleading.

West Bengal has gained an unenviable reputation for 'scientific rigging' of elections. The police, the administration, party cadres and criminals combine to do the rigging, demonstrating a capacity for elaborate cooperation which would have rightly evoked admiration had it been employed for a higher purpose. The longest serving chief minister in India reportedly appealed to the police to help his party capture power once more in the coming elections. Another very important person, himself a minister, thought fit to declare in public that his party had all along the past few decades taken care to enlist support of bogus voters. Such bold truthfulness is rare indeed, but it is mixed with an arrogance which bodes ill for the future of democracy. It is time to pause and consider the consequences of the murder of fair elections.

Democracy even with fair elections does not ensure that the best party will always win. But it does permit the people to experiment freely, to judge a party by its performance and throw it out if it is found wanting. The people of Bihar have thrown out the redoubtable Lalu Prasad Yadav and given Nitish Kumar a chance to prove his worth, with the assurance that he too will be judged by his performance. Conceding that human judgment is never infallible, it is important to leave the way open for peaceful change. This is what fair elections and other democratic rules and conventions taken collectively are expected to assure. When this expectation is killed, fear and desperation take over. Prompted by fear, some assume a posture of habitual subservience to the powers that be; driven by desperation, others secretly or even openly organise themselves for a violent conflict. The country slides towards civil war.

This is the meaning of the resurgence of Maoism in extensive areas of the country. Maoism cannot achieve in India what it has done in China. But it cannot be suppressed by simply meeting violence with violence. The party in power need not abdicate without a fight. But it has to make it patent that it rules with the free consent of the people and that it does not put its lust for power above all considerations of fair play and honest contest. It cannot do so by putting on display a blatant disregard for the rules and spirit of democracy. Such calculated cynicism can only hasten the march towards ultimate disaster. As things are shaping; democracy remains the alternative to civil war. But it has to be honest democracy. Although it is important to have fair elections, democracy is not simply concerned with electoral rules. It has to go deeper, that is to say, nearer to the roots of human association.

Maoism should be thanked for drawing attention to the rural problems in India. Since independence, the country has been ruled by an elite of which the leading component is an urban educated middle class which dominates the administration besides planning the policy of the state. The resultant bias in the development pattern of the country is there for all to see. India produces a superabundance of people trained for urban professions, of which a good number migrates abroad, while rural illiteracy stays on obstinately as a curse on our land. It is time to recognise that this imbalance has done great harm not only to our villages but also to the cities. The path to the city runs through villages. It is just not possible to create healthy cities surrounded by sick villages.

Let us pause briefly and try to understand the nature of the problem. The surplus generated in the agricultural sector provides a basis for industrial growth. This sectoral interdependence provides a theme which can be conveniently used to build models of growth dear to economists. We will adopt here a different approach which starts with rural under-employment and takes us closer to the heart of the Indian problem. Insufficient opportunities for productive work in the countryside push the rural poor to move to the city in search of jobs. But the city itself has a limited capacity to absorb surplus rural labour of which the supply is unending, thanks to rapid growth of population. Consequently, those who fail to get absorbed in productive occupations in the city are forced to choose between begging and anti-social activities. Thus, rural poverty makes the city sick and the sick culture of the city makes the countryside sicker.

The West, in the critical phase of its industrial development, found an outlet for its surplus population in the 'New World' with its abundant space and the newly conquered colonies in the Old World. Such outlets are unavailable to the industrially less developed countries today. India can export its skilled labour abroad. But surely our problem cannot be solved by simply assisting the outflow of our trained manpower. Part of this migrant manpower has already started flowing back to centres of development in urban India. That still leaves unanswered the very important question concerning the fate of the poor and the underemployed in the rural areas. Only a fraction of our rural poor can be accommodated in the cities within the limits of reasonable and tolerable time horizons. There is no alternative to rural development. In India this has to be so designed that a great majority of villagers get opportunities for productive work and decent livelihood without getting uprooted from their community.

We have to move towards that goal with a certain amount of clarity of vision and all possible speed, for time is running out. Let us think out what is strictly necessary and what is not for reaching the goal we have proposed. It will be fanatical to maintain that there is just one correct model of rural development. What is best depends on an interaction between ideals and local conditions. Past experience suggests that a flexible approach is often wiser and socially less costly. Generally speaking, family farming is a good basis for agriculture and collective farming is not strictly required except under special conditions. Granted, family farming, cooperation among different families must also find a prominent place at the village level for a variety of purposes. Let us illustrate. Scarcity of water is a problem in many villages and the remedy lies in arrangements for storage of water at the ground level. Proper storage, distribution and utilisation of water require careful cooperation at the community level. This again strengthens the argument for land reforms. Extreme inequality in the rural community acts as an obstacle to cooperation. This is just an example. Agriculture cannot be the sole basis of rural development if we are aiming at productive work for all concerned. There are other activities connected with credit and small-scale industry, forestry, horticulture and pisciculture, education

90

and primary health care, without which rural development remains incomplete. All these call for diverse forms
of cooperation among villagers. What is required then is a
broad-based programme of economic, cultural and social reconstruction. There are some who are already engaged in
such activities, building up people's alliance for reconstructing the countryside, sowing hope where there was
despair. They are the pathfinders of a new India, an India
with a future.

In carrying out these diverse activities in a spirit of local
self-help, there is no reason for rejecting all outside assistance.
But it has to be a programme of rural reconstruction in the
true spirit of democracy, in other words, for the villagers, of
the villagers and by the villagers. 'Radical' democracy means
people's self-government starting from the roots. Consistent
with this approach, people must learn cautiously to reject
excessive dependence on the state or any centralised authority
for gaining their basic objectives. From here we are led on to
a more fundamental yet practical question. Does democracy
at the village level have to be guided by the same rules and
conventions as in the city? There is really no reason why this
must be so. Some critics have blamed us for a mechanical
imitation of the Westminster model which has been strongly
influenced by the spirit and circumstances of a market
economy. The rural community may accept the highest ideals
of democracy and reincarnate them in a new form to suit its
own vital needs. What are these ideals? Democracy, as we
noted earlier, provides a peaceful method of social change. It
also stands for the right to freedom of conscience and freedom
of speech, ideals which we must cherish and preserve as best
as we can.

Organised competition and struggle for capture of power,
along with the disregard for ethical norms that these have
generated, are not part of the cherished heritage of humanity.
Some of the finest political thinkers of modern India, with
unquestionable dedication to the ideal of human freedom,

such as M.K. Gandhi, M.N. Roy and Jayaprakash Narayan, disagreed among themselves on many issues, yet agreed in their ripe old age to recommend 'partyless democracy'. Gandhi Vichar Parishad and other likeminded organisations are actively engaged in propounding and practising that innovative idea. There may be something to learn from them in making our villages safe for democracy. It is a great pity that so many of our villages have passed under a veritable reign of terror in the name of that democracy which purports to show the path of peaceful change.

The spirit of partyless democracy must precede and dictate its form. The question is not about the right to freedom of association which should stay, but its assigned role in the political organisation of society and the moral life of the citizen. The citizen must feel that his dignity as an individual demands that his allegiance to any party should only take second place to his loyalty to truth and the basic principles of public morality.

The debate on partyless democracy will take time to get resolved. Less debatable, there are other areas of concern which deserve immediate attention. Once we put faith in the power of people's cooperation, we find ourselves morally committed to a radical reconstruction of society. Traditional society has got used to barriers to cooperation in diverse forms which are unacceptable to reason and palpably harmful. Such, for instance, are caste barriers and the spirit of sectarianism or what in common parlance in India we call 'communalism'. Humanism, properly understood, is a revolt against these barriers and defects of vision which prevent mankind from comprehending its essential unity. As these barriers are rooted in and even sanctified by tradition, the spirit of humanism directs us to undertake a reasoned reappraisal of religion as actually practised in our society.

While the last century was dominated by a prolonged conflict of ideologies, the world today is in the grip of what has been called a 'clash of civilisations' fuelled by religious fanaticism. Yesterday, the great debate centred on the choice between democracy and totalitarianism. Today, the need for reconciliation between religious faiths has come to be inscribed on the agenda of history as a matter of major importance for the future of mankind. In other words, the leading task for our age is to clarify and put into practice the principles of cultural reconstruction which will make possible a creative and peaceful coexistence of different religious faiths. Faced with this situation, some earnest souls are content to declare that at the highest level all religions have an identical message.

This idea of the essential identity of all religions cannot cover up the fact that the great religions of the world have had different histories and have come to be marked by peculiar distinctions and distortions arising out of those temporal circumstances. Sickness of the mind is easier to cure when the patient himself understands its material causes. In a similar way, a clear awareness of the historically caused perversions of religion can guide and assist the purification of tradition.

Consider, for example, the cases of Islam and Hinduism. It is well known that the life of the Prophet of Islam falls broadly into two phases. In the early part, he was still a resident of Mecca, the place of his birth, where the great majority of people in power was basically idol worshippers and strongly opposed to the message of Islam. Prophet Muhammad's early followers were cruelly persecuted by the dominant tribes, so much so that they had to flee Mecca for fear of life. The second momentous phase of the Prophet's career started after he migrated to Medina in search of security. Even after he had established himself strongly in Medina, his Meccan opponents tried repeatedly yet unsuccessfully to destroy him and his followers. In this context of war, the Prophet's message combined firmness with clemency. Followers of Islam are clearly told that Allah disapproves of aggression, but when Islam is under attack, it is the duty of the faithful to fight back with all possible strength and determination. Once the attack ceases, Allah recommends forgiveness. Looking back, it appears that the Islamic consciousness has been burdened from its early years with an unfortunate historic legacy, further aggravated in recent times by new circumstances. Among Muslims spread over diverse lands, there are many streams of thought, some of which like the Bahai carry the spirit of brotherhood and the light of the spirit beyond all narrow limits. But there are the hard core conservatives, with formidable strength and influence, who strongly reject these liberal trends and feel that Islam is never safe until it captures political power and combines it with strict religious authority. Drawing inspiration from an earlier expensive phase, some fanatical followers of the faith continue to believe that Islam is destined to conquer the whole world sooner or later. The spirit of Islam has to be purged of this historically acquired paranoiac strain before it can truly fulfil that mission of peace which its name itself proclaims.

Hinduism under attack has typically reacted in a manner which stands in strong contrast with the Islamic response. Faced with a threat of aggression or encroachment by outsiders, the Hindu mind has far too often sought security in withdrawal inwards. This has resulted in a social formation with strong segregationist features. The Hindu consciousness, in its conservative Brahminical variant, is tainted with the spirit of apartheid, the upper castes anxious to protect their purity by maintaining ritually prescribed distance from others lower down. The traditional Hindu has got so used to this negative code of conduct that he practises it without much thought and often sees nothing wrong in it. He refuses to recognise that it amounts to a callous rejection of the idea of coexistence with one's neighbours on terms of equal dignity for all men.

True, there have been protests against this narrow and discriminatory creed from within the Hindu faith itself, notably in the form of the Bhakti movement which proclaims pure love as the essence of true spirituality. However, this movement has had only limited influence in traditional Hindu society.

It is only fair to note that other religions can equally well be submitted to a similar historical scrutiny. The perversion of Christianity under the influence of imperialism from the time of ancient Rome to modern America is there as a stern reminder of the corruptibility of all faiths.

Let us now move beyond specific case histories and consider in a more general way the question of religion and its reform for the advancement of human freedom. Criticism of religion, Marx insightfully observed, is the beginning of all criticism. There is, however, a lack of clarity about the scope and nature of that criticism. It is unquestionable that religion requires to be purged of superstitions. As far as that is concerned, a secular and rationalist approach can be confidently recommended and deemed to be adequate. However, superstitions are not the only obstacles to the progressive realisation of human freedom. Narrow collective loyalty presents a particularly stubborn problem and secularism does not show here an easy and assured way out. For instance, Stalinists were and, to the extent they have survived, continue to be secular. But they are fiercely loyal to the party to which they belong and also to the nation as long as they are in power. It is not easy to lift people above narrow sectarianism and it is doubtful if they can be inspired with active human compassion by the force of reason alone. The rational faculty acts, more often than not, as an instrument of a distinctly circumscribed self-interest following the normal bent of the heart. Beyond that, one talks of that 'change of heart' which reason accepts when it happens but cannot itself readily produce. As we pursue this question, we are led farther afield.

Religion is concerned with the idea of the place of the individual in the universe. Here too there are riddles and ambiguities which challenge reason and invite the spirit of man to

cross the limits of prudence. Reason, as we normally understand, is 'this worldly'. Practical reason tends to be concerned
with the readily recognisable interests of the individual in the
only life, limited in time and space, that he can call his own.
However, man at his highest is ever so often overstepping
these limits. A person who risks his own life to save others or
in the service of an ideal which he does not expect to see
materialised in the foreseeable future is, in fact, deeply interested in a life which lies beyond the bounds of his own time
and in goods which he cannot directly share. Thus, reason has
a choice between two kinds and visions of life of which one is
directly accessible to the senses and the other 'transcendental',
available to contemplation.

This being the human condition, it is only natural that
there are alternative versions of humanism. One of these is
anxious to stress its materialistic roots; another, its spiritual
aspirations. Sometimes they view each other with misgivings.
Yet the really important contest lies not between different
camps of humanism, but between the essence of humanism
beyond distinctions of race and local cultures and that narrow
sectarianism which contradicts the idea of human unity.

We have purposely put three different themes — the problem of democracy, the question of rural reconstruction and
the dialogue between religion and humanism — all within
the compass of a single discourse. While the philosophy of
humanism is important enough to deserve separate consideration, it runs the risk of losing its vitality and effectiveness
unless it is carefully linked up with practice. Its practice
itself can take up many forms, rural reconstruction being a
principal form particularly in the Third World and, therefore,
in the world considered as a whole. It is not accidental that
both Gandhi and Tagore, despite their known differences,
accepted rural uplift as a major area of activity in the service of mankind. Sevagram and Sriniketan have a common
message. In the mottoes that Gandhi and Tagore chose for
their institutions, there was a striking similarity. It is clear

that the programmes of social reconstruction which they initiated were varying expressions of a common humanist mission. Democracy provides in our time the political framework within which the humanist mission can hope to move forward.

The form of democracy — radical democracy if we choose to call it so — should be determined by the practical requirements of the ideal of human freedom struggling to realise itself at different levels of society under varying circumstances. Within this broad movement, there should be space for a variety of people, such as writers, artists and social activists. Most of us can be active only in a limited area suiting our special abilities. But we need a shared vision of a future world to integrate these multifarious activities and give them a common direction. In its essence, this is a non-sectarian movement, patient yet persistent, towards a higher form of human civilisation, more rational and more compassionate than what we have today.

12

Higher Education in India: A Dilemma

Anybody who starts seriously meditating on the aims and objectives of our universities finds himself, sooner or later, confronted with a dilemma. Let me briefly explain the nature of that dilemma.

The advancement of learning is a principal aim of higher education. Modern science has developed through a process of visible and invisible cooperation of scientists all over the world. The frontiers of knowledge are widening all the time. Every country has to try and keep abreast of this continuous march of knowledge. Universities have a special responsibility here. We cannot let the standards of our universities decline without serious risk of falling behind the rest of the world.

Let me, for the sake of emphasis, restate the point. While models of trade are based on the principle of competition, the cultivation of knowledge, particularly modern science, provides a leading example, nationalist rivalries notwith-standing, of creative cooperation among researchers all over the world as seekers of truth dedicated to a common cause. A university hardly deserves its name unless it includes among its highest aims the spirit as well as suitable forms of participation in this common quest for universal knowledge. But such participation is only possible if and to the extent that a university maintains certain standards of quality of teaching and research and facilities for free and purposeful interaction.

Judging by this standard, most Indian universities will be found wanting. They do not function adequately at the expanding frontiers of world knowledge. The very idea seems alien to them.

But let us be realistic. Even in a country as prosperous as the U.S.A., there are not many universities of the same standard as Harvard, Princeton or Yale. Not all universities in the Soviet Union had the same eminence as the University of Moscow. In India, it will be entirely unrealistic to expect all or most universities to reach the academic standards of the best in the world. The question is whether we should have at least a few which come up to those standards. The elite in India are not seriously handicapped by the absence of such universities within the country; they can afford to send their sons and daughters abroad. In the process, the 'brain-drain' gets uncontrollable.

There is, therefore, a good case for fostering at least a few centres of academic excellence within the boundaries of this country comparable with leading universities abroad. But this inevitably raises a number of questions. It is impossible to ignore them. Indeed, they deserve serious attention. There are diverse demands, global and local, to be reconciled. We have to grasp the nature of the problem before we can respond to it purposefully.

We can start with a simple question. Granted that only a few universities and faculties can operate effectively at the frontiers of knowledge, what should be the common functions and essential features of all universities in India? The answer to that question is, at least in part, uncomplicated.

To produce enlightened citizens must be a common task of all our universities. India is reputed to be the world's largest democracy. The quality of a democracy depends — to no small extent — on the quality of its educated citizens. Education should foster a liberal and scientific outlook. Indian society is divided into castes, clans and communities.

There is, therefore, a continuous risk of long-term interests of the people being sacrificed under the influence of too narrow loyalties and destructive passions. It is one of the responsibilities of Indian universities, wherever they are, to contribute towards the creation of that broad, tolerant and forward-looking culture in which a country as heterogeneous as India can function harmoniously and with an active concern for the common good.

This is not an easy task and it is by no means clear that our universities have addressed themselves to it with much success. Rather, in the contrary, higher education has generated a new division within our society. This is something worth noting with care.

Higher education in this country is confined to a small minority. This situation is bound to continue for a long time even with a substantial expansion of university enrolment. The educated minority is cut off from the common people.

Higher education in India is caught on the horns of a dilemma. If standards of higher education are lowered, universities lose their raison d'etre. That is one aspect of the problem. With the kind of education they receive, our university graduates come to constitute an elite, standing apart from the rest of the society, a divisive rather than an integrating force. That is the other aspect of the problem. This is, indeed, a very perplexing situation.

The new education which took root in India in the last century had for its principal aim the creation of suitable cadres for different levels of the administration that came into existence at that time. Conditions have not fundamentally changed since then. To be sure, there has been since Independence a notable increase in the size of the middle class along with a very considerable widening of the range of professional and managerial skills for which training is imparted today. These skills have a national, in fact an international, market. The rewards for these skills are, therefore, related not so much to the average income of the common people of India, as to what similar skills might fetch on the world market. The new middle class in India imitates the standard of life of its counterparts in other parts of the world. As its professional skills have a foreign base, so its practical aspirations have a similar direction. Thus the educated elite stands apart from the common people not only in its lifestyle, but also in its aspirations and its perception of problems. The dilemma of higher education in India is rooted in this alienation. To overcome this alienation should be a conscious aim of the national education policy.

Measures have been proposed and adopted to open the doors of the universities to disadvantaged sections of our society. Quotas have been fixed in favour of these sections for admission to higher educational institutions. There are stipends for scholars from poorer families, and more can surely be done in that direction. Proposals have been put forward for remedial courses for socially and otherwise handicapped students, and these should be more seriously taken up and thoughtfully implemented. The national talent search should direct its attention to backward areas, where there are hidden potentialities waiting to be discovered.

These measures are necessary and important. But they are not sufficient.

A clear-sighted policy must start with some rethinking on fundamentals. Universities, we argued, must have respect for knowledge as a creation of the entire human species. But that is only part of the truth. While science as pure theory tends to be universal, technology is closely bound up with the local conditions in which it is applied. In the growth of knowledge, there is a creative interaction between theory and practice. When this is ignored, knowledge loses its dynamic character. Our universities need not be ashamed of borrowing knowledge from every corner of the world. But it must be careful to test and apply knowledge in the specific conditions of this country, observe systematically the consequences of that application and make such observations the basis of new extensions of knowledge. The search for universal knowledge must not be divorced from a concern for local problems. Universities, then, can best fulfil their mission by developing the art of an intricate interweaving of the local and the universal.

Every university should try and develop an identity of its own. In many cases, this can best be done by taking full advantage of the location or regional base of the concerned institution. Those universities which lie at some distance from big cities have very often a special advantage there. North-Eastern Hill University (NEHU) is a good example. It has an extraordinarily rich regional base, particularly for social and life sciences. With hills overlooking the plains, with diverse races and cultures living side by side, NEHU can launch research programmes which will be of deep interest to scholars all over the world. These will also provide opportunities for fruitful cooperation between local researchers and experts from other regions and countries.

NEHU is no more than an example. It is interesting that as far back as in 1926, Acharya P.C. Ray put forward the same idea in his convocation address at the University of Mysore where he said, 'You cannot go on adding faculty after faculty without due consideration to your regional needs'.

Each university should specialise in those courses of study and research projects in which it has a comparative advantage based on its location, endowments and tradition. It is also important to organise extra-mural lectures for the benefit of the local community outside the walls of the university. In this way, a bond will be established between the university and its environment and the community and the region within which it functions.

Those universities which are located in big cities are at a disadvantage in this respect. They risk being cut off from the country. They should, therefore, make special efforts to overcome that disadvantage. One way they can do this is by adopting joint programmes with those colleges and universities which have a natural rural base.

In the final analysis, it is not just programmes that matter, but the spirit which animates them. A memorable expression of that spirit is to be found in Rabindranath Tagore's conception of his university, Visva-Bharati. Tagore was not only a poet, but a great educationist. The dilemma of higher education found in his ideas the only plausible answer.

Visva-Bharati had, so to speak, two faces: one turned towards the world and the other towards the neighbouring village; the one as indispensable to the fulness of Tagore's university as the other. Santiniketan was to be a centre of culture dedicated to the promotion of 'good fellowship and co-operation between the thinkers and scholars of both Eastern and Western countries, free from all antagonisms of race, nationality, creed or caste'. At the same time, 'to win the friendship and affection of villagers and cultivators by taking a real interest in all that concerns their life and welfare' was among the stated aims and objectives of Sriniketan, which became an integral part of Visva-Bharati. The university, as conceived by Tagore, must actively mediate between the two poles, the wide world and the little village. This is a difficult mission, but Tagore made it inseparable from his broad humanist principles.

Some would find Tagore's educational ideas romantic and unrealistic. They would point out that even Visva-Bharati has failed to live up to those ideals. But that criticism still leaves the principal question unanswered. The dilemma of higher education in India — and is it in India alone? — is a stark reality. We cannot get rid of it by simply refusing to take note of it. In the final analysis, Tagore's creative response to that dilemma was closer to reality than the insensitivity of others who continue to be unmoved by it.

13

Education, Science and Economic Development

Economic development is not simply a process of quantitative growth. It involves a continuous qualitative change in the economy and society. Capital is not simply 'accumulated'; stocks are not simply 'replaced' and 'expanded'; but new capital goods are introduced and the old structure is all the time reorganised. Hours of work are not just shortened (or lengthened), but the nature of work changes. Income does not simply grow, but the way of life is transformed. The quality of goods that form the standard of life and the quality of knowledge that enters into the production of these goods change and evolve through a kind of mutual dependence.

What kind of knowledge does a developing economy need? Do we have in our country a policy and an institutional setup reasonably well adapted to providing this kind of knowledge? How well does our system of education and research meet the demands of a developing economy? Such are the questions we intend to discuss in the rest of this chapter.

Adam Smith noted that division of labour and increasing specialisation are basic characteristics of economic development. Correspondingly, the system of education and vocational training in a developing society has to provide for an increased range of specialisation. In its absence, the educational system falls out of step with the needs of the economy and the discrepancy is reflected in unemployment, lack of

correspondence between jobs and acquired skills and aptitudes and a slower rate of economic growth. This is widely
recognised in this country and, as a matter of fact, the point
has been made in several official reports. Thus, for instance,
the Sapru Committee of 1934, after an enquiry into the causes
of unemployment in U.P., came to the conclusion that 'the
real remedy is to provide diversified courses of study at the
secondary stage and to make that stage more practical and
complete in itself and more closely related to the vocational
requirements of different types of students'. More recently,
the Mudaliar Commission observed, 'At the High School or
Higher Secondary stage, diversified courses of instruction
should be provided for the pupils'. This recommendation
has as a matter of fact been adopted and an attempt is being
made to let higher secondary education flow in seven different 'streams'.

This change in the system of secondary education in this
country may seem to correspond to the inherent structural
tendencies of a developing economy. But the correspondence
is spurious; both the recommendations quoted above and their
attempted implementation are based on a misconception; and
unless the errors in this system are quickly rectified, great
harm will be done to the development of science and education in India.

Higher secondary education is properly to be regarded as
a preparation for university education. It is an error to make
it 'closely related to the vocational requirements of different
types of students' and to diversify it accordingly. Let us develop this point briefly.

There is a clear distinction to be made between vocational
training, of which the main aim is to teach a person the art of
doing or making a thing with due care and skill, and scientific
education at the university level which should teach students
to investigate causes, sift evidence and contribute to the careful building up of a body of systematised knowledge. It is no
more certain that a mechanic is potentially a true scientist than

that a housewife has an aptitude for philosophising meaningfully about life and the world. In a developing country which is interested in building up a tradition of scientific education and research and which does not have unlimited resources to dispense with, it is necessary to be careful about selecting students for university education. Since the last two or three years of higher secondary school should be a preparation for university education, it may be best to make this selection, say, at the age of 14.

Let us spell out the point more carefully. It is of great importance that primary education should be compulsory and it is a pity that this objective still remains unfulfilled in our country. With a wide base, we shall have a large population from which to choose students for admission to higher education. But if we want to improve the quality of our higher education a careful selection must be made at some stage of our secondary education. It may be a good idea to make the selection at the age of 14. A substantial section of students can profitably be directed at this stage to technical institutions. In these institutions, they can have further general education combined with specialised training in some craft or practical vocation. Still others could be attached to some industry and have training on the job. This is a point where diversification will be useful and necessary. But for those who are allowed to pass on to the last two or three years of higher secondary school preparatory to university education, there should be in the main a consolidated course with relatively few elective subjects. The languages, particularly the mother tongue and English, should be more carefully studied at this stage than is done now in most schools. The so-called 'core' subjects, particularly mathematics, which are dropped now in the last year of higher secondary school, should be persisted with till the very end and a higher standard established. Not only should the core sciences be taught, but also an elementary course in scientific methodology may do good. Little diversification should be allowed here beyond, perhaps, a distinction between the sciences and the humanities. Just as in the national economy, there is such a thing as the social and the economic 'infrastructure' on which rests a diversified superstructure of multiform productive activities, so in the sphere of learning, encompassing both the sciences and the humanities, there is a basis of common knowledge to be firmly laid if we want to build up a tradition of intellectual activity which will be vigorous and responsible, specialised and supple at the same time. If this is what the higher secondary school should aim at, the time has not yet come when it can open its doors indiscriminately to all.

In a traditional society and a stagnant economy, the state of the arts and techniques is unchanging or very nearly so. So is the state of knowledge. In a dynamic society knowledge, together with the arts and techniques, is in a state of flux. This has profound implications for methods of teaching. So long as awareness of these implications is not reflected in our methods of teaching, there will be little 'advancement of learning' in this country. Some practical measures are worth considering at this point.

The diversion of a section of school students to technical in-stitutions and training centres may come at the age of 15. In that case, the next two years of 'higher secondary' education can be taken out of 'school' and organised in 'colleges', as 'inter-mediate' courses once were. But it will suit better the means of a large section of our young people in the next 10 years if they are allowed to join technical institutions or on-the-job training at the age of 14.

In all this, we have something to learn from the experience of the Soviet Union. In the early years of planned development of the U.S.S.R., there was a tremendous increase in the number of students as well as educational institutions. The number of universities, for instance, increased from 129 in 1928–29 to exactly five times as many (645) in 1932. Simultaneously, the level of university education declined. In 1932, it was officially recognised that 'abuses had appeared, mainly apparent in the one-sided attention directed to increasing the network of educational establishments and the number of students, whilst insufficient attention had been given to the quality of teaching; the subdivision of specialisation had also been carried too far'. Subsequent reforms of the Soviet educational system make sense in the light of this basic criticism. It is significant that while the number of pupils in elementary and secondary schools increased from 21 million to nearly 32 million between 1932–33 and 1938–39, the number of universities and higher technical schools rose from 504,000 to 603,000 only. Moreover, in 1940 comparatively high fees were introduced in the three senior forms of secondary schools apparently setting aside the constitutional guarantee of free education for all. 'This measure was designed to make it somewhat more difficult to receive secondary higher education and to divert some of the school population towards Artisan, Transport and Industrial Schools' (Baykov 1948). These fees were abolished 16 years later.

In a traditional society, the teacher is supposed to know the truth and the whole truth, which he transmits to the student. The ideal relation of the pupil to the preceptor is one of unconditional trust as of a child to its parents. It is the same in the sphere of the arts. The technique of production is transformed by tradition into a hallowed ritual which is handed down from father to son without change or addition. In a dynamic society, problems and their solutions, techniques as well as products, are continuously changing. It is, therefore, not enough to transmit to young students a body of settled conclusions. It is particularly important to build up in them a capacity to react positively to new situations and problems. This can only be achieved by drawing the student into some sort of a dialogue with the teacher. Teaching has to be problem-oriented. But this change in the method of teaching cannot be made effective without a corresponding change in our system of examination. Our students would be drawn as readily to an intellectual activity unrelated to final examination results as traders would respond to motives other than profit. If teaching through discussion is to be promoted, we must discard sole reliance on written tests at long intervals and start grading students on the basis of their participation in seminars and class-room discussions and the papers they prepare for this purpose. Our examination system has often been criticised on the ground that its results are not 'just'. But the most important criticism is that the existing system is an adjunct of an outmoded method of teaching, and both reflect and help to perpetuate the ethos of a traditional society. The alternative we are suggesting here will not necessarily be more 'just'. We must try to make it as fair as possible; but it is the need for dynamism in our educational institutions, and through these in our intellectual tradition, which must guide us in our choice of a new system of examination. It is exactly like that in our economic policy too. A dynamic economy is not at every point more just than a static economy. We have to try to make it as just as possible, because a minimum of justice is needed even to sustain dynamism; but it is dynamism which we have to make our first concern whether in economic policy or in education and science policy.

Any serious attempt to change the system of teaching would involve as a necessary corollary a new programme of training and retraining for the teachers themselves, changes in pay scales and conditions of work and so on. But this is a matter into which we cannot enter here. What may still be worth adding is that if we decide to wait for all 'preconditions' to be fulfilled before the new methods are introduced, we may never get started. We had better begin at a few selected points and then push ahead through trials and errors. There is no sufficiently good reason why a beginning should not be made, for instance, in post-graduate classes in the leading universities.

While capital has been moving from the richer countries to the poorer, scientists have tended to move the other way. In traditional international trade theory, we are told that while capital is mobile between countries, unless its movement is restricted by special measures, labour is more tied to the country of its origin. Obviously, this is not so true of labour of the highest quality, the movement of which is, moreover, more difficult to restrict in a democratic society. In recent years, there has been a certain amount of discussion on the problem of outflow of talents from this country. There is, however another aspect of the same problem which has engaged less of public attention, but which is even more fundamental. It is not simply that we lose our scientists to foreign countries. But those who come back after doing good work abroad often cease to do research of any value on their return. It is possible that we lose more in this way than through any outright defection of our trained scientists. Moreover, the two phenomena are interconnected; and if we could stop the one we might go a good way towards stopping the other.

The fact is that we have not been able to create in this country a climate in which scientific research flourishes. It is this situation that we have to remedy. If we want to retain our best students and promote simultaneously a climate of creative work in our universities, the best strategy might be to select a few centres spread over the country and bring them up to the highest academic standards we are capable of. This may be better than trying to upgrade all educational institutions equally at the same time. Something like this happened naturally, without any central planning, in many pioneer countries. Japan did it consciously in the early period of her industrialisation with her select imperial universities. The main points of this strategy are simple. No student will normally be allowed to proceed abroad for higher studies until he has completed the highest courses that the best universities at home have to offer. On passing out of these universities, students will get assured jobs commensurate with their abilities. It is after they have thus established themselves in life, struck roots in their own society and formed some idea of what they want to look out for in other societies that they should make their foreign trips which, therefore, would be purposeful and not of indefinite duration. Meanwhile, the best universities of the country should be provided with all necessary equipments and facilities for study and research, a large number of scholarships of sufficient value to attract talented students, even if poor, from all over the country, and the best available teachers from all over the world. *Mutatis mutandis* — the same policy should apply to our leading research institutes.

It is widely felt that there is too little team work in our research institutes. A brief comment is made here on one aspect of the problem only. In our institutes and other seats of learning, the head is usually a senior member of the team. In a traditional society, where experience is another word for knowledge, and men, like old wine, are deemed to mature and gain in value by being preserved longer, promotion is naturally by seniority. In a progressive society, men are more like fruits that first ripen and then decay. One is continually running to keep pace with growing knowledge and one ultimately falls behind. This does not necessarily mean that research institutes should be headed by young people. It may be better not to embarrass a young researcher — and the same holds good for a young teacher — with administrative duties in the most productive period of his life. Moreover, the brightest man in a team is not necessarily the best fitted to be its head just as the brightest member of the cabinet will not always make the best prime minister. Age does confer a few advantages: an older man, for instance, would be less likely to arouse envy. But in the peculiar situation, of a growing society the head should have a proper conception of his role. He may or may not be the best scientist in the group. He should not be perturbed if he is not; for his task is not to compete but to coordinate. Where other members of the group are often his superior in their own lines, coordination demands mutual consultation. In some cases, it

111

may be best to form a small committee at the top with the post of the chairman rotating. Even if this is not acceptable, there should be firmly established conventions to make joint consultation effective. More generally, it is important to foster among scholars, research workers and teachers a sense of belonging to the institution where they are enrolled and of pride and responsible participation in its work and achievements. Further, an attempt should be made to promote simultaneously specialisation and interdisciplinary dialogue. It is by these methods that creative teamwork can be developed in depth.

A few words may be added here on the vexed question of promotion in educational and research institutions. In research institutions, promotion should go by research output, in published form or circulated otherwise, the evaluation being done wherever possible by an independent and competent body. In educational institutions, both the quality of teaching and the output of learned work should count. The former is particularly difficult to assess with any show of objectivity: a possible aid to assessment might be a vote of, say, the best one-fifth of the students who have passed out of the institution in the previous five years or a certain proportion of this population taken at random if the total is large. Whatever one may think of this, the main point is quite straightforward. If advancement in places of learning appears to depend on adventitious considerations, these will be plagued by what in India we call 'politics', the essence of which is the substitution of a skilful combination of sycophancy and factional intrigues, a game with a negative sum, for the more productive work of pursuit of knowledge.

A section of our teachers wants to keep 'politics' out by making promotion depend on 'experience' or 'seniority' more than on anything else. But this is to perpetuate in educational institutions the rules of a traditional society. The problem is to evolve a clear-cut criteria of efficiency, and teachers should strive and agitate to formulate and get accepted such criteria.

It is usual to make a distinction between scientific discovery, invention and innovation or development. That in the long run there is a vital connection between scientific discovery and industrial development is easily understood. But the lag between an important development in pure science and its repercussions in productive enterprise can be long. In general', writes J.D. Bernal (2006), 'the industry of the nineteenth century depended on the scientific and technical achievements of the late eighteenth century'. Similarly, the great discoveries of the 19th century in the physical sciences, resting essentially on the law of conservation of energy and the interchangeability of its different forms, took decades before they made a notable impact on industrial processes. It is true that the lag between advance in pure science and industrial development has, generally speaking, narrowed in our century. But the relation between the two is still sufficiently remote to make it potently unwise to leave the organisation of scientific research to private initiative. Even in matters of invention and development, where the link between science and industry is closer and where industries should be both expected and encouraged to make investment in research, public funds must supplement private. Private investment is bound here to fall short of the social optimum for a number of reasons. The social value of an invention would often be greater than its value to any individual firm because it is of use, directly or indirectly (for example, by making other inventions easier), to a much wider range of enterprises than the one where it is originated. Also the funds necessary for organising research on an effective scale are often beyond the means of individual producers or productive units. This is best illustrated in agriculture. As Nurkse (1962) rightly observes, 'innovation in this sphere (that is, agriculture) cannot be relied upon to happen in response to market incentives alone. Even in the United States the agricultural extension service has long been a classic example of a non-market method of development policy in a progressive and market-oriented economy.'

In India, where most intellectuals are by no means partial to private enterprise, these propositions would be readily accepted and it is unnecessary to dwell on them longer. But there is one point that does need to be enlarged upon. It is possible to have, with or without government aid and encouragement, a good deal of research and cultivation of science at the top and yet very little material development at the bottom. Let me use an illustration to drive the point home. In Japan the Imperial Agricultural Experiment Station and its branches were established in the 1890s. In India, the Imperial Agricultural Research Institute was founded not much later by Lord Curzon in 1906. In the mid-1920s, a historian could truthfully report that 'since its establishment, during the thirty years of its activity and development, the Station has contributed remarkably to the rational management and rapid progress of Japan's agriculture'. The Agricultural Research Institute in India had several important discoveries to its credit, but the food-producing sector of our economy remained a classic example of stagnation which we have not yet quite broken at the end of 60 years of organised agricultural research. Our research, like our administration, has remained curiously suspended in mid-air.

In industry too, we come up against a similar problem to which a complete answer cannot be found simply in more public investment. What is also needed is that enterprise- and government-sponsored research and training institutions should develop a special kind of fruitful collaboration. This should extend to both manpower training and industrial research proper.

Evidently, we need a system of links or lines of communication by which scientific knowledge at the top can pass to common people engaged in the ordinary business of life. In agriculture, for instance, local adaptations are necessary before the results of research at higher levels can be used in the field. Our agricultural research organisation seems to have lacked local links to help on with such adaptations. Another major difference between India and Japan is, of course, that while Japan eradicated mass illiteracy at the beginning of this century, we have still to achieve this. This brings us back to the question of education. Our society cannot afford to carry on with a few eminent scientists at the top and colossal ignorance at the bottom. The contrast between Russia and the United States in the 19th century helps to bring out the point forcefully. In natural resources, the two countries have a certain resemblance. Russia in the 19th century produced scientists of the highest calibre, such as Lomonosov, Jacobi, Lobachevski and Mendelev. The tradition of scientific work in her academies was, if anything, superior to America's. But the Russian masses remained ignorant while in America education spread rapidly. This is one of the handicaps which the Soviet Union determined to remove.

The Middle Ages evolved a priestly class which mediated between God and man and explained the scriptures in simple terms for simple people. If science is to be brought to the common people we need a class of dedicated intermediaries. Even after mass literacy is achieved, a large section of people will go without university education. Most people will not be specialised in science. A major objective of science policy in this country must be to promote a varied scientific literature for such people. It is quite obvious that such literature must, for the most part, be in the regional languages. It is also not enough to have popular scientific literature. There should be organised guidance for people who need such guidance outside of their working hours. We need, for instance, night schools fitted with libraries and laboratories, at least, in all the bigger cities to begin with, where working adults will be able to take science courses. By such means interest in science can be made to percolate through a society. It is in such society that new knowledge finds ready acceptance. Given also a tolerably good system of incentives to productive work, development of knowledge can enter into that process of interaction with material needs by which economic develo-pment is sustained and quickened.

A sound science policy needs to be rooted in an appropriate philosophy. To this statement, an objection can be raised im-mediately. Science has grown in combination with diverse faiths. Pascal was a devout believer; Cavendish 'non-religious'. America, by and large, has believed in a divine purpose from the days when the Pilgrim Fathers founded a settlement in New England; the U.S.S.R. believed in history's broad design, but not in God's. It might seem that the growth of science is unrelated to any particular philosophical conception of life and the world. This is both true and untrue. Wherever the scientific revolution has taken place, an adjustment of the old tradition in a particular *direction* has been found necessary. What science demands of its devotee is not that he accepts or renounces faith in God, but that he believes, broadly speak-ing, that the universe in its measurable aspect is subject to measurable laws. Science is intolerant of magic. It calls for a critical scrutiny of religion itself to rid it of pre-scientific, magical remnants. Much of the philosophical–religious revo-lution in the West from Occam through Bacon down to Kant can be explained in these terms. A properly conceived science policy must be friendly to a similar philosophical revolution in this country. Let us face the fact that religion in India is permeated with magic. Many of us seem to think that it does not matter. The leaders of the Indian renaissance, such as Raja Rammohan Roy and Vidyasagar, thought differently. Perhaps they knew better. The path of scientific progress is strewn with trials and experiments gone wrong, and the scientist too needs a faith to sustain him through the journey. Even when superstitions retreat from the field of the physical sciences, they continue to impede the advance of the biological and social sciences. In their own ways, both the West and the U.S.S.R. have faced this problem. Science policy in India cannot afford to ignore these facts. It must give the country a sense of direction.

A few controversial measures have been suggested above. Some of these will possibly be opposed on the ground that they are 'impractical'. The existing system is always practical. Through years, its rough edges have been polished off and the whole system works with an impressive interdependence of parts and the whole. Change is always 'impractical', for all things do not change equally readily and discrepancies arise between one part and another. How, for instance, can we make a success of the new system of teaching? Where do we get the teachers? Where are the books? Where are the conventions that make such a system work smoothly? Let these come first. And, of course, they just cannot come first. There is a point in the practical man's objection. But beyond a certain point, in social life as in economics, the glorification of equilibrium is the hallmark of conservatism.

References

Baykov, A. 1948. *The Development of the Soviet Economic System*. The Macmillan Co. pp. 219, 346, 355.

Bernal, J.D. 2006. *Science and Industry in the Nineteenth Century*. Routledge. p. 6.

Nurkse, R. 1962. *Patterns of Trade and Development*, Oxford: Blackwell. p. 42.

14

Tagore's Philosophy of Education*

Only those who are incomplete or imperfect need to be educated. A being, who is perfect and self-sufficient from birth, if we can imagine such a one, has no such need. On the other hand, a person so grossly imperfect as to be incapable of improvement will also be incapable of education. For him too, education is unnecessary.

Education occupies the middle ground between the antipodal states of full self-reliance and irredeemable deficiency. The incomplete man must set up relationships with others to complete and perfect himself. Education is fundamentally concerned with the setting up and fostering of these relationships.

Tagore's philosophy of education too is based on the sense of such relationships — between man and nature, between man and his fellow-men and finally between man and the universal humanity.

Let us start with nature, for Tagore's educational project took shape at a place where man could enter into intimate communion with nature. There are two aspects of the relation between man and nature, and therefore of the conception of man and nature in educational theory. First, nature can

---

*Based on a lecture delivered at a special session of the Bangla Academy, Dhaka on 24 May 1986. Translated from the original Bengali by Sukanta Chaudhuri.

be viewed as a machine ruled by iron laws. Science and technology investigate how this machine works or how it can be made to work. If we view nature in this light, our educational process will be formed accordingly. Of course, education can be rendered still more mindless and mechanical. Often the teacher resorts to empty pedagogic rituals within a conventional system. But this is not true education.

There is another side to the relation between man and nature. Nature can be a medium for the growth and extension of man's love. The education that does not recognise this fact is incomplete: it is un-Tagorean. The poet-teacher had a simple but profound perception of the nature of a child's love. We can observe this for ourselves when we look at a child. A child commonly cries for a specific reason, be it hunger, discomfort or something else; but its delight or happiness is often without cause. A child dances with joy for no apparent reason. This is a fundamental truth. Man has a spontaneous sense of joy in nature and the universe. Each of us shares in this joy to the extent that he is a man.

As we grow worldly wise, we come to consider this causeless joy as a form of madness. Not only do we learn of practical affairs, we come to regard them as the only thing worth knowing. There are thus two ways of looking at the world: as matter for practical use and 'useless' unpractical joy – a joy without purpose, a love without motive. Tagore did not reject the practical side of a child's education, but he laid stress on the unpractical side. This is a basic premise of his philosophy of education.

We must next consider a related issue. We have distinguished between the practical and the unpractical; but there is also a link between the two. Nature meets certain of our needs: she nurtures and fosters us. But nature is also a source of joy, as to the child or the artist. This is how the mother stands to the child: she fulfils some of its wants, but she also provides it with a source of causeless joy. (Conversely, she too finds such joy in her child, otherwise she is not a true mother.) The

119

two functions are related. The mother who cannot meet any of her child's material wants is unlikely to inspire it with a joy of spirit. In the field of education too, man must be taught to build up a relation with nature whereby she fulfils some of his needs, while he in turn, like a child or an artist, discovers in her a source of joy and love.

Practical necessity plays an important part in the matter. Tagore realised this perfectly well, especially after he saw rural poverty face to face. The helpless, destitute villagers had to be educated to satisfy their wants with nature's aid. This is a goal of science. Tagore resolved to use science, especially in order to eradicate rural poverty. While at Santiniketan we are first struck by the joyful relation between nature and the child, Sriniketan illustrates the effort to bring science to work upon nature to meet the villagers' needs.

I said at the outset that nature embodied iron law in one respect and purposeless joy and love in another. Neither of these aspects can be dismissed. We must discover the rules that bind nature. This is what Tagore has brought out clearly at Sriniketan. If we have not grasped the laws of nature, our minds fall easy prey to superstition and blind fear. These are dispelled by an understanding of nature's laws. Such understanding is necessary for freedom of the mind. At the same time, this understanding enables us to apply the forces of nature to our needs even in simple everyday matters. There is rule and science in the growing of crops and the use of manures.

When the rural development wing at Sriniketan was first being formed, Elmhirst played a leading role. In his letters to Elmhirst as well as in his other writings, Tagore has said very clearly that science is needed in rural development for two purposes: to free the mind from blind fear and to teach rational methods of farming and manufacture.

This leads on to the question of man's relation with his neighbours. So far I have chiefly talked of his relation with nature. But the individual man also interacts with other men

120

and extends his own being thereby. Hence come both the literal and the philosophic *atmiyata*: a shared selfhood, a shared existence of the soul. The word vulgarly implies a tie of blood, but its deeper philosophic sense is a spiritual extension of being. He towards whom I cannot extend my being is not my *atmiya* in this deeper sense, though he may be related by blood. The *atmiya* is one whom we know to be our friend and neighbour.

We often call people by the assumed cognomens of 'brother', 'sister', 'uncle' or 'aunt'. Here the terms do not imply a tie of blood; but they often indicate real ties, as long as they are not reduced to lifeless formalities. 'Neighbour' is another such word. 'Who is my neighbour?' Jesus asked. One can offer many answers. There is an ideal conception of the 'neighbour'. Like our relation to nature, this assumes two aspects. One is a practical workaday relationship and the other a festive kinship of joy.

The cooperative offers the finest form of practical interaction: here neighbours join hands to fulfil their common needs in an organised, equitable, constructive manner. But at a festival, people gather for joy and joy alone. The two relationships together create neighbourliness; they fulfil themselves in the life of an ideal rural community. In our country, the traditional fair provided another such union of the two impulses, a meeting-ground of the needful and the joyful.

This is the finer spirit and form of the *palli*: a village, neighbourhood or community. We cannot form direct acquaintance with all members of the human race. Our range of acquaintance and relationships makes up the social unit of the *palli*. Actual village life incorporates a great deal of spite and enmity, quarrels and scandals. Obviously, we must know and accept this reality. But if we accept that alone and entirely discount the ideal, we reject the possibility of education. What can we progress towards if not an ideal? For what are we to build ourselves anew? I have earlier said that education begins with the imperfect; but it is made possible, and successful, only if we admit an effort towards perfection. Hence while we must experience village or community life as it is, we must also picture for ourselves its ideal form. Tagore was not ignorant of the reality of village life. He knew it from within, as his short stories and many other writings testify. But in his essays like the famous 'Swadeshi Samaj' we also find a picture of ideal village life. He gave the village community an important place in his philosophy of education, drawing upon science and the cooperative movement to transform the actual into the ideal, while also invoking a deeper sense of joy, love and expansion of the self. Sriniketan is as much a part of Visva-Bharati as is Santiniketan, and rural organisation is its first and most basic principle. School education must be in harmony with rural organisation, or rural regeneration as Tagore sometimes terms it. Many of us are aware that Tagore founded a school at Sriniketan besides that at Santiniketan and even judged the former to be more important, as answering more closely to the country's needs.

Next comes the question of relating the individual to universal man. What we have called the relationship of *atmiyata* commonly operates within a small group. The village community is a ready instance, but many larger bodies are held together in the same way. A form of *atmiyata* is fundamental to identities based on race, nationhood or religion. There is nothing unusual in this; but there is cause for caution, for these enclosed or limited relationships easily attract the hostility of those outside the fold. This leads to a battle between two opposed social groups, destroying all deeper notions of social relationships. Whenever we contemplate an ideal, we must remind ourselves of its opposite reality. Tagore knew of the militant face of nationalism: how Japan attacked China, how the nations of Europe rose to the savage stimulus of war. This convinced him that while education must incorporate the indigenous and the patriotic, it must also embrace the notion of universal man. This is why he called his university Visva-Bharati. He set it up in his native land, but opened it to the *visva* or world. His vision extended in one direction to the neighbouring village of Surul, the object of Sriniketan's efforts; in the other to the whole world and universal man. Learned and gifted men came from all over the world to his little abode of peace: from China and Japan, from the nations of Europe and America. These citizens of the world were needed to complete his ideal of education.

Let us now bring together the points I have made. Through education, man perfects his relation with nature. It is a relationship of joy in one respect, of study and observation in another. Education also teaches man to relate fruitfully with his neighbour. It expels poverty by the use of science as controlled by cooperative effort. But Tagore also wished that through education, man might raise his simple and spontaneous joys to the level of a celebration or festivity: as instances, he has left us some ordered and finely wrought practices and ceremonies. He also had care that a small group or community may not find its *raison d'etre* in conflict with an opposite group; that each segment of humanity might learn to fulfil itself through joyful service to a greater fellowship of man. The concept of a native community must be linked to the common religion of humanity.

Tagore did not readily admit politics to the campus at Santinketan. He had a reason for this. He was not ignorant of politics: he can be credited with some memorable political statements and activities. But he wished to keep Santiniketan free of party politics. This was partly because politics almost inevitably led to factionalism. Also, the chief purpose of politics is the struggle for power. Our first struggle was to wrest power from foreign rulers. Later, the chief purpose became for one group to wrest power from another. Whatever the merits and demerits of such a struggle, whatever the need for it, Tagore knew that there was a greater purpose to life. Just as Gandhi had a constructive programme alongside his politics, Tagore undertook the task of rural reconstruction and the setting up of certain precious ideals of humanity, not only as philosophic concepts but also as established realities. He knew that these deeper purposes could never be fulfiled through politics. Others might concern themselves with political activity. Tagore realised that he could best employ his genius in the service of man through constructive and creative work kept free of politics. The question is not whether education is superior to politics; it is whether politics should control education. Tagore thought it best to keep the two apart and tried to run Santiniketan accordingly.

It is arguable that Tagore did not always succeed in his aims. No man, and particularly no great man, is ever wholly successful. It is easy to argue that Jesus Christ was a failure. Whether Tagore fully succeeded or not is unimportant. It is important to realise that his views have a relevance for the future. His ideal of education is an epitome of humanism.

15

Power of Religion

The word religion has been used in a variety of senses and there is, in fact, a yawning gap between the theory and the practice of religion. Ideally, the aim of religion is to foster a feeling of union and the brotherhood of men. In practice, it promotes sectarian conflicts all too often.

There are two courses open to a man of goodwill. Either he can reject religion on account of the protection it has given over a long period to fierce fanaticism and obscurantism; or he can choose to be respectful towards 'true' religion which promotes the spirit of compassion and union and can reject as false a religion which contradicts that spirit.

The name of the creed one professes is of small importance; more important is the manner in which it is practised. As a matter of fact, the same remark applies to atheism as a creed. Stalin was an atheist; so in his own way was Bertrand Russell. But there is a world of difference between the two. Even among Gandhians, there were some outstanding atheists. For ethical purposes, to divide the world into two camps, theists and atheists, does not make much good sense. Christ was a theist; the Buddha was not one; that his followers deified him is another matter.

Marx said that criticism of religion is the beginning of all criticism. One must add that the rejection of fanaticism in all its forms is the beginning of all fair criticism. Although Truth, in an abstract sense, may be one, its manifestations in time and space are partial, manifold and pluralistic. The idea that there can be only one correct ideology, code of moral conduct and social order is untenable. The problem is to make possible a tolerant and mutually respectful coexistence of these diverse expressions of truth in the practical affairs of the world consistent with some basic values. The task can be best illustrated in terms of the coexistence of religions.

In China, coexistence of religions is a marginal problem. In India, it is a major problem. Every major religion of the world is represented in this country. How can we evolve unity out of this diversity? Some high-minded people have come up with a simple answer to that question: if we cut out the in-essentials, we find that the essentials of all religions are the same. Now, this statement is neither wholly wrong nor wholly right.

Faith in God is an essential part of Islam, Christianity and some brands of Hinduism; but it is not an essential part of Jainism or Buddhism. Among those who profess faith in God, some strongly reject idol worship, others do not. So there is the problem of deciding what are those essential ideas, if there are any, where all religions find a common ground. A war of religions today, open or veiled, a violent confrontation, is fraught with terrible consequence. What is the attitude we should promote through words and deeds to replace con-frontation with a reconciliation of religions?

A clue to an answer to that question can be found in some-thing remarkable that the head of a Buddhist religious order, the Dalai Lama, once said. It does not matter, he said, whether you take the name of the Buddha, or you call yourself a Buddhist; what matters is whether you believe in the value of compassion. How many other heads of religion would make such a statement? Are there leaders of *Hindutva* who would proclaim that it did not matter whether you called yourself a proud Hindu, that it only mattered whether you cared for equality and union among all men? Are there heads of Islamic communities who would declare that it did not matter whether or not you took the name of Prophet Muhammad, what is important is whether you believe in word and deed in the brotherhood of men? Are there Christian priests who would say that it did not matter whether or not you took the name of Jesus Christ, the really important thing is whether you believe in what Tolstoy called the law of love? The Dalai Lama has set an example of the language and spirit of religious reconciliation which others would do well to emulate.

It is a cardinal feature of Buddhism that its founder presented his religious teachings in notably rational language. This, I submit, is the common ideal towards which all faiths, despite their differences, should seek to converge if human civilisation is to be saved from violent disorder and destruction. This sounds simple. But there are complications.

There are dilemmas in human existence to which one can reasonably respond in diverse ways. There are saints and religious teachers who lived and preached under different circumstances and these differences have left their marks on the style and content of their messages.

In every major religion as preached and practised, there are some ideas of perennial significance and others which are time-bound and require to be critically examined and, where necessary, amended or discarded. A good example of the need for such critical review is provided by the question of sex and relationship between the sexes. Most religions somehow believe that men are superior to women and religious injunctions are framed on that basis. In a general way, the idea of social equality gets greater recognition in Islam than in Hindu society where the caste hierarchy is deeply entrenched.

Yet on the question of sex, Islam departs from the idea of equality all too clearly. 'Men are in charge of women', the holy Quran declares*, 'because Allah hath made the one of them

---

*All extracts from the Holy Quran reproduced here are taken from the standard English translation by Mohammed Marmaduke Pickthall.

to excel the other, and because they spend of their property ...
So good women are the obedient ...' (4/34). This presumption
of the superiority of men is not confined to Islam, but shared
by other religious traditions quite as unquestionably. Surely
it is time to rethink.

Quite evidently, a principal cause of male dominance is
economic. In traditional patriarchal societies, men are in
charge of income-earning activities and property and women
have to depend for their subsistence, as the Quran pertinently
points out, on what 'they (men) spend of their property'. While
this was the position particularly among the ruling classes
over a long period, things have started changing in recent
decades.

More and more women, particularly in the cities, have
started working outside the home. This seems to be an irreversible trend. Orthodox ideas regarding the place of women
in society have got to change. The process is not going to be
smooth, with many broken homes strewn along the way. But
fundamentalist attempts to return to the old order can only
make confusion worse confounded.

This makes it imperative to reconsider the question of sex
and morals with an open mind. This is not an easy task, for
sex occupies an area of life which rationality finds hardest to
penetrate. We can offer here only a few brief comments. One
thing is certain. There can be no single moral code which will
suit all temperaments. The social problem in question cannot
be solved by forcing uniformity.

In some religions, including Hinduism, *bramacharya* or total
abstinence from sex has been held in very high regard. This
idea, if it is universally adopted, might prove disastrous. With
limited application, it can produce some exalted characters,
particularly when it is accepted with humility and not with a
holier-than-thou attitude. Monogamy provides an alternative
code of ethics which is strictly prescribed by many religions,
but not all. The advantage with this code is that its presence
provides psychological security and stability within the

family, while its absence often breeds suspiciousness and other complications arising from a feeling of insecurity.

A friend of mine once told me in defense of the Islamic permissiveness of polygamy that its intention was to legitimise what would otherwise lead to a clandestine hypocrisy of life with no dignity for women. The underlying assumption seems to be that a substantial section of men is naturally promiscuous. However, even the liberal must pause and ponder. It is obviously unfair to have two sets of rules contradicting each other, one for men and another for women. It is not fair to demand absolute fidelity from one party and to claim exemption from such restrictions for the other party. The rights one claims for oneself, one must be prepared to concede to the other. This is what justice demands.

Whether human nature can be so moulded as to make it possible for the family to coexist with this relaxation of moral codes is a moot question. But one should grant that it is not reasonable to make exclusive fidelity the principal criterion of the goodness of a person's character. It is easy to illustrate this point. Neither Bertrand Russell nor Albert Einstein nor Martin Luther King was free of the taint of 'promiscuity'; but they were admirable specimens of the human species, dedicated to great causes that should make us feel proud of them.

What then are the basic values by which sexual relationship, or for that matter any human relationship, should be judged? Underlying any such relationship, there must be a bond of goodwill. Sex, or what men call love, can lead to an agonised state of bondage when it is dominated by the spirit of possessiveness. But love combined with a kind of non-attachment, evident in the work of great artists, can be infinitely precious. Sex cannot be purged of what is based within it by simply branding it as sinful. Sex education must include within its compass the building up of an awareness of certain dangers and pitfalls which an immature infatuation is likely to encounter; as well as an adequate understanding and appreciation of that spirit of non-attachment and goodwill which can include sex and open the door to a world of incomparably rich experience.

Let us now widen the scope of our inquiry regarding the function of education. Ideally, our system of education should be carefully related to the kind of man and society we want to have; in other words, it should have a man-making and society-building mission. Judged by this criterion, the system of education we have today is clearly unsatisfactory. It has got distorted in two ways.

More than half a century has passed since we adopted a constitution which directed the state to endeavour to provide, 'within a period of 10 years', 'free and compulsory education for all children until they complete the age of fourteen years'. Since independence what has taken shape is a system of education oriented towards the aspirations of a relatively prosperous urban middle class and, therefore, unrelated to the needs and requirements of the majority of our rural population. Moreover, the party in power is more interested in using our educational institutions for consolidating its political power than in providing education of the required quality and quantity. Naturally, the promise held out in our constitution remains grossly unfulfilled.

It so happens that my own thoughts on this subject of where our system of education stands, what is lacking in it and what needs to be supplied largely coincide with those of J.P. Naik, the most knowledgeable person on education in India that I ever met. It will be useful at this point to offer some extracts from his writings. In an essay entitled *Reconstruction of Education*, Naik writes:

> ... the ideas of the national system of education evolved between 1906 when the Indian National Congress adopted its Resolution on national education and 1966 when the Education Commission submitted its Report were conceived in very different social–economic and political contexts... the dominating concept between 1906 and 1947 has been that of winning political freedom between 1947 and 1978 we were

obsessed with bridging the gap between our elite and the international elite.

Elsewhere he writes:

... the existing model of the primary school favours the well-to-do...and harms the interest of the masses, the bulk of whose children are converted into "failures" and "dropouts". If primary education is to be made universal, the traditional model of the primary school should be radically modified ....

In the same paper titled *The Functional Primary School*, Naik makes some significant recommendations regarding the content of primary education. He writes:

The introduction of a single set of textbooks uniformly in all primary schools...tends to standardise content and to make variations to suit local conditions almost impossible. It is necessary to give up all such trends to centralise authority in curriculum construction and to give freedom to schools to adjust the curriculum to the local environment.... This will make it possible to have a curriculum for every primary school which stimulates children and attracts the support of the parents.

These observations are worth very careful consideration. It is not enough to plead for universal literacy. It is not all that important to make the right to education a fundamental right enshrined in the constitution. It is essential to relate education for the people to an aim and a programme clearly understood and accepted by the people. If integrated rural development is the aim, as it ought to be, the methods and content of education for the villagers must be so framed that they subserve and are seen to subserve that aim. Also people themselves should be able to freely cooperate and participate in the implementation of such programmes of education and reconstruction. A spirit of self-reliance rather than excessive dependence on a centralised authority should be cultivated.

This virtually amounts to an agenda for a radical reconstruction of our society. Our villages are divided into castes
and classes and sects, with ancient superstitions sanctioning
divisive barriers. These are obstacles to cooperation for integrated development. It is necessary to overcome these obstacles. Conflicts in village society can be effectively overcome
only through a positive commitment to a common task of rural
reconstruction. Customs which sanctioned division have
to be replaced by a cultural renaissance which glorifies the
union of free individuals. But that means a critique of tradition.
What is needed primarily is a revaluation of old values rather
than a victory for one political party or another. Party politics
is concerned with a struggle for power, and a political revolution tends to keep that struggle alive in one form or another, thus creating new barriers to cooperation. A change
in property rights is necessary; but that will itself have to be
justified in terms of a clearly understood programme of constructive work.

The culture we need would stress the value of ever-expand-
ing union. Besides articulating itself through an appropriate
social philosophy, it should find a creative expression in festivals which rejoice in and celebrate the widening of union
among men and with nature. These must be festivals in which
all people can participate without distinctions of castes and
creeds. It was one of Rabindranath's signal contributions to
produce such festivals of great aesthetic appeal. This is illustrated by seasonal festivals which celebrate man's union with
nature. Some of them have revealed a deeper significance with
the passage of time than what was originally recognised.

Consider, for instance, the tree planting ceremony. Trees
are things of beauty. But that is not all. Additionally, an awareness is growing about the destructive consequences of ecological imbalance and the importance of protecting forests
for averting such imbalance.

Rabindranath himself clearly recognised this when he introduced this ceremony, as the song which he composed on

that occasion clearly reveals. It is a beautiful example of that union of love and reason on which alone human culture can safely rest.

In sharp repudiation of an earlier concept which over-stressed man's struggle against nature, his ambition of lord-ship over nature, it symbolised a reconciliation, acceptable to both theists and atheists, which represented the spirit of Tagore's Religion of Man. The gains made through conflict are temporary; it is through reconciliation that humanity is finally saved.

16

Ambedkar: A Rebel with a Cause

If there is a modern and distinctive Indian variety of social democracy, Babasaheb Ambedkar is its foremost and most authentic expounder. The struggle for equality takes different forms in different countries and historical situations, but it has also some common features. We have to try and understand both the universal elements of Ambedkar's social philosophy and its local characteristics.

The causes of inequality are various. But once inequality is established in society from whatever cause, it gives rise to an ideology favourable to its perpetuation. Plato espoused the idea that slaves were intrinsically inferior to their masters. Since then there has never been a dearth of similar myths all around — blacks are inferior to whites, natives to colonial rulers, women to men, Sudras to Brahmins. The idea that all men are equal is a dogma which cannot be exactly verified by facts. But it is valuable as an anti-dote to myths of natural inequality.

The slogan of liberty, equality and fraternity may have had its origin in a 'bourgeois' revolution. But its wider significance clearly transcends its limited historical origins. Ambedkar was deeply impressed and inspired by the motto of the French revolution. He realised that the three components of that motto were integrally interrelated. Equality, which derives its moral worth from the idea of human fraternity, itself becomes forced and mechanical, an obstacle to man's creativity, unless it combines with liberty.

Ambedkar found in the caste system a complete contradiction of the triune ideal of liberty, equality and fraternity. He came to the conclusion that the emancipation of Indian society was impossible without abolition of the caste system. The depressed classes, by breaking their bondage, will be emancipating Indian society.

This is where Ambedkar's difference with other nationalist leaders lay. For them, the supreme objective was winning India's independence by ending British rule; for him his life's mission was gaining freedom for the 'outcasts' by ending the caste system. The symbolic value of making a bonfire of foreign cloth during the non-cooperation movement was matched by the public burning of the *Manusmriti* under Ambedkar's leadership in 1927. The difference of approach was fundamental and it continues to have relevance to this day.

Our nationalists of yesterday were content to blame all the major ills of Indian society on foreign imperialism. Many of their diverse descendants, of the Right as well as the Left, are never more pleased with themselves than when they do the same even today. Ambedkar, by stark contrast, was concerned to point out that the roots of our ills were deep down in our own tradition. To pretend otherwise, he thought, was to serve upper caste interests.

Ambedkar was a Mahar, an untouchable. His knowledge of the condition of the depressed classes was not bookish; it came to him from within and not without. He knew from personal experience the humiliations and denial of elementary rights that these classes had to suffer all the time. From experience again he came to certain firm conclusions. Justice to the untouchables, an effective recognition of their human rights, could only come through the organised strength of the deprived people themselves; it could not come as a gift from the upper castes.

Ambedkar, therefore, struggled to build up separate and independent organisations for the outcastes. He demanded

separate representation for the depressed classes on legislative bodies at different levels. Nor was it enough that the
laws should be just. Since the effectiveness of laws depended
also on the hidden sympathies and prejudices of the people
charged with their execution, Ambedkar wanted that the deprived castes should be suitably represented in the administrative services.

These ideas led to a predictable estrangement between
Babasaheb and the majority of nationalist leaders. Ambedkar
was accused of imperilling the unity of Hindu society and the
nation. But he was convinced that it was less important to
preserve and maintain an appearance of outward unity than to
secure justice and freedom for the oppressed castes. It will be
wrong to say that he did not care for the unity of India; rather
the contrary. But he was of the view that it should be unity
based on equal rights for all.

Although Ambedkar, an eminent scholar and lawyer by
training, attached importance to just laws, he also knew that
something more was necessary to establish a good society. In
a famous address in honour of Ranade, another great leader
of the Indian renaissance, he said, 'Rights are protected not
by law but by the social and moral conscience of society'.
Political revolutions give primacy to the struggle for power.
But social revolutions are never even nearly complete without
a moral and cultural revolution. Ambedkar firmly believed
that a fundamental critique of *chaturvarnya* was an essential
prerequisite of a cultural revolution in India.

Three elements of that critique deserve special notice. In
theory, the *chaturvarnya* system was originally based on individual distinctions of natural worth and aptitudes. However,
in practice, it has come to rest for a very long time on the
accidents of birth. This makes the system in its present form
totally indefensible. A critique of the existing system cannot
be countered by a theory which has no correspondence with
practice.

We come now to the next point. Is *chaturvarnya*, even in its theoretical and ideal form, defensible? Ambedkar cogently argues that it is not. The system carries specialisation too far. It is not good for society and its individual members that some should specialise exclusively in acquisition of knowledge and learning, others in martial occupations and still others in manual labour. A radical separation between intellectual and manual labour is educationally wrong and socially undesirable and unhealthy. Nor is it consistent with the ethos and requirements of a democratic society that military training and military power should be the monopoly of an exclusive caste.

Third and final, the caste system is detrimental to healthy social development because it weakens and destroys unity by strengthening and elevating divisive caste loyalties at the expense of a larger and more comprehensive social consciousness. Ambedkar forcefully argued that this had made Hindu society incapable of defending itself and responding unitedly and effectively to those major challenges which were beyond the capacity of any single caste to face and combat. In that deeper sense, it is not Babasaheb who was the enemy of the unity of Hindu society. Rather it is the caste system, sanctified by orthodox Brahminism, which has all the time prevented the emergence of real unity.

Ambedkar's opposition to Brahminism was total and uncompromising. He said he could not reconcile his self-respect with a system so fundamentally inhuman. It is this which led him along with his followers finally to renounce Hinduism and embrace Buddhism. This has hurt the sentiments of many Hindus. But even here we should not miss the significance of his final choice of faith. On the eve of his conversion, he declared that he had told Mahatma Gandhi that when the time came for his renouncing Hinduism, 'I will choose only the least harmful way for the country ... I have taken care that my conversion will not harm the tradition of the culture and history of this land.'

Let us make no mistake about it. A rebel against the society in which he was born, Ambedkar's feeling for the unity of India and the Indian people was still strong and positive. In December 1946, he sensed civil war, and yet looking beyond he declared:

> We are in warring camps and I am probably one of the leaders of a warring camp. But with all this I am convinced that, given time and circumstances, nothing in the world will prevent this country from becoming one, and with all our castes and creeds we shall in some form be a united people.

And he went on to add, 'Notwithstanding the agitation of the League for the partition of India, some day enough light will dawn upon the Muslims themselves, and they, too, will begin to think that a united India is better for everybody.'

Thus Ambedkar dreamed of a united India founded on the solid rock of humanism and social democracy. We are still far from that culmination. But surely the birth centenary of Bhimrao Ramji Ambedkar is a fitting occasion for people of goodwill in all parts of this divided subcontinent to rededicate themselves to that high and noble objective.

It is important to make a distinction between what is abiding and what is temporary in the message left behind by any great man of the past. Ambedkar, himself no stranger to politics, knew the limitations of what can be achieved by political methods. In recent times, caste has got mixed up excessively with the idea of 'vote banks'. The question of 'quotas' and 'reservations' has virtually monopolised the debate on the reconstruction of Indian society, and Ambedkar's vision of a new India has got all but lost. The spirit of social democracy cannot be enthroned through legislative measures alone. A principal architect of the constitution of independent India, Ambedkar was still fully aware that a legal document cannot be a substitute for that spirit of brotherhood and vibrant sense of justice which can provide a firm foundation for the India of his dreams. Legislation has its place in social reform, but it needs to be constantly reviewed to find out what steps have yet to be taken to supply what is still missing. In the unfinished struggle for social equality in India, the best part of Babasaheb's ideas can be of inestimable value at this juncture.

17

On Gandhism

It is wrong to attempt to assess the merits of the Gandhian technique of struggle and the associated ethics and philosophy without reference to the conditions in which the technique and the philosophy developed. To a large extent the Gandhian technique of non-violent struggle made a virtue of necessity. It may, at least, be urged with considerable force that the technique would not have received the wide acceptance and whatever success it came to enjoy unless it had been rooted in necessity. When Gandhiji appeared on the Indian political scene, discontent against the British raj had already become a force in the ranks of the middle class. But this discontent had carved out for itself only the fruitless channels of terrorism, and possibly in large measure terrorism was getting inwardly diffident about its potency. When Gandhiji began his experiments with *satyagraha* against the vastly superior powers of suppression of the imperialist government, the method of violence used by the terrorists seemed futile. The argument that violence begets violence seemed to carry a decisive weight only because people came to realise that every act of violence by the local anti-imperialist forces could only provoke ruthless and effective retaliation from the enemy. It is always the victim of violence that comes to feel intensely that violence is wrong. The man with superior power of violence rarely recognises it.

It is in the nature of man to moralise. When India came to fear the might of British arms, she felt the psychological need of raising her fear to a moral plane, of explaining to herself that she was not really afraid, but was only indignant at the use of violence, and that the source of her indignation was her conscience which had the fineness to recognise the baseness of violence. It is only by going through this psychological process that the nation could hope to rehabilitate its self-respect. Gandhiji's philosophy of non-violence helped the nation to experience this invigorating psychological process. It infused into the nation a new sense of self-respect; it gave the Indians a sense of moral superiority over their violent oppressors; it made the people courageous with this sense of superiority, courageous even to face violence. It is impossible even for opponents of Gandhism to deny, consistently with observed facts, this elevating influence of Gandhiji's teachings on the masses of Indian humanity.

To state that the Gandhian glorification of non-violence found support in a widely felt emotional need of the Indian people is not to assert that the Gandhian philosophy lacks a rational basis. The psychological source of a belief neither confirms nor repudiates the possibility of establishing that belief on a purely rational basis. For the purpose of arriving at a rational estimate of Gandhism, it is useful to undertake a two-fold investigation, trying to find out, first, how far the Gandhian *technique* of struggle is efficacious, and, second, how far the Gandhian *philosophy* of life and society is valid and acceptable.

The Gandhian technique of political struggle as applied, for example, in the early thirties has been criticised by leftists on the ground that it was really dictated by the interest of Indian capitalists, that it insisted on strict observance of non-violence only because it intended to avoid revolutionary upheaval by insurgent masses. Spratt, in his book *Gandhism*, gives an interesting rejoinder to the leftist critic. He says that it is true that if Gandhiji had intended to avoid revolution in the interest of the capitalists while maintaining opposition to the British regime, the policy he actually adopted would have fitted in with his purpose; but at the same time, objectively speaking, revolution was not at all a serious possibility during the great years of the struggle in the early thirties, and it is a mis-representation of reality to suggest that Gandhian leader-ship was responsible at that time for holding off a right royal conquest of power by the people. If Gandhian leadership were more inclined towards violence, there could only have been greater disorder and chaos; there could not have been any revolution in the accepted sense of the term. A violent move-ment would undoubtedly have been repressed by the govern-ment quickly and effectively and could only have left behind among the people a mood of widespread depression. Re-covery from that depression would not have been easy or rapid. The quickness with which recovery actually took place after the failure of the Civil Disobedience movement of the early thirties is a tribute to the quality of the method and spirit of *satyagraha*. Non-violent non-cooperation could not, indeed, produce great results; but, Spratt suggests, every alternative method was, under the prevailing circumstances, bound to fail at least in equal measure. While concurring with this conclusion in large measure, it is possible to suggest that from a long-term point of view the results of the C.D. movement might have been better if, while retaining the general non-violent basis of the struggle, the movement had placed smaller reliance on Gandhian mystic appeals and greater reliance on formulation and propagation of the basic rights of the people. The objection may be raised that clear formulation and propagation of the rights of the people would have alienated the landlords and other privileged classes whose support Gandhiji was unwilling to lose at that stage. But here perhaps a bold, clear lead would have given the move-ment a healthier complexion and a more fruitful direction than compromise covered up with mysticism.

That the non-violent method of struggle was found eminently suitable to Indian conditions in the past is not any proof that it will remain desirable or acceptable in India in the future. Certain considerations against the adoption of violence will, however, remain strong even in the future. For one thing, a modern government is so well armed with the latest weapons of destruction that it is bound to be an extremely hazardous adventure for any group of people, however well organised, to seek to defeat an established government in an open trial based on violence. Moreover, the introduction of violence in political struggle is bound to destroy certain established codes and habits of social decency and toleration which are undoubtedly of no mean value. Violence, whether it brings victory to the one side or to the other, can hardly fail to charge the atmosphere with hatred and intolerance, to lead to the suppression of all opposition and to prepare the field for the rise of dictatorship and the eclipse of whatever is best in the liberal culture. It is the awareness of these vices of violence that persuades the intellectual Gandhian to stick to non-violence as the only proper method in a struggle for a free society. The exponent of revolution will possibly point out here that hatred of what is bad is quite consistent with love of what is good, and that a fighter for a free society who allows himself to grow indignant against the enslavers of man does not thereby do any harm to himself or to future society. This argument is not without some force, but it is vitiated by excessive naivety. Hatred, as it grows, has an inexorable tendency to overstep the limits of propriety. It is bad, indeed, to allow toleration to grow to a point where it paralyses all action, but it is equally bad to allow toleration to fall so low as to make possible the ascendency of the despotic tendency in human nature. The balance is always difficult to strike, and it is certain that will be quite wrongly struck when people are guided by glorified hatred. The emphasis on the desirability of keeping up toleration even in course of struggles against political opponents is, within limits, a highly desirable emphasis.

Gandhiji's insistence on love and non-violence calls for two other mutually unrelated but independently important comments.

While, as already pointed out, emphasis on toleration is useful, and the disregard (bordering often on contempt) for it expressed by extremists of the 'right' as well as of the 'left' is unfortunate, the absolutist Gandhian dictum that nothing done in hatred can have any real value is palpably false. Gandhiji made that extreme type of statements on a number of occasions. On a sober view, it appears that judgement on the value of any particular act depends on the balancing of many contrary considerations. There are material barriers to the good life, and it is good to break them down. Hatred is also a barrier to the good life, and it is good to do without hatred. If in a certain case people break down important material barriers to the good life and derive the energy for this act mainly from the spirit of hatred and bitterness, we may only say that the act would have been of higher value if the destruction of the material barrier, which by itself is desirable, were brought about without reliance on hatred, which by itself is undesirable. It is wrong to say that, bad and good aspects considered together, the act on the whole must necessarily be without value. In personal life as well as in social history, it is possible to find instances of acts done in bitterness producing results that on the whole are good. It must, however, be conceded at once that in matters like this, the past is not as sure a guide to the future as historically minded people may sometimes suppose. Organised application of violence is bound to be incomparably more costly in the future than it was in the past. The discovery of atomic energy has, so to say, added a new aspect to the controversy on non-violence. Even without subscribing to the Gandhian philosophy of non-violence in its absolute form, it is possible to hold that *satyagraha* as a technique of struggle represents today an experiment of great value.

The second comment on Gandhian non-violence has reference to a paradox. Many Gandhians, including Gandhiji himself, exhibit, in spite of their philosophy of love, a strange lack of open-mindedness. Many have felt—and some have registered that feeling—that in speaking before Gandhiji, they were speaking before closed doors. It is necessary to recognise here that love and understanding are not interchangeable terms; the one helps the other, but is never a complete substitute for the other. Gandhiji had enough of love and affection; but he lacked open-mindedness because he did not have a strictly rationalist temper and possibly made no serious endeavour to understand the changing course of social life, social thought and social relation. He often expressed quite clearly his distrust of reason and his disregard for scientific treatises. He relied on love and intuition. In a static society, in which people are largely agreed on the basic postulates of social ethics, conflicts between persons arise generally from selfishness and not from differences in intellectual presuppositions. In such a society, resolution of conflicts requires not any re-examination of basic beliefs, but only a 'searching of the heart' and a readiness to adjust interests in conformity with commonly shared moral principles. In such a society, it is truly love that is the most important solvent of discords. But in a changing world of ideas, open-mindedness and the critical spirit are essential for progress without undue friction and bitterness. The Renaissance in Europe released two great spiritual forces of immense importance, a new emotional devotion to man and nature as well as an eager scientific enquiry into the nature of things, a humanist as well as rationalist movement. The humanist movement is not really complete without rationalism. Gandhian humanism, otherwise lofty, has been vitiated by its link with mysticism and unreason, its failure to combine with the critical spirit of rationalism. It is desirable to preserve and propagate the magnificent emotional kernel of Gandhian humanism, but it is necessary to purify this kernel with the spirit of reason. Unless this is done, Gandhism in practice will produce results which may be quite shockingly anti-humanist.

Gandhiji's lack of understanding of the course of evolution of the world in which he lived, his preoccupation with a static model derived largely from a past society, produced serious drawbacks in his social philosophy. His theory of trusteeship illustrates this point. He could not think in terms of a radically different economic order in which there shall be no place for the landlord and the capitalist. For all practical purposes, he took the permanence of these classes for granted and thought of harmonising the interests of these classes with the welfare of the people through a process of moral conversion. The tendency to think instinctively in terms of harmonising conflicting interests was strengthened by the exigencies of the anti-British struggle which produced in him an unflagging eagerness to maintain the solidarity of nationalist forces. Professor Bose, in *Studies in Gandhism,* suggests that Gandhiji was wedded not to the theory of class-collaboration, but to the theory of peaceful and voluntary class-liquidation. This seems to be a representation of Gandhism as better than what it really is. A theory which cannot envisage a new order in which landlordism will be not simply purified, but will be quite out of place, is by no means a complete theory of the liquidation of the landlord class. In actual practice, the Gandhian theory lends itself to being employed as a shield against any movement for overthrowing the dominant classes in existing society.

In India, Gandhian theory is being made to serve purposes which true Gandhians deeply dislike. Its insistence on non-violence is used to impress the duty of obedience on wronged and resentful employees; the spirit of *satyagraha* is invoked to glorify contentment with suffering by the oppressed people; its mystic temper obstructs a rational reconsideration of the fundamentals of social ethics; the very greatness of Gandhiji is employed to inject into the minds of the people a fantastic national superiority complex. In short, it is used as a friend of conservatism, even of reaction. That is the tragic price that Gandhism has been called upon to pay for its failure to link itself with a dynamic view of society and rational ethics. That tragedy may only be avoided if Gandhians — more than any one else — pluck up courage to undertake a drastic revision of their creed in order to save and preserve its splendid humanist core.

18

What Gandhi Meant by God

Gandhi had an intense desire to see God face to face. Sometimes he expressed that desire in memorable words. But he did not claim to have seen Him. 'I have not seen Him', he once said, 'neither do I know him, but I have made the world's faith in God my own.'

It is doubtful if he really believed in a personal God. He wrote, 'I do not regard God as a person. Truth for me is God, and God's law and God are not different things. He and His law abide everywhere and govern everything.'

I have quoted Gandhi above. Now, quotations are not always a firm basis for settling points about a person's fundamental ideas and beliefs. The same person, even a great man, says different things at different phases of his life. But it still seems safe to maintain that, for Gandhi, the quest for God was a quest for God's law.

What then is God's law? For Gandhi, God's law is the law of love or, better still, the law of truth. He said, 'This law of love is nothing but a law of truth.' But why is it better to call it the law of truth?

It is better to call it so because God is not confined in space; He is everywhere and in everything. Truth has this quality of universality. What about love? 'Without truth', wrote Gandhi, 'there is no love; without truth, it may be affection, as for one's country to the injury of others; or infatuation, as of a young man for a girl; or love may be unreasoning and blind, as of ignorant parents for their children.' So love is a slippery word; it is shaky; it has to be fixed by being joined with truth. This is also the reason why Gandhi adopted the word *'ahimsa'* rather than 'love'. *'Ahimsa'* is steadier and it is rather more obvious that it must mean absence of *'himsa'* towards all. It is true that the word 'love' has the advantage of a more ready appeal; but *'ahimsa'* has been, on the whole, less contaminated by the evils of the world. That word has retained a purity of its own, or so Gandhi thought. *'Ahimsa'* obviously should not be used to describe a situation where there is *'himsa'* towards anybody. Once the basic idea is grasped, it matters little whether one talks of 'love' or *'ahimsa'*. Love is a beautiful word; but if it is to be used interchangeably with God, it must be free of all taint of jealousy or ill will against anybody. It must mean active goodwill for all.

This also clears up a point in the controversy between atheists and people like Gandhi who profess faith in God. Gandhi did not see God. The atheist may feel tempted to jump on that statement. If it is a matter of preaching love, why talk of God or spirituality. One does not have to go beyond the bounds of nature to talk of love. In a sense, this may be true. But there is this grave risk. When one talks of love within the confines of nature, love tends to get tainted. When one wants to talk of the purity of love, as an ideal, it helps one to understand and to communicate the point if God or spirituality is brought into the picture. Yet the word God, in turn, has to be continuously referred back to love and truth, or it is emptied of all energy, of what gives it life, and so God is left dead and cold. Gandhi wanted to stress this mutually supporting relationship between God and love and truth.

This tells us something about his idea of God. But it still does not say enough. Gandhi wanted to go one step further. He wanted to dynamise the idea of God by putting it into action, by activating it. Philosophers have interpreted the idea; men of religion have meditated on it; for Gandhi the point was to apply it, to make it work. When an eminent American missionary approached Gandhi and asked for his advice, the Mahatma said, 'emphasise love and make it your working force, for love is central in Christianity'. He chose his words carefully. He did not simply say that love was central to Christianity. That would amount to interpreting Christianity. But he stressed that love had to be made a 'working force'. He emphasised work.

Gandhi appreciated missionary work for spreading education or tending the sick or bringing relief to suffering humanity in other ways. But he had serious reservations about organised efforts for religious conversion. It will be interesting to find out the reasons. Some of these are of a temporary or special nature, others are more general and more fundamental.

One temporary reason for Gandhi's objection to Christian efforts towards religious conversion was simply related to the fact that the British were in power in India of his time. They were, therefore, in a position to distribute rewards and penalties. A programme of religious conversion tacitly backed up by the temporal authority looked unfair and morally suspect under those circumstances. Whether the missionaries wanted it or not, those who opted for conversion to the faith of the rulers might be influenced by expectations of material gains. Conversion based on such expectations would lack moral merit. With the emergence of India as a sovereign state that objection would no longer hold. But there would still be a complicating factor left. Within India different communities compete for power and position. In a democracy numbers count. Conversion on a large-scale may tilt the balance in favour of one community or another. Thus the drive for conversions may get mixed up with the competition for power. A particular community may grow in size and put forward demands on the basis of their numerical strength and this may lead to political and social tensions. This will not generate love.

Suppose that these complications did not exist. Would conversion be justified then? There are reasons to believe that Gandhi would not have objected to a conversion which was free of these complications and rooted purely in moral conviction. He would not have objected in individual cases on those abstract suppositions. But he would still have a reservation expressed in general terms. His argument would be simply this.

There is a sense in which all religions are equal, or so Gandhi thought. At the heart of all the great religions, there is a message which is universal and of equal value wherever it is found. It is better for a person to go deep into his own religion and discover its ethical and spiritual core. Moral restlessness should prompt a Hindu or a Muslim, for instance, to explore further his own faith rather than to change over from one organised faith to another. The truth of religion, of all religions properly so-called, of God, is one and the same. This is where Gandhi and the missionaries failed to agree.

All great religions are, in their essence, about love and truth. The really serious business is not to change outer labels, but to deepen one's understanding of this truth and to practise it. This is a point which we may now stop to consider. Knowledge is power. This is what Francis Bacon taught, and a whole age received that teaching and believed in it. The focus then was on knowledge of the physical laws of nature, the kind of knowledge which created new technology and so gave man greater power to produce wealth, that is material goods. Gandhi too was thinking of power, but power of a different kind. He, too, attached tremendous importance to experiments, as the practitioners of the physical sciences did. It is not without significance that he called his autobiography *My Experiments with Truth*. He had a very experimental attitude towards religion. But it is with the law of love that he experimented, in personal life, in small groups in his ashram and on a national scale. It is impossible to understand Gandhi without taking into account his strikingly practical and experimental attitude.

There is one point which needs clarification here. Spiritual experiments are not a new thing in India. As a matter of fact, yoga itself is an experimental method and it has a long tradition. The yogi sometimes acquired great power. But he was not involved so much in a social experiment. The yogi was primarily concerned with his own salvation. That was more typical. Gandhi made the law of love an instrument of social action. Perhaps some branches of Buddhism come closest to the Gandhian outlook. But Gandhi was born at a different stage of human history, his methods were different and he has more immediate relevance for us.

Of the law of love, we shall presently speak briefly of two aspects.

It is important to understand love both as an ideal and as something existing. In its pure form, it is an ideal, just as some of the concepts of mathematics have only an ideal existence. But this does not make love, or those concepts, operationally invalid. As a matter of fact, their justification lies in their operational validity. Love is not simply a dream or a distant ideal, but it permeates life and creates and sustains life.

This is easy to illustrate. We have simply to think of a child which was cut off from all love and consider the consequences. Or think of a grown-up person locked up in a solitary cell, provided with sufficient food and the other material requirements for the body. Under these conditions, a normal human person will soon disintegrate psychologically; he may simply go mad. Thus love is the minimum condition of mental sanity. The absence of love that we witness all around becomes tolerable only because there is some love still left somewhere. Even a little love saves. Cut off all love and you have killed life. Love, then, is a condition of humanity. We have to assume that the need for love and the capacity for it exist in all men, although it may have suffered atrophy in some.

There is in every man a spiritual energy. It exists mixed up with many impurities. It can be purified and the purer it becomes the more powerful it is. In its pure form, it manifests itself as the power of love. Just as electricity can be made to work so too the power of love. Gandhi used it in two ways. In the first place, he used it for his programme of constructive work. But he also used it in a second way. That was the most striking thing he did. Love can be used as an instrument of war against injustice. In fact, it is the most potent instrument. This is the other manifestation of the power of love. Gandhi called it 'soul force' or 'truth force'. *Satyagraha* is 'truth force' organised and applied for combating injustice.

The basic idea is quite simple. We should not withdraw love, for love must be all pervasive and made to work. All we do is to refuse to cooperate with what we consider to be evil, without ceasing to love the evil-doer. This is what a true friend does to a friend. And this should be enough. Injustice cannot last when those on whom it is perpetrated refuse to cooperate.

Here Gandhi discovered and demonstrated something new. We know of some great religious teachers who enjoined on us to return good for evil or to respond to anger with love. But nobody before Gandhi had organised passive resistance on such a large scale and demonstrated before the full view of humanity that it worked. This was something unprecedented.

The principal axioms on which the theory and practice of passive resistance rest can now be stated. In the first place, evil is parasitic on good, inhumanity on humanity. Second, no man is entirely devoid of humanity. Third and final, suffering, rightly practised with a purpose, can restore to a person his lost humanity. These ideas may now be briefly expounded.

Exploitation is made possible by the willingness of the exploited to render labour under the person who exploits him. It may be forced labour. But the worker has the ultimate choice of deciding that he will not work under the terms offered, which he judges unjust, and then face all consequences unflinchingly. If injustice in whatever form is done by a minority, the majority can bring it to an end by refusing to carry out the orders of that minority. In fact, even a minority can practise *satyagraha* against a majority, for a wrong can equally be perpetrated by a majority.

That no man is entirely devoid of humanity, that is a capacity to love or be touched by love, is an idea which we have already encountered above. But now it is a question of putting it into practice. Here Gandhi fastens on the idea of the potency, the secret power, of suffering. By taking suffering upon himself, the non-violent fighter strives to awaken the dormant humanity of the evil-doer. The *satyagrahi* fights with his power of suffering, arouses his opponent's power of sympathy and so restores him to humanity while restoring to himself the justice so long denied.

As man is fallible, so the *satyagrahi* himself may have made a mistake. He may even be fighting for the wrong cause. But then a non-violent struggle has the advantage that, if it is properly conducted, it leaves behind no trail of bitterness. With fallible men, a non-violent struggle is, therefore, the best course to follow. If a dispute arises which cannot be decided by other peaceful means such as arbitration, *satyagraha* should be the method of last resort. It is the best method because its costs are minimum and the value added is maximum.

That *satyagraha* works was Gandhi's great message of hope. New technology intertwined with the delicate texture of modern civilisation has brought mankind to a point where a war, fought by violent means, can produce catastrophic consequences. It may even result in the annihilation of mankind. But disputes between individuals, communities and countries are there and will continue to be. If human society is to survive, what is needed is a method of settling rival demands which works without threatening all concerned with total destruction. History has been moving in a dangerous direction, faster in our century than ever before, producing all round a mood of black despair. It is in this situation that Gandhi came and made his momentous experiments.

Either there is a non-violent alternative to war or there is no hope for human civilisation. Gandhi's gospel, the good news he brought for the world, is that there is, indeed, a non-violent alternative to war, provided a sufficient number of men prepare themselves for it. Gandhi brought this good news when mankind needed it most. As Stanley Jones said in his book, *Mahatma Gandhi: An Interpretation*, in the fateful year of 1948, 'If the atomic bomb was militarism's trump card thrown down on the table of human events, then Mahatma Gandhi is God's trump card which he throws on the table of events now — a table trembling with destiny.' India itself is a world in miniature. Here too the forces of violence are surfacing again, their protagonists often swearing by false gods. It is time now to remember what Gandhi meant by God.

19

Kumarappa's Critique
of High Industrialisation

Although 'globalisation' bids fair to conquer the seats of power all over the world today more completely than any great religion ever did in the past, there is some consolation to be derived from the fact that the venerable tradition of economic thought from which it draws support has not gone unchallenged. There are signs that a body of unorthodox ideas represented by thinkers like Ruskin and Gandhi, which used to be treated in academic circles with scant respect till recently, is now receiving more attention than it did earlier in the 20th century. Professor Mark Lindley's admirable work, *J.C. Kumarappa: Mahatma Gandhi's Economist*, provides evidence of this new development. It is worth presenting the matter in a historical perspective.

The mainstream of traditional economic thought is usually traced back to Adam Smith (1723–90), Ricardo and J.B. Say. The academically acknowledged opposition to this tradition starts with Sismondi followed by Karl Marx and his disciples.

Although one part of the orthodox stream of thought came to accommodate in course of time analytical innovations of sufficient importance to break loose from classicism and establish a neo-classical school, it clearly retained an unbroken identity of its own by virtue of its steadfast support for industrial development based on the market system. It is only fair to add that those who reposed faith in the efficacy of the 'invisible hand' of the market were careful enough to leave room for a supplementary role to be played by the state, which Smith had himself approved under the rubric of the three-fold duties of the sovereign which included the maintenance of 'institutions which may be in the highest degree advantageous to a great society ... though they could never repay the expense to any individual or small number of individuals.'

As far as Marxian thought is concerned, it should be noted that although its identity is based on a critique of capitalism, it is not opposed to high industrialisation. This is what sets the peculiarly heterodox ideas represented by Ruskin, Thoreau and Gandhi clearly apart not only from the orthodox stream of classical economic thought but also from its accredited Marxist critics who have been appreciative of the Industrial Revolution as a manifestation of the forward march of the 'forces of production' even as they have been critical of the exploitative capitalist 'relations of production'. It is in this context that we have to try and understand the significance of the Gandhian challenge.

Let us restate the basic point. Recognising that mankind, divided into 'tribes', has a common and interrelated history and, for better or for worse, a common destination, if we now seek to gain some understanding of the general design of history in the modern age, we may with reason find it, as Arnold Toynbee did, in the inexorable drive towards industrialisation in different parts of the world with certain time lags in the last couple of centuries. In that design are included the diverse histories of England, Germany, the United States, Russia and Japan and several countries of the Third World in more recent times. This leads up to a crucial question. Why did all these nations, so different in their cultural background, feel persuaded to opt for industrialisation?

This is a question I raised when I was invited to deliver the Tagore Memorial Lecture 2000 at the Indian Institute of Technology at Kharagpur. I apologise for being so personal, but this helps me to come straight to an answer to that question. 'The choice in favour of industrialisation was made', I ventured to suggest, 'not because industrialisation (of the kind adopted) seemed to guarantee greater welfare, higher culture or anything of that kind, but because ... it guarantee(d) greater military power (to the nation concerned) to resist the threat of subjugation by other industrially advanced countries.' It is military power for the sake of national security or national glory which has been the decisive consideration and that is how a large part of the history of our time has been moulded. It is important to grasp this point for a proper understanding of the Gandhian critique of modern economics. The question of industrialisation is intimately linked up with the deeper question of violence and non-violence.

There is, in fact, a two-way connection between industrialism and military power. Search for military power has strengthened the national resolve to launch forth on the path to rapid industrial growth. The requirements of industrialisation have dictated a high degree of centralisation of power, economic and political, notably in the form of the national state. Even if a programme of economic development with accent on large-scale industry is adopted from non-military considerations, it usually requires for its efficient execution a highly centralised administration. The nation state, by its very form and spirit, tends to sharpen the struggle for power, thus creating a vicious circle of violence. This has its social costs which escape all accounting. This is the heart of Kumarappa's critique of modern industrialism. Let me quote from Kumarappa to substantiate this point. Gandhi and Kumarappa had occasional disagreement. But they substantially agreed on what follows: 'Under mass production, whether under capitalism or communism, every person becomes a 'Hand' or a 'mouth'... We have invented machines that have become masters.'

While the plant that transforms raw materials into consumable articles is located in someone place, the ... raw materials are gathered from the places of their origin and brought together to feed the machinery... at a speed demanded by the technical requirements... (And then) when the goods have been produced they have to be sold. ... Exchange, customs and other financial and political barriers have to be regulated... All this can be done only at the point of the bayonet.

The nation pays through the nose for its armaments program, holds raw-material producers in political bondage, and sacrifices its sons. When the cost of production includes all these, who will say that centralized production is cheaper?

These extracts are taken from Dr Lindley's carefully compiled work. Kumarappa's argument bears the marks of the Indian experience and is not equally applicable to other countries at all points. But the general thrust of the reasoning deserves careful consideration today as much as it did when it was first presented in the second quarter of the 20th century. It will be an error to ignore its universalist significance.

Let us try and investigate the problem a little more deeply. Where do the roots of evil lie in contemporary society? There are rival hypotheses in this regard. Marxists and many orthodox socialists have long maintained that private ownership of the means of production is the principal culprit. Gandhians put the blame on overcentralisation of power and excessive mechanisation of production along with failings of human nature, such as greed, fear and hatred. The Marxist hypothesis was tested by the leaders of the Bolshevik revolution as best as they could and it did not come out gloriously. Private ownership of the means of production was extensively abolished in the Soviet Union. But this did not result in the abolition of injustice and the establishment of freedom in the new social order. The Gandhian hypothesis had never a chance to be seriously tested. It still needs to be closely examined.

What are the grounds for the Gandhian indictment of modern technology? We have already noticed a few things that Kumarappa had to say about it. For one thing, mass production robs the worker of his personal identity: 'every person becomes a hand'.

There is also something more to be considered seriously. When production is undertaken for the main part with local resources for local consumption, we get a neighbourhood economy where workers stay integrated with a stable society. Under factory production, labourers are uprooted from their homes and burdened with the uncertainty of being thrown out of job and forced to drift farther away. And so we get 'a rootless proletariat', as pointed out by Fritz Schumacher, the noted economist who was strongly attracted by Gandhian ideas.

This leads on to other points of profound cultural and political importance. When people are cut off from sources of satisfaction of natural affections, they seek compensation else where by methods which may be socially very expensive. Thus the 'external cost' of highly concentrated production can be reasonably computed to be much higher than what orthodox economists ever cared to take into account. In fact, the question of violence is closely related to this matter.

Human violence is perpetrated both against other humans and against nature. Man's cruelty towards other men is not something new; but science and technology today has put at the disposal of man's untamed ferocity vastly increased powers of mass destruction. Violence against nature has become a serious global problem only in comparatively recent times. The problem has been aggravated by a sea change in man's life style. The fast life of modern high-tech society has taken away from man the simple joys of unmediated communion with nature and intimate companionship and substituted for these a whole new world of mechanically contrived and marketable pleasures. Here we have a problem of vast magnitude which needs to be addressed with all seriousness. Uncontrolled consumerism has combined with persistent militarism to produce an assault on the non-renewable resources of nature and this threatens to undermine the foundations of the safety and the welfare of the present as well as future generations of mankind.

E.F. Schumacher, who—perhaps more than anybody else in the last half a century—alerted public opinion all over the world about the gravity of the ecological problem, remarked in an article in 1960 that 'a way of life that ever more rapidly depletes the power of earth to sustain it and piles up ever more insoluble problems for each succeeding generation can only be called "violent"'. A few years earlier he had written in a more circumscribed manner: 'The whole problem of ... the exhaustion of non-renewable resources can probably be reduced to this one point—Energy.' A few inferences readily follow. What is crucially required now is a new technology, an 'appropriate' technology, for a systematic utilisation of a source of energy which is 'clean' and 'safe'. Neither coal nor fossil fuel nor atomic energy satisfies this double requirement; solar energy does. We have to go a long way before the new technology can be put into use really extensively. Evidently this innovative use of energy will be compatible with, even require, a plan for more decentralised production. This will also call for and facilitate an appropriate change in people's way of life.

All these add up to an unprecedented global experiment which cannot succeed unless it is accompanied and supported by a 'philosophy of non-violence'. These are the goals of the Gandhian programme. There are other items too which are not equally relevant to the world today. We have to make a distinction between what is universal in the Gandhian outlook and what is more culturally bounded. The stage is set for a historic debate. Are the Gandhian goals realisable? Can anything much less rescue the world from the contemporary crisis? The debate remains titled in favour of high industrialisation for two main reasons. In the first place, it is very hard for a nation state to vote unilaterally against the use of military power. Second, national policy is framed by a 'new class' which is created by modern commerce and industry and finds it difficult to resist its many allurements. But there are larger existential considerations connected with the collective welfare of mankind which cannot rationally be ignored for any great length of time.

20

Life World: Private and Public Domains

Life has to the lived in two different domains, the private and the public. Their requirements are different, sometimes seemingly irreconcilable. The private domain turns barren when it has no room for love. But love is not a sufficient basis for justice, which is a necessary condition for a good life in the public domain.

At an elementary level, our sense of responsibility towards others arises from natural sympathy. Thus it is that the family becomes the nursery of people's moral sentiments. Neighbours and others sharing a similar culture come to be included within the boundaries of our sympathy. Thus people come together, both by necessity and by instinct, to form communities or tribes, held together by customs and a sense of mutual obligations and loyalty. At this stage a problem arises. The boundaries harden. With the growth of tribalism, what started as a process of union becomes a source of division. The role of true morality is to carry the sense of caring for others beyond the limits set by tribal solidarity.

Here is an evolutionary problem which remains still unresolved all over the world. Tribalism has many incarnations. In different parts of the globe it is found in different forms. Moreover, it often manifests itself in diverse ways even within the same society.

Let us take the case of India. Corruption is rampant in our society at all levels, the more deplorably so at the higher and middle levels. Yet this country has seen even in the 20th century some of the greatest men the world has produced. How can we explain this contradiction? Most nationalists including the 'Leftists' blame it all on India's 'colonial heritage'. Very few of us care to turn the searchlight inwards.

Yet we cannot really cure our disease by simply blaming outsiders. We have to have the objectivity, courage and determination to discover and defeat what is false or wanting within our own tradition and society. For centuries, the mainstream of the Indian tradition has lacked a clear recognition of the importance of civil rights, public duties and an impersonal dispensation of justice.

What existed instead was our own brand of tribalism, an emphasis on loyalty to the caste to which one belonged and the prescribed duties that went with it. Along with it came an acceptance of the value of familial sentiments and obligations, which traditionally included the virtue of hospitality but had little room for the idea of equality and impersonal justice. Special importance was also attached to the observance of religious rituals. Deploring the neglect of active social service by Hindu religious establishments, Raja Ram Mohan Roy very perceptively observed long ago that in the Hindu theology 'rites and ceremonies' had become virtually synonymous with 'action of moral merit'. Now, all these do not really add up even remotely to the moral requirements of modern society.

In a properly constituted civil society, a person holding a position of public responsibility is morally bound to give precedence to the public interest. In India, as long as a person stays loyal to his family and his caste, his public image remains virtually untarnished, however much he may neglect his public duties or misuse public funds. During the days when Prime Minister Indira Gandhi was trying to build up Sanjay Gandhi by dubious methods, I remember having overheard somebody arguing that if a mother would not help her son, who would? Politics has also given a new twist to the order of things. Robbing the public to help the party has come to be treated as an acceptable practice by those who are engaged in the political struggle for power. Violence is on the increase and unbridled partisanship is pushing the country towards conditions of a thinly disguised civil war.

For the ancients, politics and ethics were cognate subjects concerned with an exploration of the conditions necessary for securing justice and achieving the good society. Economics too came under the umbrella of ethics.

It is no longer the same in our time, although a few are valiantly attempting to reconstruct the broken links. Ethical issues have been thrown into a sad state of disarray by politics, with its fevered pursuit of power, and economics with its overemphasis on the importance of wealth. This makes it necessary to try and present the subject of morality and ethics in a proper perspective as concisely as possible before we conclude. What we will be attempting here is an exposition with practical implications.

Plato made a distinction between desires, passions and reason. There is an area of human relations where affective inclinations, desires and passions, normally prevail. At an early stage of social evolution, based on kinship ties, this looks natural. At higher stages of society, moral codes guided by reason become more important for the maintenance of justice and social cohesion.

Moral injunctions and activities can be divided into two categories. Some moral duties are mandatory. There are other activities inspired by goodwill which are laudatory; they may be noble, but they are not obligatory.

For instance, murder and rapes are punishable crimes and the moral injunction against such acts is absolute. If somebody risks his own life to prevent such a crime done to a third person, his moral courage will deserve high praise. But there is nothing in law which requires him so to risk his life and it is not considered a crime if he chooses not to take that risk. The mandatory duties of a citizen so sadly neglected in our society and the deepest promptings of love and compassion do not belong to the same level of reason and consciousness.

Religion is commonly regarded as a source of ethical teachings. The problem with the scriptures is that they include an extraordinary range of statements extending from the utterly superstitious to the truly spiritual. Aurobindo made a distinction between the infra-rational, the rational and the supra-rational. Racial hatred and sectarian fanaticism clearly belong to the infra-rational region of human consciousness. A cardinal weakness of the Indian tradition is that it is too inclined to take a big leap from the infra-rational to the supra-rational and bypass the rational. The service of critical reason is necessary to purge human consciousness of its superstitious elements. The cleansing mission of the rational part of our mind needs to be combined with that grand vision of the spirit which urges us to love our enemies and seek union with the universe. Not everybody can rise to the height of that grand vision, but we cannot give up striving for reason and justice without grave peril to the fabric of human society.

21

Beyond the Clash of Civilisations

Parallel with the pollution of the physical environment, there is a psychological pollution which is spreading all around. This is as evident abroad as nearer home. With the end of the Cold War, there was hope of a new beginning of peace. However, this did not happen. The old ideological war was now replaced by what has come to be called, thanks to Huntington, the clash of civilisations. Calling the upsurge of violence at the present juncture by that name does not exactly help promote peace. Rather it gives organised violence on either side a kind of justification, a sense that one is fighting for a high cause, a civilisation. However, it can also serve to make sensible people more conscious of the possibility of all civilisations being doomed by the clash of rival brands of fanaticism. If our striving for peace is strengthened by that perception, it is even possible that out of evil will come good.

In the clash of civilisations, President Bush puts himself in the position of the great leader of Western civilisation, this in spite of the fact that the only other Western country ready to follow him is Britain. President Bush has dressed up Saddam Hussein as his arch enemy. How do we explain this? At a personal level, George W. Bush is reported to have complained that Saddam Hussein is 'the guy who tried to kill Dad'. This sounds terribly tribal. Some commentators believe that America's bellicose policy is explained by a desire to gain control over Iraq's oil reserves. Perhaps this is not the whole explanation. In the 'clash of civilisations', America is on the side of Israel. If Iraq is indeed equipped with deadly weapons, it does constitute a serious threat to Israel's security. Or, so it is felt. If Iraq can browbeat Israel, it will become the leader of the Arabs and, more generally, the Islamic people. Bush would not let this be. It is true that Saddam was not a man of religion. But that does not matter so much. Jinnah was not a man of religion. Power attracts and it has a logic all its own.

President Bush has a dangerous way of looking at things. The United States does feel persuaded that it has the historic duty of ordering around keeping the peace in the world. But it will be unrealistic on its part to expect other countries, some of them important members of the world community, to agree with America's perception of its duty. Bombing Iraq, it cannot win the heart of the Islamic world nor the assent of a number of other major countries. It has indeed enough resources to buy the support of a few heads of state who do not really represent the peoples of the countries where they rule. This is not how the superpower can pave the way for a lasting peace. Nor is this the way to prevent more terrorist strikes against America and elsewhere.

There are other ways of working for peace. If the demand for a Jewish homeland deserved to be treated with sympathy, so does the Palestinian demand. The United States and the world community as represented by the United Nations must do justice and appear to be doing justice by these rival demands. Judaism and Islam are cognate religions and quite strikingly similar in a number of ways. If they can set an example of peaceful coexistence in west Asia, they will be jointly doing a great service to humanity. The Arabs must accept the existence of Israel as a settled fact and Israel must give up ambitions of aggrandisement. The vision of a confederation, an Arab–Israel Union, should guide the steps of West Asian political entities towards lasting peace and cooperation. Only by a consistent policy of helping this process can America play a positive and constructive role in that troubled part of the world.

Between a bird of prey and its natural prey, the relationship is antagonistic as part of nature's design. It is not like that between the Jews and the Muslims in West Asia. The antagonism there derives from man-made causes, political and cultural circumstances, which men can change if they have the necessary will and foresight. If the will fails in this case, it will be morally deplorable as the consequences of failure will be extremely unfortunate both for West Asia and for the international community as a whole. The same kind of reasoning, with suitable modification to allow for local differences, should be deemed valid for other parts of the world including India. There is such a strong similarity among problems the world over that one can think and act today in terms of a flexible global agenda.

Peace is what the world needs today first and foremost. As peace is a requirement for sanity and survival, other questions, though important, should not be allowed to obscure the importance of peace. For instance, it is less important whether a person believes in God; it is more important that he should talk the language of peace. If one does believe in religion, one must have a proper criterion for distinguishing between a true and a false religion. The spirit of peace can well serve as that criterion. For instance, it is more important to promote the spirit of peace in the Indian subcontinent than to build or demolish a temple, a church or a mosque. In a clash of false religions, a true believer should have the strength to rise above the battle. Equally, in a clash of civilisations, one should have the strength of conviction to rise above that clash and take one's stand on the side of humanism as the core of true civilisation.

In a good society, justice is a major objective. The most significant contribution of Gandhian thought in our time lies in its earnest endeavour to address the question of how to reconcile the spirit of non-violence with the moral requirement to oppose injustice. In the same sense, it is important to assist a process of reviewing and reconstructing our political, economic and social institutions to bring them into closer conformity with the requirements of peace and justice. For instance, we have seen politics getting shamelessly corrupted by a struggle for power in flagrant disregard of all ethical norms. Building democracy from the base and making people's power an effective instrument of social welfare is an unfinished task awaiting completion in the years ahead.

Technology has always had a strong influence on the structure of society. A programme of social reconstruction must have its technological complement. If in the past technology substantially decided for us the kind of society we have, in future it should be the other way round. Our social goals and ideals should strongly influence the orientation of our scientific research and technical experiments.

All these hold out the prospect of an exciting agenda for the new century. There is one further thought with which we should conclude. The transition to a new stage in social evolution will not be effective without an adequate and supporting change in human consciousness. There is no conceivable set of social institutions, call it by whatever name you please, which can guarantee a sufficient change in the quality of the human mind. A reconstruction of political, economic and social institutions is desirable, even necessary. But that is not enough. The terrible things that happen outside are warnings. But these cannot be relied upon to produce the necessary transformation of human consciousness any more than a child can be helped to attain a true vision of the good life by mere threats of punishment. Clash of civilisations at this late hour in human history has been made possible by a legacy of wrong ideas and a deformity of human vision.

Nothing that we can think up in terms of outward circumstances can be relied upon with certainty to bring about an inner transformation such as we need. It should be understood that what we are concerned with here is not personal salvation but overcoming a social crisis. It is in that context that we talked of the insufficiency of institutional changes and the need for a change in the quality of consciousness. Although nothing makes such a change inevitable, certain things do help by teaching people 'right discrimination'. Such, for instance, is a philosophy of life that looks beyond the principle of pleasure and ideas of moral allegiance which are truly humanistic. Compassion for the suffering heart of humanity is more important than power, a feeling of union with nature and the universe more fulfilling than pleasure. Creative writers and artists can help convey this message. However, these things cannot be planned, surely not at the state level. A state-sponsored philosophy and state-controlled art and literature can be worse than useless. The state does have a role in education, but even there it is dangerous to cross limits. Cut flowers can be no substitute for spontaneously blooming blossoms.

Common people who feel drawn by such ideas have a more important role to play than what a hierarchy of official bodies can achieve. We the people can form societies of friends. These friendly associations can discuss and disseminate ideas, render loving service in times of distress, stoutly resist the pretensions of fanatical faiths, provide warmth in an otherwise cold environment and create small models of an alternative society while things fall apart all around. From small islands, where men respond reasonably to nature's signals, the message may travel to the wider continent of humanity.

These ideas will not appeal to those who have lost faith in man. But this amounts to a meek acceptance of the idea of an inevitable doom. Does reason require that we accept such a philosophy of hopelessness? We do not know with certainty the final outcome of the evolution of human civilisation. It is more manly to keep up hope and courage and act according to the dictates of conscience as long as there is life in us. If civilisation goes under, let that not happen because we did not strive to save it.

22

The Problem of Corruption

Corruption in public life has become a cause for deep concern the world over. None of the major countries of the world appears to be even moderately free from it. How we will rank the different countries in respect of their degrees of corruption depends to some extent on our judgment regarding the forms of corruption which we consider to be most censurable and harmful for society. Despite its complicated multiplicity of forms, most of these stem patently from either money or sex. It is possible to push the analysis further back; in fact, it is necessary to do so. But money and sex provide convenient starting points for discussing the matter.

Beyond question, money serves some useful functions. These are so well known that it is unnecessary to talk about them at length. Money is useful as a medium of exchange, a store of value, a standard and a basis for accounting. Yet it has been proverbially described as the source of all evil, a proverb which cannot be simply dismissed as baseless. Here is an acute paradox. On the one hand, money and its diverse derivatives, such as instruments of credit, cannot be banished at the present stage of the evolution of our economy. On the other hand, they engender forms of corruption which, on recent evidence, are so serious that, if unchecked, they threaten to damage gravely the fabric of modern society. We have here a problem which is not easy to solve yet far too dangerous to ignore.

To some extent, the problem with sex is of an analogous nature. The attraction between the sexes serves some useful, even essential, purposes of life. It is part of the mechanism by which the survival of the species has been ensured so far. It is also a source of natural energy and joy and an important component of poetry and culture. Yet, at the same time, it is prone to take vicious forms, souring and corrupting human relations. Even from ancient times, it has been recognised as a major factor of strife and war, as even a cursory glance at the epics will attest. Property and sex match each other in their capacity to produce conflict and violence. However, the analogy should not be pushed too far. While sex, like money, is marked by opposite tendencies, benign and malign, constituting a kind of contradiction, there are essential differences between the two and it is better to consider them separately rather than lump them together.

Money is an instrument with a multiplicity of uses. For an understanding of corruption, it is simpler to look at it from a consumer's point of view. What is money desired for? A miser is supposed to desire money for its own sake. But this is uncommon. Money is commonly desired on account of its purchasing power, the power it gives to command commodities in general, including goods and services of many different kinds. Some commodities are obviously necessary to provide the bare means of subsistence, an essential support of life. Others are required as aids to creative activity. Still others are desired for pleasure. Beyond what goes by the name of pleasure, there is craving for power. Money is desired not only for sensual pleasure but also for power. This is an important phenomenon which calls for separate attention. Individuals and groups of people, including political parties, want money for acquiring and defending power. Not a small part of the corruption prevalent all around can be traced to this source. The sum total of human happiness is not enhanced by this struggle for power. But it does use up a great deal of money, often acquired by questionable means.

It will be instructive to look at the matter against a historical setting. The history of our time has been moulded and deeply influenced by three interlinked forces — the growth of industrialism, the spread of the market system all over the globe and the rise of the modern state as a formidable centre of power, military and administrative. The contemporary upsurge of consumerism is closely related to modern technology which offers ever new consumer durables and services, while the market system is naturally interested in creating a taste and strengthening the demand for these commodities. Politics is concerned with the struggle for power centering round the modern state. This struggle for power is notably unrestrained by moral scruples. Neither dictatorial regimes nor democracies are immune from the infection of politics divorced from ethics. The quest for money has followed a parallel course, though business ethics fights to survive. People find their normal income insufficient to satisfy either their craving for power or their appetite for new and attractive commodities and so fail to resist the temptation to gain extra money by morally indefensible means. This describes, in simplest terms, the process of growth of corruption.

Once we accept the preceding analysis, we find ourselves placed on the horns of a dilemma. It is unrealistic to expect the state to wither away in the foreseeable future or the global market system to disappear. But if this be so, does it not follow that consumerism and the struggle for power and the resulting evils will also continue unabated and the crisis of civilisation will persist and even deepen in course of time?

Yet we have to keep hoping that there is a way out of the horns of that dilemma, a third way, so to speak. What weakens our determination to take that course or, at least, start moving in that direction in all earnestness is a lack of genuine conviction about the seriousness of the crisis of our time. We are in the grip of a wrong philosophy about the way to human happiness and we cannot make much headway until that grip is loosened.

Next to hunger for food, man's most pressing need is what has been felicitously called 'hunger for union'. The hardest of all punishment is confinement in a solitary cell. One may feel so confined even without brick walls. The Spring 1998 number of 'Australian Humanist' carries a piece with the significant headline *We are alone: How shall we live?*

Consumerism cannot rescue man from the trap of alienation. The case against consumerism can be simply stated. Beyond a certain point, the additional pleasure that commodities can fetch starts diminishing. Overwhelmed by the external stimuli supplied by commodities, one's capacity to feel love and inner joy grows weak. But by that time, one is already in bondage to consumerism. This is a kind of addiction which is difficult, even painful, to give up. Most addictions have this common characteristic: one stays in a state of bondage because it is painful to break that bondage. A feeling of inner loneliness continues to be there. No amount of purchasable things can compensate for the loss of a positive feeling of fellowship.

The growth of 'fundamentalism', so evident all around us, can be explained as a reaction to this situation. People court a militant solidarity with some group, a new tribalism, as a way of escape from a feeling of loneliness and insecurity. Politics steps in and 'fundamentalism' gets mixed up with the struggle for power. What results from this is not a movement towards good neighbourliness, but collective hatred. This cannot be a way out of the contemporary crisis. What we need is a principle of union which leads on from smaller to larger circles, not that intensification of conflicts among local groups which must ultimately be ruinous for all concerned.

This has a message about the form and spirit of an alternative society for the future. The message is clear enough, but it is obscured by settled habits of thought inscribed in the central tradition of political economy since the time of Adam Smith. Smith wisely recognised both the value of private enterprise working within a competitive market system and the limits of that system. Whatever activities of importance fell outside those limits, he tended to include under the 'duties of the sovereign'. By and large, the market and the state have come to occupy all the space in our economic and political thinking. Whatever goods and services the market fails to deliver satisfactorily, the public expects to be supplied by the state. It is time to think constructively of an alternative social order which is not constricted by this narrow duality. In fact, new thinking on these alternative lines was already initiated by stalwarts like Rabindranath Tagore and Gandhi at the beginning of this century. But their ideas have not been included in the mainstream of our social philosophy. However, there are signs that new ideas similar to theirs will gain increasing acceptance by the force of circumstances in the coming decades. The future depends to no small extent on the outcome of this struggle of ideas both in theory and in practice.

Outside the private and public sectors, there is space for a community sector. Ideally speaking, the village is an example of the community sector. However, the Indian village today is a poor specimen of that reconstructed village that Tagore dreamt of when he set up the Institute for Rural Reconstruction at Sriniketan. Gandhi, blending politics with economics and distrustful of the power of the state, spoke of *Gram Swaraj*. The idea of the community sector can also be fitted in a vision of the future city. However, it is simpler to expound the central concept with reference to the village before we extend it farther a field.

A village is a face-to-face community, a community of neighbours. In reality, the typical Indian village is not a homogenous whole. It is divided into groups belonging to different castes and sects, segregated from one another by customs and superstitions, sometimes ancient rivalries. It is burdened by a social hierarchy which contradicts the idea of human brotherhood. The task for the future is not just to 'revive' the village, but to reconstruct it as an experiment in community building in a new form and befitting spirit. It will be proper to add here a few words on the form and spirit of the model to strive for.

The economy of the community sector will take the form of what has sometimes been called the neighbourhood economy. It will be more self-reliant than reliant on the state and its bureaucratic machinery; largely self-sufficient in its basic necessities, but not isolated from the outside world; and ready to adopt flexible forms of cooperation cutting across caste and class barriers which should be vanishing in any case in course of time. As far as possible, the neighbourhood economy should utilise the surplus labour of the village and locally available resources to produce goods and services required to satisfy local needs. This does not mean a distrust of science and technology. It only means a conscious and careful application of science and technology to serve certain social objectives freely selected on ethical grounds. Thus, for instance, neither organic farming nor alternative medicine is opposed to science. But, contrary to an earlier and still prevalent trend, they pay decidedly more attention to locally available natural resources for meeting the needs of the people for food and health. The neighbourhood economy is careful to reduce its dependence on the state and on the world market and for good reasons. That the central teachings of political economy, attuned to the rise of the modern state and the world market, have not paid much attention to these questions must be reckoned today as a deficiency that waits to be remedied.

It will be useful at this point to add a few brief observations on the concept of ownership of property, including means of production. The traditional idea, which tends to regard ownership as an absolute right of disposal of property, needs to be revised just as much as the widely accepted idea of sovereignty which associates it with the absolute power of the sovereign or the state. What we need is an idea of ownership as a bundle of rights in respect of a given resource along with correlated duties. Again this bundle of rights need not be uniform, but it may vary depending on the nature of the resource in question. Although these rights should not be absolute or unlimited, they should be wide enough to permit the person or the group of persons concerned to make experiments in good faith and learn from errors.

Since corruption in its many forms is closely associated with an unprincipled struggle for power dissociated from ethics as well as an unchecked consumerism fuelled by the market system, as the state will not wither away in the foreseeable future nor the market system disappear, the best we can do to contain the crisis in the coming decades is to promote activities for developing and expanding the community sector based on the principles of self-reliance and fellowship side by side with the market and the state. A movement in that direction has already started, although it is as yet weak and scattered. To heighten awareness about its importance is the task for the future. What we will have then and what we need is a pluralistic society breaking out of the dominant duality that rules today. The community sector, itself multiformed, will have to attain a critical size and importance before it can rescue people, a sufficient number of them, from that loneliness of spirit and desperate craving for power from which so many evils arise. What we need is a fusion of individuality and creative fellowship in replacement of that false sense of security that people expect from a display of power and militant solidarity.

Unlike power the problem of sex is complicated by a special factor, the idea of sin that has come to be traditionally associated with it. This is the response of traditional culture and religion to the strong attraction that belongs to sex by nature's design. It is an attraction so strong that people are understandably afraid of being in bondage to sex. However, a sense of sin does not do much to break that bondage. It only adds elements of deceit, desperation and cruelty to what people are unable to resist.

Sex is further complicated by a sense of possessiveness that it is apt to generate. This is what makes it a source of strife as property also does. To strife is added the desire to dominate by force. The consequences are deplorable, even tragic. A husband considering the wife as his property is less interested in whether she loves him than in making sure that she does not love anybody else. There are numberless cases of spouses living together in loveless union, yet correctly by accepted social standards. This starvation of love is a great pity because few experiences are more fulfilling than a feeling of loving union. For the common man, this is the nearest he and she can get to true felicity. By contrast, a love that is strongly infected with possessiveness generates far too often a complex of suspicion, jealousy and extreme bitterness which kill love. What then is the way out? Again, there is perhaps no one way, but different ways suited to different temperaments. As with forms of property so with forms of love, society has to learn to accept this plurality. But there is one thing which is still worth stressing. Possessiveness corrupts and absolute possessiveness corrupts absolutely. Yet society virtually puts the stamp of approval on the idea of a man's right to treat his mate as his absolute property. Our sex education does not teach us to reject that idea. It does not guide and motivate people to accept sex with a mixture of compassion, goodwill and a cultivated detachment. This does not come simply from nature; it has to grow as part of an alternative culture.

What we evidently need is an enlightened ethics with a basic revaluation of property and sex, promoting what is creative and life-giving in them and opposing what is narrow and corrupt. This should strengthen the foundations of a decent and generous human community of the future, hopefully free of the many deformities of the existing society.

23

Atheistic Idolatry

A tremendous change is under way in the socialist world. In a period like this, one would expect Leftist thought in India to be in a creative ferment. The quality of man's consciousness can be judged by the quality of its response to changes in the world. Judged by that standard, the performance of Marxism in this country has been very disappointing. A 100 years after the death of Vidyasagar and 50 years after Tagore, a strange sterility has come over the intellectual life of Bengal where a majority of our Marxists to this day know nothing better than to continue paying verbal tributes to Stalinism.

For those loyal Marxists the argument, in its simple form, runs like this. Stalin led the Soviet people in the victorious war against Nazi Germany, and it would be a singular act of ingratitude to belittle his role today. The party of Lenin emancipated the Russian people from Tsarist autocracy and, thanks to Stalin, the Soviet Union became one of the leading industrial countries of the world, at the same time providing leadership to anti-imperialist forces.

Russia before the Communist revolution, we are told, was as poor and backward as India at the time of independence and the post-revolutionary achievement, in that context, is judged to be incomparable. Mr Mikhail Gorbachov, by his hasty ideas, so it is alleged, has unnecessarily pulled down the impressive edifice of socialism built up under the Stalinist leadership. In the process, he has helped place the U.S.A. in an unchallengeable position in the world, a regrettable development for both Russia and the rest of the world.

The argument in that form has a wide appeal. In fact, it has found acceptance with many people who do not, strictly speaking, belong to the Communist movement. To the Communists themselves, it is a series of self-evident propositions. They can only regard all other views with deep suspicion. Yet the whole argument is faulty. It is not my purpose to subject it to a close scrutiny. Those who are under its spell have to free themselves by their own effort. An outsider can only invite them to take into account a few simple facts.

Despite a widespread impression to the contrary, it is simply not true that Lenin and the Bolshevik Party were responsible for overthrowing the Tsarist regime. The facts relating to the case are so elementary that I feel almost embarrassed to mention them. When the Tsarist government collapsed in March 1917, Lenin was not even present in Russia. Then a Provisional government, formed principally by the Constitutional Democrats and their non-Communist allies, came into existence. It was headed for a while by Kerensky, a man of moderate Leftist inclinations. The Bolshevik revolution occurred a few months later in November 1917. Lenin himself knew that the Tsarist empire was doomed; what mattered was the war of succession, which continued within the party after Lenin.

By European standards, Russia before the revolution was industrially backward. But the process of industrialisation had already started and some economists are of the view that Russia was evidently on the threshold of a 'take-off'. Germany and Japan, two 'late starters', were developing rapidly. It was now Russia's turn to join the race. The idea that Russia before the revolution was as poor as India under the British rule is incorrect and misleading. Per capita output of food grains in Russia in 1913 was roughly three times as high as that in India in the early years of independence. Moreover, Russia was exceptionally well endowed with crucial deposits of a variety of metals and minerals. While Stalin's leadership determined the actual pattern and methods of industrialisation, it is only fair to assume that Russia would have developed in any case after World War I, with Stalin or without him.

What can still be claimed with a certain amount of justification is that the great dictator did play an important role in building up Russia as a military power. Other positive achievements included the eradication of illiteracy and the introduction of a comprehensive system of social security. It is noteworthy that a few other authoritarian and militaristic states had similar achievements to their credit. Germany under Bismarck had introduced a system of social security before the end of the 19th century, and Japan among Asian countries succeeded in removing illiteracy early in the 20th century.

While the achievements of the Soviet Union in these areas are not to be belittled, the foundations on which these were built were not as firm and secure as they once appeared to be. One cannot lightly dismiss Mr Gorbachev's words when he writes 'We are far behind industrialized countries whose share of investments in public education, health care and other social spheres in the national income is much higher than ours'. It is safer in such matters to seek out models from some of the social–democratic countries. It is victory in war that gave the Russian dictator a special place in history and covered up his enormous crimes.

The unlimited adulation that Stalin once received for his role in World War II has now substantially waned among the Soviet people, but it remains virtually undiminished among the dictator's Indian devotees. Knowledgeable Russians remember too well how Stalin's extreme suspiciousness affected the top leadership of the Russian army. 'After the fabricated "Tukhachevsky case", the repressions had dealt the army a blow from which it could not recover by 1941', wrote Major General Vitaly Nikolsky, now an old man, in the columns of a Soviet weekly of world affairs recalling the bitter experience of that period.

If the German hordes were nonetheless beaten back, the explanation must be sought elsewhere, in the geography of Russia and the logistic problems it posed for the Germans, the combined industrial strength of the allied powers, including particularly the U.S.A., and above all the tenacious and death-defying patriotism of the Russian people. To glorify Stalin on account of the defeat of Hitler's Germany is to suspend one's critical faculty and surrender to the 'personality cult' in a form unbecoming of any true Marxist.

After World War II, China and East European countries were added to the socialist world. The defence and security of the Soviet Union were to that extent further strengthened. During wartime the highly bureaucratised command economy which Stalin had built up worked tolerably well, patriotism providing the main incentive to work. People then were also prepared to put up cheerfully with certain scarcities, controls and deprivations. As the years passed, the psychology of war weakened, the appeal to patriotism and class struggle became ineffective, much to the chagrin of some honest revolutionaries, and the Stalinist command economy became increasingly unworkable. This provided the background to Mr Gorbachev's new approach.

The Russian economy today is passing through a difficult period of transition. The old-styled command economy has lost its title to obedience. A market economy is yet to be put in shape. Neither has any practical compromise between the two been worked out. Things are out of joint. Some try desperately to restore the old order. But this is a remedy worse than the disease. It cannot work even if it is given a chance. It can only make the transition more complicated, prolonged and painful. Some are terribly angry with Mr Gorbachev, but the problems he addressed would still remain.

Mr Gorbachev wants a democratic and peaceful transition to a new order. That is the only sane way. The question is: Will sanity prevail?

With the Soviet Union in disarray, America has become, at least temporarily, an unrivalled superpower. This has frightened many people, particularly in the Third World. There can be little doubt that the position is going to change. Within the Group of Seven industrialised nations, a division has already surfaced. In the past, opposition to the Soviet Union held the Western world together. As the threat from Russia recedes, the West will cease to be a single bloc, if ever it were that. The Third World will have to adjust itself to this new situation. How well it does will depend on the spirit of self-reliance and mutual cooperation it can develop.

The era of ideological bipolarity and the excitement it generated are coming to an end. Those who were sustained by that excitement will find it a little difficult to readjust. Compulsively mouthing the old slogans, they might look a little foolish. Thinking people all over the world are groping their way towards a new philosophy of life superseding the embattled ideologies of yesterday. For those who dare there is enough challenge there.

24

The Decline of Communism

The 14th congress of the Romanian Communist Party was held in Bucharest from 20 to 24 November 1989. Elected from nearly 4 million Communists, 3,308 delegates attended the congress. The following excerpt from a report on the congress makes interesting reading:

> It took Nicolae Ceausescu almost five hours to deliver his report on the present stage of development of Romanian socialist society. The report was punctuated with applause 101 times, with the delegates rising to their feet 62 times, when the general secretary spoke about the successes achieved by Romania in the economic and social spheres.

Less than a month after the congress, Ceausescu was thrown out of power by an irresistible popular upsurge which exposed him as one of the most hated leaders of the country. 'I cannot see a place for the Communist Party in Romania in the future', declared Petre Roman, the new Prime Minister, soon after the fall of the dictator.

The manner in which all this happened was extremely painful. Friends of democracy would have preferred a more peaceful transition. However, Ceausescu's ruthless regime ruled out that possibility. This surely is an occasion for some fundamental rethinking.

The report on the 14th congress of the Romanian Communist Party which appeared under the highly evocative title, *Towards a Radiant Future*, and the hysterical applause and unbounded adulation received by the leader of the party, sound deeply deceptive and utterly ridiculous today. But nobody who is at all familiar with reports on conferences of the Communist Party of the Soviet Union prior to glasnost, and particularly in the days of Stalin, can help noticing a strong and unmistakable similarity between them and the very style and idiom of reporting from Romania.

One of the slogans raised at the 14th congress was, 'Ceausescu — heroism!' Why was such 'heroic' and blatantly untruthful propaganda, so reminiscent of Goebbels, adopted as common practice over many years? Why did Communists all over the world put continued trust in it, so much so that all those who refused to be persuaded by such propaganda were suspected to be agents of Western imperialism?

How did limitless trust in partisan and one-sided propaganda become a revolutionary virtue? A large part of the answer to such questions is provided by the psychology of war. Goebbels used untruth, the big lie, in the service of war. In his case, it was war between nation and nation. What mattered was not so much whether an idea or a statement of a deed conformed to truth, as whether it strengthened the nation's will to fight on the side of the leader and the party which led the war. In the case of Communists, it is the same logic which worked; one had only to put 'class' in place of 'nation'. In countries where the Communist Party was in power, the greater glory of the party and its leader also meant the greater glory of the people and the nation.

Marx was a humanist; though not the first. Rammohan Roy, who was born nearly half a century before Marx, was considered a friend of humanity, and he too derived his humanism from a tradition which existed before him. Marx's real distinction lay in regarding history as class war. To the faithful, his message was very clear. It is only by fighting the class war to the end, till the working class wins all over the world, that a free human society can be established for all mankind.

Is that argument valid? You cannot wish away class conflict. What, then, is wrong with the Marxist–Leninist idea of proletarian dictatorship and the leading role of the Communist Party?

Granted the reality of class conflict, it is still a matter for legitimate doubt whether the interests of that class are best advanced by any single party arrogating to itself an exclusive right to lead that class. This is a question which can be finally settled, not by theory, but by reference to practice. The testimony of recent experience is very important and should, indeed, serve as the basis of new theorising.

In a climate of militancy generated by harsh material conditions of existence, further fuelled by the theory of class war, a unified leadership for the working class looks justified and even necessary. But the dilemma of large organisation soon asserts itself. This is particularly the case once the party captures the state apparatus. On the one hand, a large organisation seems necessary for effective power and planning; on the other, as the revolutionary fervour subsides, what emerges is an elaborate bureaucracy which, even as it speaks in the name of the proletariat, provides a new basis for exploitation. To this is quickly added cultural and psychological factors conducive to unfreedom. The class is a collective entity. What nationalism does, particularly in times of war, to the 'collective ego' of the nation, the theory of class war does to that of the class. In that atmosphere, all dissidence is treated as conspiracy and the individual is sacrificed at the altar of collectivity. Mass hysteria and the muting of dissent make a mockery of democracy.

Even within this constrictive framework of the so-called dictatorship of the proletariat, a certain amount of industrial development does take place, at times quite rapidly, as happens during war. But this material development itself creates a new consciousness and new aspirations which are in increasing conflict with the institutional and cultural basis of the totalitarian regime. A 'contradiction' thus develops between the 'relations of production' of the Communist state, as embodied in its over-centralised economic and administrative system, and the 'forces of production', including the new consciousness evolving in that society. How to handle this contradiction within socialism now becomes the great question. Those who do not know better than to blame the capitalist system for the crisis of socialism fail to cope with the new situation. The crisis intensifies till it explodes.

Are the interests of the classes basically contradictory? The answer is both yes and no. It is a mistake to make too sharp a distinction between conflict and cooperation. All cooperation takes place under certain terms. In most cases, these are not to the entire satisfaction of either party, though accepted by both. Conflict is quite often only a temporary breakdown of cooperation. The actual relation between the classes is a mixture of conflict and cooperation moving hopefully towards larger freedom.

Even Adam Smith took note of the unequal bargaining power between masters and their workmen. Employers have kept wages low by tacit or open agreement among themselves. At any given time, the size of the national dividend is fixed and the more the capitalists take, the less left for the working class.

But it is also the common experience of all industrially developed nations that the standard of living of the working class has risen in the long run with the progress of industrialisation. True, a great deal of distress and deprivation remains even in the industrially advanced countries. But this is to be found mainly outside the ranks of the organised working class. It is noteworthy that, in the advanced capitalist countries, the militancy of the working class movement has decreased with the progress of industrialisation. This is by no means to ignore some very serious problems which, arising from industrialisation, torment civilisation today.

But something wider than the class approach is necessary for a proper understanding of these problems.

As between the classes, so too between nations; the actual relationship is marked by conflict and complimentarily, rivalry and cooperation, all at the same time. This is as true of the relationship between socialist and capitalist countries as between the Third World and industrially advanced countries. The Third World wants more trade, not less, with the rest of the world. In their own perception, both sides have something to gain from such trade.

In a recent issue of New Times (Moscow), a contributor to the Discussion Forum points out contradictions between socialist theory and practice. In practice, socialist countries today seek to set up joint enterprises with Western companies, but Marxist theory teaches that this is a way of working people being exploited by foreign private capital. This is happening nearer home too. The need for cooperation is accepted in practice, but conflict and class war continue to dominate theory.

The discrepancy between Communist theory and reality has long since been widening and it will be 'madness' to ignore this fact any longer. In 1952, a year before his death, Stalin confidently wrote in *Economic Problems of Socialism* about 'the ever-increasing decay of the world capitalist economic system on the one hand, and the growing economic might of the countries which have fallen away from capitalism — the USSR, China and other people's democracies — on the other'. Equally boldly he spoke of the 'inevitability of wars between capitalist countries'. These pronouncements were hailed at that time as signal contributions to Marxist theory.

Stalin's anticipations of 1952 were strongly contradicted by subsequent history, putting Marxists everywhere under an obligation to do some hard rethinking. The idea of the absolute superiority of the Soviet system and Stalinist ideology became patently untenable. Within the Soviet Union, new ideas started taking shape fairly soon. Already in the 1960s, Andrei Sakharov, that great scientist and forerunner of the historic pro-democracy movement in the Communist world, declared that 'any action increasing the division of mankind, any preaching of the incompatibility of world ideologies and nations, is madness and a crime'. This new line of thought, so pregnant with possibilities for the future, failed to arouse the least bit of enthusiasm among Indian Communists who continued to think that Stalin had spoken the last word.

Looking back, it is easy to see the strong affinity between the forward-looking policy enunciated by Mikhail Gorbachev in the second half of the 1980s and the ideas expounded by Sakharov, and others like him, against heavy odds during the previous two decades. Also in tune with these same ideas is the revolution which swept across East Europe in 1989. Again, Indian Communists in general, and Bengali Communists in particular, have been unable to respond to these events in a positive sense. Their incapability for creative thinking makes them a party of the past.

The situation in East Europe and even the Soviet Union still remains full of uncertainties. There may be cruel setbacks in the movement towards freedom. But it is certain that the old order can no longer be restored and perpetuated. A new orientation of thought is necessary for a new world order. Will Marxism survive? But that is not the really important question. What is important is to have a system of ideas which does not glorify any collective entity as the basis of totalitarianism of any variety, nor uphold a one-sided view of the inevitability of war between classes or nations. What we urgently need is a view of man which reposes faith in basic human rights and fundamental values rather than rely on fixed ideologies.

25

Reason, Revolution and Social Progress

'The time will come', prophesied Condorcet, the 18th-century French philosopher, 'when the sun will shine only on free men who know no other master but their reason'. This is the great idea which inspired the philosophy of the Enlightenment. Reason is first applied to nature, and its fruit is the increasing mastery of man over his environment. Soon it comes to be applied to social institutions. It undermines superstitions and dissolves myths which sanctioned ancient tyranny. It sets human society on the road to indefinite progress and wider freedom. If this theory of progress has turned out to be deceptive, we still have to regard it with respect even as we subject it to critical scrutiny.

The rationalist movement in the 18th century did not equally penetrate all layers of society. If it transformed the mode of thought and feelings in Paris, it did not affect the rest of France similarly. After the revolution, the breach between the capital and the country was revealed with brutal clarity. If an atheistic, revolutionary, anti-royalist tradition came to characterise large parts of Paris, the country remained Catholic, conservative and a dupe of lost grandeur. Repeated attempts at revolution came to grief, not because of capitalist intrigues, but because France prevailed against Paris. If Robespierre belonged to Paris, Napoleon spoke for the French people. When de Gaulle said he was France, he spoke with a deep sense of history.

The war between the two traditions had grievous consequences. In France the movement in the name of reason
went beyond good-tempered agnosticism and hardened into
militant atheism. When rationalism became an ideology, de-
manding conformism from its partisans and hatred against
its enemies, it ceased to be reasonable.

It was otherwise in England. From the Great Rebellion
in the 17th century and its aftermath, England learnt not
only the wisdom of government by consent but also a lesson in religious toleration which was of great value to her
in subsequent history. The clash of interests between the
'classes' did not disappear; in fact, it was at times quite acute.
But the intellectual climate discouraged extremism, and
the integration of urban and rural elites worked against a
revolution. At the time of the Great Rebellion, the city of
London was against the king. Since then there has never
been in England the same radical split between the city and
the country as in France.

This contrasted tale of two cities gives us an important
insight into social evolution. There are certain 'contradictions'
that develop in the transition from traditional to modern
society. Orthodox socialists have stressed particularly on
the clash of interests between capitalists and the proletariat.
But no less important is the rift between the 'city' and the
'country'. Many things appear in a different light when we
look at them from this point of view. It throws a new and
penetrating light on history and offers guidelines for the
future. There is something common between this and the
Gandhian approach. But labels are deceptive and it will
be better to avoid them. The conflict between the city and
the country is both economic and cultural. Unless it is held
in check, it can produce serious unrest and even turn into a
civil war, in which the best values of the Enlightenment are
jeopardised.

The forces for a secular and libertarian society may be im-
perilled in two ways. The movement may be weak all around

and, therefore, unable to defend itself. Or, being unequally advanced in different parts of society or between different communities, it may give rise to a schism that threatens to overwhelm it. If the struggle against obscurantism is to show desired results, it is not enough to pursue it with a certain degree of enthusiasm, but one has to be mindful that no significant section of society is left out of it. It is also necessary that the movement should be linked with productive activity in the city as well as in the country, for there is no other way of making it broad-based and confident about its powers. Let us note here a special point about the interconnection between economic and cultural factors. A purely economic disequilibrium corrects itself relatively more easily. But when economic disparities are reinforced by cultural barriers, the rift within society is not only difficult to overcome but tends to get wider.

Viewed in this perspective, the limitations of the 19th-century Renaissance in India are all too evident. The movement was city-centred; it left the country untouched. It failed to link up with productive activity in industry and, more particularly, agriculture. This particular failure of our Renaissance was even more pronounced in Bengal than it was in Bombay. The city produced its own culture, which gave rise to a one-way traffic of talents. In the process, the outlying districts were impoverished. These in turn took revenge by sending out a swelling stream of employment-seekers and misfits, who eventually made the city sick. Here are the roots of our social malaise.

I do not agree with those friends who register their disappointment with the results of our Renaissance by denying that we had one. The Italian movement by that name was also city-centred; it did not initiate what we call today self-sustained growth; and it left the peasants untouched and steeped in superstitions. We do not improve matters by waging war against accepted nomenclature. We have reasons to be proud of the leaders of that 19th-century movement in which the Renaissance and the Enlightenment blended, who impressed on us ideas and ideals which were virtually unknown in our society before and are still hardly known in those parts of the country which the movement failed to reach. But the limitations of the earlier movement should be clearly recognised.

The task today is to evolve a new language and extend the Enlightenment beyond the limits of yesterday. Objectively speaking, this should be possible. There is already a new stir of expectancy in the villages of India. Mass illiteracy, still existent, is no longer the same insuperable barrier as it was in the 19th century. The farmer is infinitely more receptive of new ideas today. I visited a science club in a rural area the other day and was greatly impressed. What is needed is leadership. Will it come? Can it make itself effective through a new adjustment between individual initiative, so vital for agricultural innovation, and social cooperation? The aim of land reform should be to help this adjustr ent by providing security to the village poor, encouraging agricultural co-operation and rewarding the successful innovator. How to combine these objectives is a matter for social experiment.

There are also larger problems. The movement we need at this moment must be practical and philosophical at the same time. It has to be practical because science can commend itself to the common man, not as a form of pursuit of pure knowledge, but by its fruits. Yet this is not enough; technology does not suffice to provide a basis for social solidarity.

In India the impact of the West has been variously felt in different parts of the country. On the whole, the coastal areas, or regions which were more easily accessible from outside, are now readier for modernisation than the heartland of Hindustan. The rift between the 'city' and the 'country' is reproduced here in a different form. Either we overcome this 'contradiction' on the basis of a liberal and critical outlook on our inherited tradition or attitudes will harden on either side in a hostile encounter. Thus a philosophical readjustment to the new situation is an essential precondition of 'national integration' in India.

There are those who tend to think that industrialisation is all we need and the cultural problem will solve itself. This goes counter to historical evidence. 'Modernisation' is a process with many dimensions. It involves the acceptance and application of modern science and technology. But a theory which suggests that we have only to take care of the economic structure of society and it will select and develop the culture it needs is grossly inadequate. Industrialisation has combined with democracy in some countries and with dictatorship in others. Contemporary history, since the beginning of Industrial Revolution, shows how critically variable is the intellectual climate in which economic growth can take place.

In different parts of the world, industrialisation and the kind of education which is essential for it have made progress, with or without revolution, with different degrees of reliance on terror to hold society together. The important question is how to preserve social solidarity by civilised methods while the transformation of the technological basis of society is under way and how, at the same time, to permit those 'manifold unlikenesses', to borrow Mill's felicitous phrase, which are the characteristics of a liberal society. Terror, as Solzhenitsyn points out, 'reduces to mediocrity whatever it touches'. It drives underground differences which come to surface again as soon as the pressure at the top is put off. Terror fails because it avoids an honest confrontation with the problem of modern society by refusing to admit its existence.

The modern mind does not consider society as something completed and given beforehand to which individuals have to be fitted, but as something continuously striving to complete itself through individuals experimenting with their lives. Despite what we have said about the split between the 'city' and the 'country', the hold of modernity thus interpreted is weak in the Indian middle class. The average, educated Indian, where he professes to be most radical, is a curious mixture of social conservatism and political revolutionism. He is divided from the common folk by a barrier of language, a more pronounced cynicism in everyday life, a proneness to jargon, a deeper inner 'contradiction', sometimes a rooted defeatism in practical affairs interlaced with moods of utopian exaltation and, in special cases, that destructive energy with which revolutionary conception celebrates its divorce from practical morality. This is what makes ideological fanaticism irrelevant to the deeper issues of the day. The growth of political extremism has only made more difficult a genuine confrontation of modernity and tradition.

How does the Naxal movement come out of this analysis? This is not the first time that agrarian discontent has assumed a violent form. The movement has many facets. But there is one feature of the activities of the CPI (M-L) which is truly extraordinary and deserves special comment. There was a time when destruction of busts and portraits of the leaders of the Indian Renaissance became a revolutionary ritual in Kolkata. The spokesmen of this movement are not sons of peasants; they belong to the culture of the city. Why were they so infuriated by all visible signs of the creators of this culture, while they remained mercifully tolerant of the worship of graven images of God? The Naxal movement in Kolkata appeared to represent the self-hatred of city culture. By the paradox of hatred, it has only succeeded in strengthening the worst and most inhuman features of the culture it purports to hate.

It will be a long time before the sun shines on free men who know no other master but their reason. In the meanwhile, the task before us is to help a rational outlook grow out of an old tradition as by an organic process, as Vidyasagar, for instance, strove to do in his time. Simultaneously new techniques will have to be evolved with the cooperation of social scientists, educationists, engineers, industrialists and others to strengthen productive links between towns and villages. It is by such methods that the problem of unemployment and the misery of a floating and rootless population in our country can be relieved within a democratic framework.

This is the only way to preserve that minimum of social cohesion which provides an atmosphere in which fundamental issues can be constructively and rationally discussed. The language of civil war, intolerance dressed up in brave phraseology, can only put off the day when a purposeful dialogue can be resumed on the basic questions concerning human freedom. The crisis of developing societies cannot be overcome by imposing upon the country 'the dictatorship of industry' or by surrounding the cities with armed squads from villages, but by allowing the city and the country to interpenetrate creatively and thus produce a new civilisation which will embody a synthesis of the two. It is time to stop and wonder if we have not moved far in the wrong direction.

26

The Limits of Hedonism

Man makes his own history. But he does not always make it wisely. This is quite apart from the fact that he is not entirely free to act just as he pleases, for he has to act within the constraints of a given environment. Even within those constraints, there are alternative possibilities and man does not always choose the best available course. A correct philosophy of history should make allowance for this failing. Human beings considered either as individuals or as collective bodies such as tribes, classes or nations do not follow steadfastly their best interest, for they fail to understand clearly what it is. For instance, what is attractive in the short-term may run counter to what is best in the long run and people may go astray ignoring warnings.

This is as relevant for understanding personal life histories as for interpreting larger movements of society. Nature as manifest in history strives to guide human evolution through a system of rewards and punishments. It is instructive to note how people respond, positively or negatively, to nature's signals. While trying to do that we will move from simple down-to-earth illustrations to relatively more complex propositions.

When an activity is necessary for sustaining life and guaranteeing its continuation, it is one of nature's methods to make it pleasant. This is illustrated by the attraction of food. The normal human being responds to this attraction positively. However, people tend to overstep nature's designs. The pleasure of eating is accepted as something worth cultivating for its own sake even beyond what is necessary for sustaining health and vitality. There is nothing necessarily wrong in this. Culinary art is part of high culture.

One cannot help being impressed by the amount of experimentation and inventiveness that has gone into the development of culinary art. However, the signs are clear that this search for pleasure has overstepped the limits in utter defiance of nature's signals. In the more opulent societies, more people die from diseases aggravated by overeating than from insufficient intake of food. Also the contrast between the indigence of the poor and the expensive merrymaking and conspicuous consumption of the rich, arrogantly displayed in public on certain occasions, disturbs social harmony. In India, we are treated all too often to an odd spectacle of socialist pretensions combining with feudal demonstration of waste and extravagance. Expensive consumptionist habits carry with them the badge of social respectability, while the skills and resources of a commercial civilisation are assiduously employed to support and promote this trend.

This is the case of a wrong response to an evolutionary problem buttressed by a defective pleasure-seeking philosophy. In fact, its defects are evident at all levels, personal and social. Every major epoch in history has its own characteristic concept of man, its philosophy of the most valid objective of life and some kind of theory of the most dependable methods and instruments for achieving that objective. It is by a comprehensive criticism of this complex of ideas that the ground is prepared for the transition to the next stage of history. Our commercial civilisation has produced the idea of the 'economic man' to do duty for the whole man, considered it rational to accept pleasure as the basic goal of life and concluded that purchasable commodities are the principal avenues for attaining that goal.

Now, this is a treacherous train of reasoning. When it is accepted as the basis of practice in the life of any individual or society, some major pitfalls turn up on the way. These appear simple as soon as they are openly stated. But they are all too often ignored, thanks to the seduction of a theory predicated on pleasure which has a strong subterranean hold on our psyche.

As a rule, a pleasure-giving object loses its capacity to yield positive pleasure as we come to have more and more of it. This is as true of a single commodity as of a collection of commodities. Economists admit this when they concede, as they often do, that money has a diminishing 'marginal utility'. It is generally not true that a rich man with an annual income, say, hundred times as large as that of a person of moderate means, is hundred times happier. As a matter of fact, he may not be any happier at all. If he still clings to his vast wealth, it is mainly because he has formed habits which he is unable to shake off. Possessiveness is not particularly productive of happiness. But one is chained to it and these chains are not easy to break. The psychological indices of mental stress are not particularly low among the rich. That they still do not want to part with any appreciable fraction of their property, even when they do not really need it, is a different matter.

It is useful to make a distinction between pleasure and happiness although the two words are sometimes used more or less interchangeably. Where a distinction is made, pleasure stands for something more passing and unsteady, akin to a state of excitement, and happiness is steadier, closer to a state of peace and equilibrium. Happiness comes from union, such as the feeling one has when one is united with old friends or people so regarded. By contrast, pleasure is derived either from gratification of the senses or from the defeat of another person or group of persons looked on as an opponent. More generally, pleasure belongs to a world or area of existence where the feeling of separateness dominates, while happiness stresses a view of the world where other selves are regarded as opportunities for one's self-realisation through an expansive sympathy. To be sure, nature's designs have space for the principle of pleasure and there is no question of totally rejecting it. Basically it is a question of orientation, a matter of deciding in which direction one should strive to move and how far.

All activities use up some limited resources. In some cases this is a major problem. There are other cases where pressure on limited resources should not be a problem unless human perversity leads us up the wrong way. Let us take up an obvious yet important example.

Just as nature has implanted in human beings an appetite for food so too man is attracted by knowledge and its fruit. Judging by the Biblical story about Adam and Eve, this is a strong attraction. It operates at two levels. There is the practical level where men face problems and make a search for knowledge to overcome difficulties. But there is also a second level, that of pure curiosity, when teased by apparent inconsistencies in the working of nature, men seek to discover a deeper harmony in the universe. Some of the greatest among men have been profoundly attracted by this possibility of an intellectual comprehension of the universe. However, at the beginning of what is called the modern period of history, people came to be attracted by knowledge for a different reason: 'knowledge is power'.

Just as nature equipped man with a pleasure-hunting propensity, so too it planted hunger for power. Both these tendencies had a certain place and justification in the rude state of nature where the early man struggled to survive. But conditions have changed since then and what looked necessary for man's security in the past has become a threat to global security today. Warnings are not wanting, but the wisdom to heed them is not evident in sufficient measure.

Nations armed with new technology have gained increasing dominion over nature including men. This has been a dubious boon. For if power gives dominion, it also corrupts. If the principle of pleasure has produced the contemporary tide of consumerism, the principle of power has produced both centralised militarism and, as an appendage to it, scattered terrorism. Consumerism, militarism and terrorism are interrelated phenomena; together they constitute the basis of what is called today the crisis of civilisation. Men have created this crisis; but they hardly know how to handle it. Instead of turning the searchlight inwards, we blame it on obscurely perceived enemies outside.

The pursuit of pure knowledge is not a particularly expensive enterprise. It does not make a heavy draft on the resources that nature has put at the disposal of man. But the development of high technology and its industrial application for consumerist and military purposes are a different matter altogether. These have been using up nature's resources at an alarming rate with dire consequences that are getting clearer day by day. Supplies of essential and non-renewable resources are getting exhausted. The human environment, including the earth and waters and the atmosphere, is becoming dangerously polluted with an increasing accumulation of noxious gases.

Signs of a serious ecological imbalance and nature's signals of an impending disaster are so clear all over the globe that they cannot be overlooked any longer by any prudent observer. What is surprising is that people who know rush to international conferences to discuss these issues, as they did at Kyoto in 1997 and at Johannesburg in 2002, and then it becomes evident that the world is not yet ready to do anything very effective at the practical level. Concern for a safe future for mankind pulls in one direction, considerations of national power in a competitive world pull in a different direction and it is the pull of power which proves to be stronger. Nature's signals are clearly ignored or played down.

27

Beyond the Welfare State

In what follows I propose to offer three rather different kinds of comments, partly on the concept of the welfare state and partly on welfare economics. I believe the time has come to reconsider and reassess the uses and limitations of what goes under those names.

The idea of the welfare state was first developed by the social democrats or moderate socialists in Europe. By now it has come to be widely accepted even by non-socialists although there are differences of opinion about the extent of welfare that the state should provide. There is no conflict between social security and the market mechanism, the two can comfortably coexist. The really important difference of opinion is about the desirable size of the public sector and the nature and extent of controls that the state should administer in relation to the private sector. People have even started talking of market socialism. More and more people, including the less doctrinaire socialists, have come round to the view that it is better to allow private enterprise to function within the framework of a reasonably free market system in view of its greater 'efficiency', the state retaining the power to appropriate a part of the wealth so produced to finance welfare measures and other essential activities.

All this assumes that the state is the most suitable instrument for dispensing welfare. But is it? Only extreme exponents of the market economy raise that question in academic circles today. But this need not be the case. There was a time when the major part of what goes by the name of social welfare was provided by institutions other than the state. It is only with the erosion of these other institutions that the state came to assume principal responsibility in this field until citizens had no option but to depend helplessly on the state.

It will be pertinent at this point to recall Rabindranath Tagore's views on this subject. It is well known that Tagore strongly deplored the callous neglect of social welfare on the part of the British government in India even in respect of such essential requirements as water supply, health and education. What is less well remembered is that he also spoke clearly, forcefully and at great length of an earlier time when people were not reduced to such helpless dependence on the '*Sarkar Bahadur*', the state, for the supply of these basic needs. He also made it abundantly clear that he regarded with great fear and anxiety this enormous increase in the power of the state. It is indicative of the temper of our time that this critical note is missing from most of our academic and political literature.

This is regrettable, as a moment's reflection should show. What the state can provide is often useful, but never enough. There is no substitute for cooperation among free individuals. A state can very well have an impressive record of providing an elaborate system of social security and it can yet be unquestionably despotic and militaristic. In fact, this comes rather naturally with modern totalitarian states. Surely the cardinal fault with the Stalinist regime was not that it did not care to provide social security for the Soviet citizens. Social security is good and desirable as such. In the absence of an alternative arrangement, the state should look after it with all the care it deserves. But it is better to develop autonomous social institutions at the base with sufficient power and resources to help people look after their own needs as far as possible. This is healthier even for those countries which have a system of representative government. If political economy today is insufficiently mindful of this problem, this only means that its political vision is obscured by the dominant ideology of the modern state or what Tagore called 'statism', miscalled 'socialism'. It is also possible that the tools and techniques of analysis fashioned by what goes by the name of welfare economics are not equal to the task of providing the guidelines for the construction of a radically different economic and social order.

This is just not enough, the more so for a country like India. It is all right to urge and try to impress on the government of India the need for building up social security in this country. The government ought to take careful note of such recommendations. But the problem is that the system of social security developed in the West does not, in some important respects, fit the conditions in India. Take, for instance, the pressing problem of unemployment. In the developed capitalist countries, the system of assistance in this respect was devised to meet principally the problem of cyclical unemployment. Unemployment in India is not so much cyclical as chronic, aggravated by a growing backlog. It is not always open, but quite often 'disguised'. The larger part of it of takes the form of underemployment. This is not a situation where a system of doles can take care of the problem. Even income-generating projects of work financed from above, whether by the Centre or by the state governments, administered either by the bureaucracy or by the cadres of the ruling party, develop very serious leakages and prove to be largely ineffective and uneconomic. They cannot cure the disease of chronic under-employment. A principal component of a durable remedy must lie in a movement for 'rural reconstruction', to use again Tagore's terminology, through the organised initiative of the villagers themselves backed by a system of education closely related to local needs and not simply literacy in the ordinary sense. Welfare economics, as taught in our universities, has little guidance to offer here. In other words, we need a new approach to welfare, different even from what goes by the name of 'new' welfare economics.

There is yet another problem which calls for a radical re-orientation of welfare economics. Many years have passed since Pigou wrote his celebrated book on welfare economics. Though outdated, its basic premises have not been seriously challenged and it will serve well to illustrate the point I want to make. Pigou made a valuable distinction between private cost and social cost. A similar distinction lies between private benefit and social benefit. Private enterprise is concerned only with private cost while he who is interested in social welfare will take note of social cost. A smoking chimney provides the simplest illustration. The cost to the surrounding locality inflicted by the smoke does not enter into the calculations of the individual producer and so does not normally influence his business decisions. But society can still try and protect its interests by imposing a countervailing tax of sufficient size on the firm or firms concerned, perhaps using the proceeds of the tax to keep the environment reasonably clean. Arguably the remedy lay within the power of the local authority or the government. But now the situation has changed radically. The hazards to the environment are altogether of a different nature and on a different scale.

Consider, for instance, the consequences of global warming. We will ignore for the moment the differences among scientists on the estimates of these consequences. The particular example cited does not really matter. The point is that there are activities of which the consequences are not confined to any particular country, but they are still so grave that they cannot and ought not to be ignored. The problem is that no effective remedy is within the power of a single government. This opens up an altogether new perspective. Political economy as developed so far has been concerned with policies of national governments. Ecological problems today force us to break out of those limits. This would involve devising new methods of estimating costs and benefits and, what is even more complex, developing norms to decide the shares of the costs to be borne by different governments at different states of economic growth. The Kyoto conference of December 1997 illustrated how difficult it is for nation states to arrive at a consensus on questions of this nature.

Thus the perspectives of welfare problems have shifted in a direction different from the horizon set for them in earlier decades. At any given time, the established methods of a science determine the range of problems it is ready to recognise and deal with. But finally it is the problems that matter. How far can welfare economics reorient itself to address the emerging problems of a new age? The old problems have not lost their importance, but as time passes there will be fewer really new things one can say about them. To a branch of science which is alive and growing, it is the new challenges which matter most as determining factors in its future development.

The nation state will survive for yet some time to come. But its power as an instrument of welfare is going to get attenuated in two very different ways in the coming years even as the air gets thick with cries of critics from the 'left' as well as the 'right' protesting vociferously yet vainly that some party or other—in fact, any party which happens to be in power—is diluting the sovereignty of the nation. On the one hand, policies relating to some vital questions concerning human welfare and their implementation have to be decided, so to speak, by an emerging 'world union'. On the other hand, the nation state, within its own boundaries, will be under constant pressure of insistent demands to cede power in favour of regional and local constituents, so that it itself becomes a kind of union of smaller self-governing communities.

We live today at the high noon of the sovereign state. But very soon, it will be past noon and it is time for opinion-makers to take note. For reasons that have a profound bearing on questions of welfare, we have to go beyond the nation state both inwardly and outwardly or face a crisis which cannot be resolved in any other way. It will take time for people and politicians to get adjusted to this new perspective. But the choice is clear for whoever cares to look ahead. It is a compulsion of history, and we have to bow or to break. There are those who see in it nothing deeper than an imperialist conspiracy and others for whom openness to the world market is all that is required. We have to steer clear of both these fallacies.

28

The Future of India's Polity

The Constitution that independent India gave herself in the mid-year of this century marked an important stage in our history. Our Constitution is in many ways an admirable document. It seeks to combine justice, 'social, economic and political with liberty of thought, expression, belief, faith and worship'. In a country with a long and deeply entrenched tradition of caste hierarchy and grossly unequal access to wealth, it proclaims 'equality of status and of opportunity'. It aims at reconciling 'the dignity of the individual' with 'the unity of the nation'. Our Constitution is a constant reminder to us of how far we have fallen behind the objectives that we as a people have set before ourselves. It can serve to illumine India's path of development for a long time to come. In spite of our many failings, we can be justly proud of our Constitution.

Yet our experience since 1950, and particularly during the last few years, has brought to light problems which the authors of the Constitution had not clearly foreseen. It will not serve any purpose to draw up a comprehensive catalogue of these problems. It will be more to the point to focus on some outstanding issues which have not received the kind of attention they deserve. As the challenge to the nation takes a new form, it becomes necessary to give fresh thought to some questions relating to the form and spirit of India's future polity. We begin by drawing attention to two areas where actual facts have diverged from common anticipations.

India's independence came with partition. Although the vivisection of what was once conceived to be an indivisible nation came as a deep disappointment to many Indians, it was hoped that the two sovereign states which came into existence at the moment of independence would each have firm foundations of unity. Islam, it was thought, would be a strong cementing force for Pakistan, while the shock of partition would strengthen in India the resolve to resist any further division or weakening of the unity of the country. These hopes have proved to be largely unrealistic.

Both in India and in Pakistan, strong centralising tendencies as well as counteracting forces have been at work since the early 1950s. The consequences are now part of history and no serious student of politics can afford to ignore them in arriving at an assessment of what is sound and practicable and what is not in building stable polities in the Indian subcontinent. India can draw lessons from Pakistani experiments as it is easier for this country to view with a certain amount of detachment the experience of its neighbour. Pakistan can similarly learn from India.

In 1952 Pakistani authorities declared Urdu to be, as one commentator put it, 'the unifying and Islamising national language'. As part of a determined plan for centralisation, provincial boundaries were removed in 1954 and West Pakistan adopted the 'one unit' system of national administration. The attempt to impose one language on a polyglot people led to an open rebellion in what was then East Pakistan, which resulted eventually in the break-up of Pakistan and the birth of Bangladesh. In what remains of Pakistan, there is strong resistance to Punjabi domination and it is extremely doubtful if normalcy and stability can be achieved without satisfying in large measure the Sindhi, Baluchi and Pathan aspirations for autonomy.

Something not altogether dissimilar has happened in India too. The demand for the creation of new states within India on a linguistic basis started soon after the adoption of

211

the country's new constitution. The States Reorganisation Commission was appointed towards the end of 1953. A large number of new states have been created since then.

There are critics even today who do not understand the significance of this development and in fact, question its wisdom. So let us stop and consider the question for a moment. Jawaharlal Nehru himself did not like the idea of linguistic states. But he had the instinct of a democrat. He realised that the longer the demand for linguistic states was resisted the more violent it would grow. Out of violence comes bitterness and this will eventually weaken national unity and not strengthen it. In his own time, it was Nehru's instinct for democracy rather than his pan-Indianism that helped preserve the unity of India.

However, the problem has not been finally solved. It has persisted and reappeared in new forms. Now and again events have taken a dramatic turn and crises exploded in Assam, in Punjab, in Darjeeling or elsewhere. More quietly yet persistently the states have demanded more power and more resources. This demand cannot be safely ignored.

If that is one part of the story, there is also another. The partition of the subcontinent of India has created stupendous problems. I am not thinking of the suffering and misery and bloodshed that came at the time of partition. That has become part of history and we cannot change the past. It is with the present and the future that we are concerned in a practical way. It is also arguable that some good has come as a result of the partition. In East Bengal before independence, the Muslim community was overshadowed by the Hindus both economically and culturally. There is a large middle class of Muslims in Bangladesh today. It could not have grown to its present size and leading role in the social and cultural life of the country without overthrowing first Hindu and subsequently Punjabi domination. Whatever the inherent limitations of this middle class, it serves a historic purpose.

The kind of problem that the partition has created for the present and the future is most pointedly illustrated by the position of the military and the burden it imposes on this poverty-stricken subcontinent. By the logic of the partition, the emerging sovereign states are compelled to maintain rival armies, dangerously dependent on the supply of foreign arms at enormous cost to themselves. Instead of one army for the whole subcontinent, we have now at least three. In terms of the welfare of the people, this simply does not make sense.

The position was bad enough till recently. But now it has taken a qualitative jump for the worse. Pakistan is ready to produce an atomic bomb. If that happens, it will be difficult to restrain India for long from matching Pakistan with its own programme of atomic weaponry. It will be infinitely tragic if two of the poorest countries of the world with large, hungry populations embark upon senselessly expensive programmes — of the production of weapons of wholesale destruction.

This is a new challenge thrown up by history. It cannot be adequately met except by arranging the affairs of this subcontinent on a new basis. This is a task for the new generation to take up and accomplish. People who came to power in 1947 are now mostly dead. Their children and grandchildren today are coming up fast to positions of leadership. They should be able to look at the landscape with fresh eyes. What is needed is a new union, a confederation, with a common defence for the whole subcontinent. The movement in that direction must be based on methods of democracy and non-violence; otherwise it will fail and problems will multiply. Wise men of India have spoken of unity in diversity. The phrase has a philosophic ring. But it has also a practical significance. It points the way to a large union with autonomy for its diverse constituent parts.

The details of the new order cannot be settled in advance. These can only be settled through a series of experiments and wide-ranging democratic consultations. It will be idle to expect instant success. What is needed is a blend of caution and courage, courage to conceive new ideas and principles and caution in giving them practical shape. There are those to whom the very idea of a new order for the whole of our subcontinent will appear highly utopian. But is there really any other way, a conventional way, out of the crisis that is fast developing all around us?

There is, in fact, a parallelism between our problem and that of the world as a whole. India is a world in miniature. There is a real threat of extinction for mankind as a whole unless relations between the superpowers are reorganised on a new basis and the race for nuclear arms halted. From this arises the practical importance of principles of peaceful coexistence. It is not an accident that a statesman as practical as Gorbachev has started pleading for avoidance of violence in dealing with conflicts the world over. The threat of atomic war has qualitatively changed the situation for India and the world.

It is in this new historical context that the idea of World Union is being discussed today. It is a distant ideal, but it gives us the right sense of direction. How can the desired unity be achieved? We do not know for certain. But we do know the paths to avoid, the methods that have been tried and failed. Imperialism set out to conquer and unify the world; it has failed. There have been attempts to conquer the world on behalf of a great faith, religion or ideology. We know today that the world as a whole cannot be converted to any one faith or ideology. The unity of the world must be founded on a recognition of its essential diversity and the principles of justice and liberty.

The subcontinent of India epitomises the complex problem of the world as a whole. Here too there is the same unconquerable diversity. In fact, there is no other country with quite the same diversity. With the high Himalayas in the north and the seas lapping its shores in the south, geography has fashioned this land into a world by itself. Numberless tribes and races and religions arrived here through the centuries and settled down side by side. Thus we came to have, by the force of history, a remarkable experiment in cultural coexistence. The challenge we face today is in many ways very different from anything we faced in the past. In order to succeed, we need new principles of social and political integration. To work them out will be the task of a whole new generation.

The ideals enshrined in our constitution will still be of value. But they will have to be interpreted and applied with an effort of imagination that measures up to the requirements of the new situation. For us this is a great responsibility. If we fail, we expose the entire subcontinent to risks of chronic terrorism, mutually abetted, war and the possibility of total destruction. If we succeed, we will have set an example for the world. This is no easy task; it may take long to accomplish it. But a new century has just begun and it is time to set our sights high.

29

People's Power

Since democracy is a living force and whatever is living is subject to change and evolution, it must be an error to identify democracy with any fixed and unalterable form. Thus it is that Athenian democracy was different from parliamentary democracy as we know it today and, again, the spirit and form of some ancient Indian republics can be easily distinguished from the Republic of India of which we are citizens now. There is a French proverb which, rendered in English, reads 'the more it changes, the more it is the same thing'. Obviously this is not always true; for instance, something may so deteriorate that it is no longer the same thing. But there is a hard core of truth in that celebrated proverb. As attendant circumstances change, the same spirit must manifest itself in changed forms in order to preserve its essential character. We have to distinguish carefully between what is essential and worth preserving and what is fit for change.

What are the basics of democracy? This is not just a philosophical question. It should be of interest to any common citizen who is truly interested in the democratic ideal as he or she ought to be. Sooner or later, there are bound to be some changes in our political structure in India and all over the world. We have to make sure that these changes deepen and strengthen the democratic tradition, or man's quest for larger freedom, rather than subvert it. That is why it is important to go to the fundamentals.

The basic problems that democracy tries to overcome can be simply stated. The first among these is the problem of power. It is the democrat's faith, born of long experience, that power has a corrupting influence and 'absolute power corrupts absolutely'. The democrat is, therefore, deeply suspicious of the rise of absolutism and strongly inclined towards decentralisation of power.

Yet this is difficult to achieve as it has to battle against some persistent forces which are not easily vanquished. Perhaps the most important contribution of Marx to political economy was his formulation of the law of concentration and centralisation of capital. In truth that was a partial statement of a wider tendency which we may call the law of concentration and centralisation of power. Capital is only one of the sources of power. Stalin did not owe his enormous power to command over capital alone. Any ideology which presumes that an attack on property will solve the problem of power is an incomplete theory and it risks installing tyranny in an alternative form. Democracy rightly believes that tyranny can be best contained and restrained by organising people's power. But how best to organise people's power in the service of freedom still remains a vital question to which the answer must be sought through endless trials and experiments. Like the search for truth, it is an unending quest.

This leads on to a second question which relates to the procedure for arriving at common decisions for the society as a whole or large groups within it. Since we see the truth in fragments and different people have different perceptions, there is the question of deciding how to make a choice from among these non-identical views. Under a dictatorial regime, there is a simple solution: the view of the dictator prevails. But how about democracy? The democratic solution is to count heads so that the view of the majority gets accepted. But this still leaves a few problems unsolved. Unless we pay attention to them, our view of democracy remains grossly incomplete. Let us note some of these problems.

In the first place, a decision backed by a majority at a given moment is not necessarily the wisest decision. It is adopted on the valid consideration that counting heads is better than breaking heads. However, in a healthy democracy, minorities still retain a certain amount of autonomy and the right to propagate their dissident views. What starts as ideas held by a minority may get accepted by the larger society in course of time. This is essential for the progress of ideas. It is a mistake to equate democracy with crude majoritarianism deprived of the spirit of tolerance and mutual accommodation. An intolerant democracy is a contradiction in terms.

In recent times, the situation has been complicated by certain special circumstances which demand attention. In India we have been witnessing a remarkable proliferation of political parties.

Each party claims to be based on some real issues, but the alacrity with which they enter into and depart from temporary alliances makes a mockery of that claim. Quite obviously these shifting alliances are based mainly on tactical considerations of real or imaginary advantages in the struggle for political power. However, this introduces an element of political instability which is highly disadvantageous for the country as a whole.

We need to develop a different kind of political culture to save India's democracy from getting discredited in the eyes of the people. The right to freedom of thought and conscience is, indeed, valuable. But postures of artificially accentuated hostility among political parties do not do any real service to democracy. What is rather required are rules and conventions to promote constructive dialogues and to widen the scope for cooperation even as the debate on honest differences goes on and democratic forms of protest are treated with due respect.

There are obstacles to the growth of the new culture we need for the functioning of a healthy democracy. These arise from vested interests, from superstitions and even from intellectual sources. Certain influential interpretations of history find a place among them. There the focus is on violent conflicts, making history look almost like a history of wars between classes, nations, races and organised religious sects. History lends itself to alternative interpretations. Undoubtedly wars occupy a prominent place in human history. Perhaps due to their spectacular character, or something in human nature which makes them specially attractive, they have received more attention than what they strictly deserve. Had violent conflicts been the main stuff of history, human society would have got destroyed long ago. Violence alone cannot hold society together. If human society still survives, this must be because the force of violence has been counter-balanced, quietly yet effectively, by the force of non-violence.

Indeed, it is instructive to look at history from this particular angle and read it as a long account of the struggle between the forces of violence and non-violence. Thus human culture evolved, haltingly yet unmistakably, towards a conscious recognition of the value of love and sympathy holding together the basic units of society. Personal and tribal vengeance came to be replaced, however incompletely, by habits of reliance on adjudication and conciliation. A system of justice based on law arose to settle disputes. The growth of democracy is a significant example of a search for peaceful methods of social change.

In all these experiments, there were setbacks and obvious imperfections. Yet the central message is clear enough. Deep down in human nature, there is a strong streak of aggressiveness which cannot be completely erased. But the resources of sympathy, fellowship and reason are also present there. Human society has struggled even for its very survival to mobilise these resources for a rational management of its affairs. This is a view of history from which the democrat can derive guidance and support. If democracy needs a philosophy of history, the halting yet persistent struggle of non-violence to conquer violence might provide the groundwork.

But then we have to go beyond philosophy and talk of praxis. What is the source of corruption of democracy in our time? Ironically democracy, which bases itself on the postulate that power corrupts, has itself been deeply corrupted by 'power politics'. This is a process of which we are all living witnesses. The rise of the modern state, complete with militarism and representing a higher degree of concentration of power than what was achieved by any earlier institution, has provided the historical context for this dangerous process. It has produced habits and expectations appropriate to its perpetuation. How do we come out of this situation?

The modern state, or political parties speaking on its behalf, promise too much and deliver too little. And what are delivered are too often goods of the wrong kind. Revolutionary parties, affected by the same *zeit-geist*, make the capture of state power an essential pre-condition for building a higher form of democracy and end up by creating a new tyranny. Surely it is now time to recognise that a radical reconstruction of democracy cannot come from the top, but must start from the base. What goes by the name of *panchayati raj* in India does not exactly fulfil the requirement. Too often it is dominated by a particular caste or controlled by a centralised political party. Where this happens, it introduces a new division within the village instead of preparing the ground for fair and effective community self-help.

There are, indeed, inequities in rural society as also elsewhere against which a movement of resistance is necessary. It is not an easy task to combine people's cooperation for constructive work with determined resistance against prevalent superstitions and injustice. But that is the way to deepen and strengthen the foundations of our democracy. The system of education, including informal education, has to be remodelled to heighten people's consciousness and bring it in line with this alternative approach to development.

Fortunately, efforts in this direction have already started. To cite simply one instance, Tarun Bharat Sangh is doing extremely good work in the Alwar district of Rajasthan where villagers, sick and tired of depending on the state to ameliorate their conditions, have combined to mobilise their own resources and capacities, supplemented with outside assistance and expertise as required, to initiate and sustain a remarkable change in the rural landscape, overcoming obstacles on the way and making new hopes sprout where despair once prevailed. They have also set up their own panchayat where every family of the village is represented.

Speaking more broadly, there are similar instances of positive initiative involving local communities to be found all over the land. Taken individually and in isolation, these experiments may look small and peripheral. But they are the forerunners of a new movement, more deeply significant for the future than many glittering establishments that hold the centre of the stage today. In them we find the fusion of a new philosophy and a new praxis to replace the tired ideologies of the past. We need many more *Tarun Bharat Sanghs* to restore to India's democracy health and vitality.

There is one final point which can only be delicately hinted here, for it cannot be adequately explained within a brief compass. Between philosophy and praxis, there is a dialectical relationship. For practical work, we have to get tied up with a bounded group or community with which we may, in fact, be very deeply involved. Yet our loyalty to that group ought to be only conditional since our ultimate allegiance must be to values which are universal. What is wrong with so-called 'fundamentalist' movements is that their adherents ignore this higher principle, swearing an unconditional loyalty to a bounded community in blatant disregard of those truly fundamental values which do not divide mankind but can only help unite.

If democracy is linked with an upward evolution of reason and non-violence, it can only recommend a system of graded loyalties. One starts working with a local community which, ideally, serves as a base in thought and aspiration for creative union with ever-widening circles of humanity. The outward structure of democracy should, as far as practicable, reflect this inner idea.

It is to be hoped that democracy, leaving behind a century of imperialism and war, will lead the world in the years ahead towards a practical realisation of a just and harmonious and expanding union. It will be a great pity if we the people of this subcontinent fall behind unable to look beyond their narrow and divisive loyalties. There can be no greater tragedy befalling democracy than the coronation of intolerance.

30

The Spirit of Indian Democracy

We live in uncertain times and look towards the future with mixed feelings of hope and fear. When we try to figure out the possible shape of things in the years ahead, a few special areas of concern and urgent questions, with ancient roots and deep contemporary relevance, claim our earnest attention. Each of them deserves separate treatment, yet they are so intimately interrelated that there is something to be gained by taking them up together. The functioning of India's democracy provides at this moment a major area of concern. It is not always realised that our experiment with the parliamentary form of government is truly extraordinary in some ways. No other country with as large and diverse a population, as economically handicapped and educationally limited, ever entrusted its future to representative government based on adult suffrage.

At the dawn of Independence, with the subcontinent bleeding from a cruel partition, our leaders put their faith in the people of India to hold the country together and carry out programmes of economic and social development. That was extraordinary and yet it was a wise decision. We have to try and understand the grounds of its rationality.

A distinctive feature of the society and culture of India is its incomparable diversity. There are a number of other countries which are physically much larger in size and our great neighbour, China, has an even bigger population spread over a more extensive territory. But in terms of language and religion, not to mention other cultural divisions, India has a distinctly more pluralistic society. Maoism gave rise to a totalitarian political system which China's more homogeneous society was ready to experiment with. Aided by a talent for orderliness and executive efficiency, qualities with which our neighbour has an advantage over us in the same way as Germany has had over Italy, China is now close to attaining the status of an acclaimed superpower, a dubious distinction that her leaders have long craved for. The Chinese way is not a route that India could have taken even if she wanted to.

The straitjacket of totalitarianism would be too cramping for India's invincible diversity. A dictator from the north would not be long tolerated by Tamils in the south while southern hegemony over the north is unthinkable. Any serious attempt to impose a totalitarian political system in India would lead to an endless civil war, inflicting a tragic setback to all decent hopes for the future. Our leaders had, therefore, good reasons for adopting a democratic constitution when the British left.

For one thing, it appeared to offer the best way of avoiding Balkanisation, in other words, further fragmentation of an already partitioned subcontinent. There were other considerations too. Peace and development were high on the agenda of independent India. It is a cardinal virtue of democracy that it aims to provide peaceful methods of social change and development.

Moreover, certain liberal values are an essential part of the idea of freedom as understood by the finest minds among our leaders and these values require the support of a democratic form of government. Political democracy is not all that one wants, but it provides a framework within which both constructive activities and movements of protest against the established order can hope to find their rightful place for a brighter and more secure future under conditions of freedom.

We have recounted briefly the benefits of democracy as a precaution against complacency as well as misconceived criticism. Our society suffers from many maladies and short-comings. These have to be removed through the organised initiative of the people. Democracy provides a system of rights and duties under which people's initiative can be effectively organised. This has its risks. It is not uncommon for the democratic system itself coming under attack and people not taking sufficient notice until it is very late. There are a number of cases of this happening with tragic consequences. There is a wise maxim which has been distilled from that recurrent experience. Eternal vigilance, it has been said, is the price of liberty. It is time for India to take notice.

Representative government is under attack in the world's largest democracy. The assault comes in diverse ways. It will suffice to get an indication of the nature of the threat and its probable consequences near home. West Bengal, for example, has been rigging elections regularly with the help of government machinery. Some members of the government had also admitted this publicly. Such bold truthfulness depicts an arrogance which is bad for the future of democracy.

India's democracy has been blamed for imitating the British model influenced by market economy. Democracy provides one freedom of conscience and speech. A few prominent political thinkers such as Mahatma Gandhi, M.N. Roy and Jayaprakash Narayan, disagreed on many issues but recommended a 'partyless democracy' for India.

For a proper experiment with partyless democracy, its spirit must precede and dictate its form. The question is not about the right to freedom of association which should stay, but its assigned role in the political organisation of society and the moral life of the citizen.

The citizen must feel that his dignity as an individual demands that his allegiance to any party should only take second place to his loyalty to truth and the spirit of democracy. Ignorance of this moral imperative has frightful consequences. There are signs that a crisis is building up and may explode in the near future. It is time to wake up, for it is already getting late. The debate on partyless democracy should not distract attention from the immediate goal, which is free and fair elections. It does not matter which party wins; democracy must win or the country will perish.

While free and fair elections are a basic requirement and a matter of immediate concern, reconstruction of the Indian polity is a historic task of profound significance for the long-term evolution of democracy in India and other developing countries. Democracy can take different forms under different circumstances without sacrificing its basic ideals. It will be useful to discuss this matter with reference to alternative forms of social organisation.

A distinction can be made between the familial model of social organisation and the commercial model. While the commercial model has grown in the city, the familial model is embedded in rural tradition. Each has a contribution to make in the unfolding of human culture. India is predominantly rural, even though the process of urbanisation is steadily advancing. The spirit of the familial model is part of the Indian tradition, although the old tradition is itself changing. Between the two forms of social organisation just mentioned, there is a basic difference. The familial model starts with the assumption of a shared interest of the whole family. In the commercial model, the parties to the deal have separate and competing interests. Thus, for instance, those who sell labour and those who buy it are two distinct parties and all that democracy requires is that there should be freedom of association and differences should be settled through peaceful bargaining.

The familial model in old societies has been traditionally authoritarian. Democracy requires that each member of the family should feel free to offer his or her ideas fearlessly and an effort be made to reach a consensus through a friendly exchange of ideas. Democracy at the village level does not require a division of rural society into rival parties. All that it requires, or aims at, is a community of neighbours where 'the mind is without fear and the head held high'. This itself would constitute a social revolution. If India can achieve this, she would be creating a model of democracy of which she could be proud. It would hold up in miniature the form and spirit of a free and egalitarian human family.

31

Quest for the Ideal

The insistence on the sovereignty of the Truth is designed to bring home the importance of the right philosophy of life. No social revolution can be complete without it.

Gandhiji called his autobiography *My Experiments with Truth*. The use of the word 'experiments' shows how careful he was in his choice of words. In relation to truth, a good citizen has two duties so different that it is difficult to stay bound to both. He must stoutly bear witness to truth as he sees it. He must also steadily recognise that his perception of truth may be only partial as it is not easy to see the whole truth. He who ignores the first of these two imperatives is a dishonest citizen, he who ignores the second is a fanatic. One has to be careful.

'For its next future the world needs the reign of the Truth'. This is the message of the Seventh World Council meeting at Pondicherry in 2003, a theme selected for a seminar on that occasion.

It is a message that needs to be considered with a combination of hope and caution. We have to take into account the ground reality.

What is the ground reality? Madmen in power imagine they possess the Truth. Each of them has a mind devoid of doubt, a heart empty of mercy. He may be a religious fanatic or a secular head of the state. We have them all around; it is unnecessary to name them. One ought to keep in mind this contemporary reality as one strives to reconcile the many voices of wise men of the past.

There is a dilemma here concerning the use of words. The higher ideals of humanity are difficult to express except abstractly. Only small minds abhor abstraction. Yet, at the same time, there are good reasons for abundant caution. High ideas dressed in abstract phrases have often a peculiar power to spread intoxication. They can be dangerous. We have to balance our reverence for the Truth at the highest level with a practical understanding of how truth, bounded in time and space, which is what a reigning authority is concerned with, can only be approached gradually with a proper appreciation of the ineluctable diversity of admissible forms.

Let us spare a few moments to note nature's way of guiding the human society in its practical affairs in the search for the truth. Disputes arise from conflicts of interest backed up by differing perceptions of the truth. Violent ways of settling disputes are socially wasteful. This is nature's way of impressing on society the need for peaceful ways of resolving conflict. When two parties disagree, it may be right and expedient to let a third mediate or arbitrate. From such simple considerations, one can trace the gradual development of the judicial system, the idea of the rule of law and democracy as the foundation of justice, peace and liberty. There is a point here which needs emphasis. The opinion of the majority is not necessarily right and democracy does not guarantee discovery of the truth at every step. No system of government suffices to establish the reign of the Truth. Democracy recognises the fact of human fallibility and attempts to devise a socially decent way of moving towards the truth. A system of government with a higher claim is likely to achieve even less. This is well attested by history.

The world as constituted today is divided into a large number of nation states, based on a multiplicity of cultures, religions and economic interests. While reason points towards the need for world union, there are stubborn differences which divide nations. The United Nations provides a platform for dialogue among nations for peaceful resolution of conflict. Here is a method which conforms to the democratic ethos. But a powerful nation, with sufficient military strength, can reject this method and try to impose its will, its perception of the Truth, on the rest of the world. This is the ground reality today. It conforms to an ancient idea of imperial hegemony as a glorified foundation for peace. If this idea wins out, we will get a world where power is effectively centralised, a unipolar world held together by one mighty nation. But this is a false ideal and it is bound to fail in the long run. To proclaim its falsity is the duty of all those who believe in the right kind of World Union.

Sri Aurobindo's own ideas, his incisive analysis of ancient history, for instance, provides an impressively strong basis for rejecting the pretensions of the apologists for a new imperialism today. It is not simply by a mechanical repetition of his noble words, but by a simultaneous and sustained effort to relate them to the current reality of the evolving world, that we can best help to keep Sri Aurobindo's philosophy alive and meaningful to the young generation.

Let me offer just one example of his luminous interpretation of past history. In *The Ideal of Human Unity*, he wrote:

> The weakness of the old empire-unities created by conquest was that they tended to destroy the smaller units they assimilated, as did imperial Rome .... Gaul, Spain, Africa, Egypt were thus killed, turned into dead matter and their energy drawn into the centre, Rome .... When the Roman grasp loosened, the world which it had held so firmly constricted had been for long a magnificently organised death-in-life incapable of self-regeneration; vitality could only be restored through the inrush of the vigorous barbarian world ...

He does recognise the positive contribution of the historical forces which help create unity. But what he pleads for is not a unipolar world, but 'the idea of a federated nation'. This should set the right perspective both for the Indian subcontinent and the world entirely.

Just as one speaks of a federated nation so too one can visualise a federation of faiths and cultures. There was a time when one religious faith, Christianity or Islam, for instance, dreamt of conquering the whole world. By now it is clear that this is not going to happen. Different faiths and cultures, religious as well as secular, are going to coexist and so they should. A feeling for a common core of values (and perhaps of perplexities too) shared by these diverse faiths and cultures does facilitate amicable coexistence. But this can only take the form of a sympathetic and perennial search, an unending quest. We do not all share a common language and in any case, language only approximately expresses our innermost feelings and thoughts. It is therefore inevitable that approximately the same truth will be differently expressed by different people. We have to learn to accept this gracefully even when we talk of the reign of the truth.

Granted the need for a tolerant approach, there is still a special point to be made in favour of a declaration of the sovereignty of truth. No system of government, no institutional arrangement however cleverly contrived, can prevent the infiltration of vices into politics and corruption of society. What is clearly required at this hour is a change, an uplift of the level of consciousness. How can this be secured? The best minds of ancient civilisation stressed the importance of sports and music and the teaching of philosophy. Among these, philosophy rightly holds a position of pre-eminence. In the absence of a sound philosophy of life, sports may soon lose the sporting spirit and music degenerates into revelry.

The insistence on the sovereignty of the Truth is designed to bring home the importance of the right philosophy of life. No social revolution can be complete without it. The Truth the world needs, whatever its verbal veil, has to satisfy two essential conditions: to each it must secure a sense of inner freedom; for all, a commitment to peace. For such is 'nature's holy plan', a design made manifest by the conditions of human survival in the future. Perfection one may never attain, but to be released from bondage to greed and vindictiveness is a goal worth pursuing.

32

A New Radicalism

Three hungers have strongly influenced the history of mankind all along and determined its course: hunger for food, hunger for power and hunger for love. While food is commonly recognised as necessary and power seen as covetable, love is often considered as something dispensable, not quite essential for the sustenance of life. This is an error and it may be just as well to stop for a moment to correct it.

Confronted with the ancient vision which teaches us that man does not live by bread alone, some are very pleased with the commonplace retort that man cannot live without bread. Here is a case where what is affirmed and what is apparently contradicted are both true. Some propositions are true but trivial; others reveal their truth on deeper thought. It needs no special effort or imagination to get at the idea that man cannot survive beyond a limited time without taking food in some form or other. It needs some deeper thinking to realise that love in some form or other is an essential support of life.

Let us consider the matter first in its simplest form. Think of a person, a human being, who has been entirely deprived of affection in childhood, of the love of the opposite sex in youth, of companionship of friends and sympathy of neighbours. Think of a person who is kept well supplied with bread, but forced to live in a solitary cell all the time. Is there much doubt that he or she will soon mentally disintegrate, cease to be a human being and perhaps be driven to insanity or suicide?

To be totally deprived of love is a state which is barely endurable for a strictly limited period, but not for long.

The link between food and love and power is provided by possessiveness. At least in common love, one seeks to possess the object or objects of one's love. This means power of a sort, the power to possess. Once love and possessiveness get mixed up, the latter tends to become dominant. In a situation like that, people would rather sacrifice love than give up power. It is a common enough experience how love turns into its opposite, hatred and bitterness, under the strong influence of possessiveness. This surely is unfortunate. Power and possessiveness cannot add to life that joy and consolation which flow from a sense of loving union through fair weather and foul.

Power, the kind of power that pits one fragment of humanity against another, has played a crucial role in history. We will have something more to say about that a little later. There is just one word that one should add before that. That is about the power of love. Even in its imperfect form it helps to hold families and societies together. But for it, human society would have disintegrated long ago. As Tagore once wrote, 'The perpetual process that is going on in the world around us is a struggle for the victory of love. If that were not true and if victory were not always achieved by goodness and beauty, then long before this everything would have been devastated.' Violence hits the headlines. The silent power of love works most of the time unnoticed by reporters.

But the headlines also matter. Power in its more aggressive form has changed the shape of the world almost beyond recognition. This has happened more rapidly than ever before since the onset of industrialism. Industrialism and the rise of the nation state are closely related historical processes and taken together they constitute a major, arguably the most dominant, feature of the modern age. It has taken hold of a steadily increasing number of countries of the East and the West, outwardly divided by divergent cultures and political ideologies. While one or other ideology has advanced or receded, industrialism has, despite temporary setbacks, continued its triumphant march in the last couple of centuries. This leads us to a basic question. What has made industrialism such an invincible force in the history of our time?

A complete answer to this question must include many things, some of which more or less debatable. But one thing is fairly certain. What a nation derives from industrialism is power, military power, above all. For some of the pioneer countries, industrialism was an outcome of a preceding period of commercial growth. But the late-comers typically opted for it from a cluster of considerations which included military power as its principal component. Such, for instance, were the cases of Germany, Russia and Japan and a number of other countries which joined the race still later. Whether industrialism with its promise of removal of poverty increased the sum total of happiness of the people for any particular country or for the world as a whole is highly questionable. What is beyond question is that any country which lagged behind risked being subjugated by an industrially more powerful nation. It is not an accident that in the last half a century military expenditure and defence research have claimed and received larger allocation of funds than basic welfare measures. This is true for all the superpowers and the world as a whole.

The attraction of industrialism has been further enhanced, first for the ruling classes and then for the lower orders of society, by its capacity to offer ever new and highly alluring consumer services and consumer durables. Consumerism is the name given to this new trend. It is matched by a philosophy of life that attempts to justify it. Happiness is equated with pleasure which depends on gratification of the senses by purchasable commodities. In course of time, the power of these stimuli to yield definite pleasure diminishes, but by then the consumer develops such a strong attachment to them that it becomes painful, almost insufferable, to do without them. Thus, in a misguided quest for pleasure, people end up with new sources of frustration and boredom which they ineffectually struggle to avoid by increasing reliance on expensive forms of excitement which further weakens their inner creative powers.

From this welter of confusing experiences, a simple yet profound truth peeps out. When hunger for power claims and receives so much that there is little left for love to live on, an inner emptiness of soul seeks relief in wasteful distraction which is not its proper food. Beyond the minimum that is required for replenishing our physical energy and protecting ourselves from gross physical harm, our true happiness and creative powers depend not so much on the power to command commodities or purchase other people's labour as on our capacity to look at men and things around us with a loving, or perhaps a half-loving and half-mocking, detachment which is the way that artists at their best look at the world. It also depends on our power of communion with nature and the universe at large. The trouble with the kind of industrialism we have known is that it has promoted an outlook on life which is at variance with this deeper verity. The roots of the contemporary crisis of civilisation lie in a wrong idea of what man should live for. It is possible to pose this as a question of personal salvation. But public discussion is best conducted in a social context, keeping in view the pressing problems of the world.

Let us come back to our central theme. We have noted the dangerously misdirected striving in modern society for power of the wrong kind. What can be done to stop this? For all we know, this will not be easy. Desire for power is strongly embedded in human nature. It is more difficult to conquer the craving for wordly power than to give up wealth. There are dictators who avoided lux wires but retained a strong appetite for power. Some people think that a change in human nature can be brought about through a change in social institutions. This is a simplistic view. While a change in institutions is normally accompanied by a revision of rules and outward habits, it does not by itself produce a basic change in human nature or cure man of the desire for power, a fact painfully illustrated by contemporary socialist experiments. What is needed is a passage, a transition, from a lower level of consciousness to a higher level by some kind of an evolutionary urge that can only be half explained and is half mysterious. What we can still do is to build up a movement of ideas, a climate of opinion which will make this transition expected and welcome and the contrary tendencies censurable.

Granted that institutional changes are not sufficient for our purpose, they are necessary. So let us say a few words about them. At the political level, it is a question of taming the power of the state, of humanising it. As war is divorced from ethics so too is modern politics which is a form of war among rival parties for the capture of state power. People's power can only be built from the base and rests essentially on voluntary cooperation where party politics, with its fierce and unscrupulous loyalties, can be a formidable stumbling bloc.

A new political structure requires a new economic structure to match it. In other words, decentralisation of political power cannot be effective unless there is also a substantial measure of decentralisation of economic power. This is not a recommendation for wiping out large-scale industry which will continue to have its place in modern society. But side by side the basis has to be strengthened for an alternative economy depending chiefly on local resources, evolving new forms of cooperation of locally available manpower and producing, though not entirely yet for the main part, for meeting local needs. This is, in fact, possible to a much larger extent than most people in the city are ready to grant.

An entrenched society creates and supports an educational system designed to perpetuate the existing order. If we seriously want a new social order to be built up over the next few decades, we have to redesign our system of education. At least at the lower levels, the contents and methods of education must be imaginatively related to local needs and requirements, moderating the enthusiasm for a uniform system of national education. At the higher levels of education, the horizons must widen. We have to combine diversity at the base with greater unity at the top. There is no other way of building a stable base consistent with a wisely and creatively coordinating centre.

A multilevel approach is also appropriate for research as it is for education although it will be improper to stretch the comparison too far. At one level, the level of pure theory, scientists all over the world can well be thought of as belonging to one single community. But technology is more closely related to practical needs and these can be widely different from one locality to another. Such differences are more important in some circumstances than in others. There is talk of globalisation and there is a sector of our modern enterprise that needs to be carefully oriented towards the world market where it is wise to take into account, assimilate and adapt the latest technology that the industrially advanced countries have to offer. But there are other areas where we have to apply our reason and ingenuity to develop a radically different technology suited to our local requirements. This is as true for engineering as for health and medicine or fuel research, to name just a few areas of concern.

To act and think in terms of local resources and local needs is not necessarily to be insular and close one's mind to the rest of the world. Ancient India developed an indigenous system of medicine. So did China and Tibet. But even in those early centuries, despite difficulties of transport and communication, there was a good deal of exchange of ideas and information among the medical practitioners of these countries. An appropriate technology developed in response to rural requirements in India, Bangladesh or Pakistan may be of interest not only to one another but also to countries in other parts of the world. In fact this is only to be expected. We may have very good reasons to pay special attention to rural reconstruction as part of a vision of an alternative social order and still retain a universalist frame of mind. An outstanding example of this approach is provided by the social philosophy of Rabindranath Tagore. An objective analysis of the crisis of human society today shows that Tagore's approach has great significance for the future even though it had only limited success in his own day.

Already there is a new radicalism abroad. There are people trying to do their little bit inspired by a vision of an alternative social order and a new way of life. They firmly believe in the need for a radical decentralisation of political and economic power, a technology and an approach to education consistent with such decentralisation, new ideas about a more creative relationship between man and his natural environment and a new emphasis on the power of love rather than love of power. Revolutionaries of the old vintage look askance at the new radicalism. No wonder West Bengal, citadel of the old idea of revolution, lags distinctly behind some other parts of India such as Maharashtra, where the pioneers of the new age draw inspiration more from Gandhi than from Lenin. The old 'leftism', with the tremendous importance it attached to capture of state power by any means and a leaning towards violence, was, despite its international pretensions, overpowered by the temper of its age, the age of the rise of industrialism and the nation state. The new radicalism goes beyond that discredited idea of revolution. In its own way, it represents a new idea of revolution. It is so different from the dominant culture of present-day society that it cannot in all fairness be described as anything less. Those who adopt this outlook are humanists in the sense that, in any conflict between hostile fragments of humanity, they give primacy to the welfare of mankind as a whole and refuse to identify themselves totally with any of the warring camps. Yet at the same time they go beyond humanism in the sense that they are less interested in asserting the superiority of the human race over all living creatures than in fostering a creative communion with the universe both as an object of knowledge and as of love.

The new radicals are still small in number. But they are to be found all over the world. They are part of a rising movement for a more hopeful future. It is a movement which will take time to spread. The more desperate the present situation grows, threatened alike with nuclear annihilation and ecological disaster, the more sharply we are faced with a decisive choice of alternatives to make or mar history. For the young, it is a great time to be alive and seek release from a gnawing sense of the insignificance of trifling pleasures.

It is a great time to start building a new world. One may start with oneself, a small community of friends or a single village. It may be only a small work of mending, limited reform, a little improvement, moral and material and so on. But outwardly small, the work must be sustained by an idea of something greater, an idea which gives to one's energies at a lower level an upward direction, an impulse to be united with something larger and brighter.

33

Socialism Reviewed

I n the debate on the relationship between the individual
and the society, we risk running into error whichever side
we take. On the one hand, the individual is the focal point
of all significant thought and experience. Truth cannot be
lived at second hand. The individual must articulate and act
upon the truth as he himself perceives it and suffer the consequences and learn from them. Yet, on the other hand, the
individual cannot effectively serve the truth in a vacuum
outside society. 'It is astonishing', J.M. Keynes once wrote,
'what foolish things one can temporarily believe if one thinks
too long alone'. The search for truth is a social and cooperative enterprise. When we elevate the role of society or of the
individual in that enterprise to the status of an ideology,
calling it by the name of socialism or individualism, we possibly import a one-sided emphasis and do less than justice
to the full dialectical relationship between society and
the individual. Yet the debate must continue as an aid to
clarification of ideas under changing social conditions. For
words have a chameleonic character, and as conditions
change so do words and their shades of meaning.

The dichotomy between capitalism and socialism is also
beset with somewhat similar problems. How does one
explicate the meaning of capitalism? For some, the heart of
the matter lies in the overwhelming importance attached to
'accumulation of capital', the extraction of 'surplus' and its

investment and reinvestment. This led some to call the Soviet economy under Stalin by the name of 'state capitalism' in view of the overriding importance attached to just that process for the sake of rapid industrialisation. For others, capitalism is concerned, above all, with the question of ownership of property, more particularly, the means of production, and, by that token, the U.S. economy and the Soviet economy are supposed to stand at opposite poles. Still others make the meaning of capitalism turn on the idea of the 'free' market economy. Socialism, too, displays a similar diversity of meanings. Socialism, said Arthur Lewis, economist and Nobel laureate, is about equality, which reflects a widely shared notion on that subject. In fact, one of the principal Indian words for socialism (or communism) is connected with *sāmya* or equality. Others take the question of ownership as the central question and, at least until recently, this was quite common, particularly among Marxists, and so was the idea of central planning of leading economic activities. Still others have more loosely thought of socialism as a system under which social welfare and social preferences are allowed precedence over private profit and individual preferences.

Some recent events have been interpreted to signify a historic defeat for socialism and an impressive vindication of the case for capitalism. The tested models of socialism have failed to deliver the goods. Capitalism, by contrast, with its market economy and the profit motive, has established itself as a more dependable engine of economic growth. To the usual objection that growth does not guarantee welfare there is the equally oft-repeated rejoinder that without growth, there is no stable basis for increased provision of welfare. But this still leaves the debate quite inconclusive. The proposition that without growth there can be no welfare does not provide sufficient ground for the inference that the presence of growth necessarily produces welfare.

In fact, there are two contrasted sets of errors which need to be avoided in this connection. Let us note them briefly one by one. On the one hand, economic growth propelled by the profit motive, unless supplemented by other well-designed measures, does not provide the surest way to welfare, particularly in a culturally heterogeneous and traditionally hierarchical society. Moreover, there are certain consequences of economic growth, beyond what is intended by individual consumers and producers, both in material and moral terms, which may be of questionable value or even definitely undesirable. These, therefore, deserve special attention. But, on the other hand, there are errors of an opposite kind which require equally to be guarded against. While it is true that the profit motive is careless of social welfare, it is an egregious error to believe that discarding the principle of profit implies accepting 'the authority of the good'. What might result is not simply inefficiency and waste, which is bad enough, but the authority of war-lords or a feudal bureaucratic spirit which is something worse. When Keynes wrote in the concluding notes of the celebrated *General Theory* that 'it is better that a man should tyrannise over his bank balance than over his fellow-citizens; and whilst the former is sometimes denounced as being but a means to the latter, sometimes at least it is an alternative', he was not just giving expression to a passing thought, but stating with due deliberation an idea that had formed in his mind over the earlier two decades.

Meditating on the German war-economy during World War I, it occurred to the English economist that industrial economies which were not organised for profit might still be organised and centrally planned for power. Keynes was so struck by certain ideas propounded by Professor Jaffé A at that time that he summed them up in an article in *The Economic Journal* in September 1915, in the following significant words: 'The old order of industry, which is dying today is based on Profit; in the new Germany of the twentieth century, Power without consideration of Profit is to make an end of that system of capitalism.' It is hardly necessary to add that a system of 'etatistic planning' for power, under which dictators and bureaucrats tyrannise over fellow-citizens, may very well adopt also a whole range of welfare measures without any substantial change in its basic character. Moreover, many capitalist economies have already assimilated certain features of rival etatistic economies which have appropriated the name of socialism.

An ideology of any worth and durability is born of a cross-fertilisation of some relatively permanent values embedded in long tradition and certain conditions, conflict of interests, hopes and frustrations, which are more time-bound and constitute special characteristics of the epoch in which that ideology presents itself. Although academic discussion of an ideology should be conducted with a certain amount of detachment, this does not offer sufficient reason for abstracting the debate from the contemporary context. However, even as we pay attention to the temporal context, we should be careful not to allow ourselves to be excessively influenced by such temporary factors as the political success or failure of the ideology in question. To take an outstanding example from this century, the victory of the Russian Bolsheviks in 1917 and the political–military gains made by the Communist movement after World War II produced unbounded enthusiasm among many adherents of Marxism and led them to believe that the verdict of history had been finally given in favour of their creed and that it was only the bad faith and perversity of their opponents which kept the argument going. Judged by the same standards, the year 1989 can again be treated as a terminal year, though in an opposite sense, and it may be thought that it is time to bring the debate on socialism to a close. But, of course, it is going to continue and there are some good reasons why it should. It is still useful to assess the socialist tradition, to judge and decide how much of it should be modified or rejected and how much retained and in what language should what is still valuable in it be clothed.

To the on-going debate on socialism, Michael Luntley, who teaches philosophy at the London School of Economics, and belongs to the younger generation of socialists, has recently made a notable contribution. His book, which appears under the title of *The Meaning of Socialism*, was published by Open Court, La Salle, Illinois, in 1990. In the next few lines, an attempt will be made to give very brief indications of some of the ideas expounded in that book.

Michael Luntley's central concern is with what he calls 'the good life'. His is a search for ways and means of establishing in society 'the Authority of the Good', or, at least, moving resolutely in that direction. There are lots of people all over the world, including many believers (with faith in God) and quite a few atheists (believing in the authority of Reason), who would sympathise with his central concern but might not choose to call themselves 'socialist'. Now, there are some definite reasons why Luntley makes that ideological choice. He is deeply distrustful of 'the rampant individualism of liberalism'. He wants to give the notion of the community, as 'the repository of the good life', an essential place in his system of ideas. He finds in the socialist tradition powerful support for that notion.

Why does Professor Luntley assign such an important place to that notion in his model of socialism? The idea of the good has a social dimension. Moral values are rooted in the positive concern, the good will, that a person feels for other persons. This feeling of concern comes when we see others 'as like ourselves'. But this comes naturally within a 'face-to-face' community, a 'reference group' with which one has so identified oneself that within it one's own good and the good of others tend to coalesce into a common good. It is within such reference groups that the search for the good comes most unforced, as a manifestation of man's innate moral nature.

As a socialist, Luntley is a bitter critic of capitalism. 'Under capitalism', he says, 'life is lived not under the Authority of the Good, but under the aristocracy of capital'. With the rise and spread of capitalism, old community ties have been disrupted. A capitalist economy must have the freedom to rearrange resources, both human and material, in such a way that profit on investment is maximised. Capitalism, therefore, cannot be friendly to stable community bonds. The destructive role of capitalism is most evident in that it leads inexorably to 'the fragmentation of the reference groups grounding our moral traditions'. Capitalism is the enemy of the good life. By contrast, socialism offers the principles of moral reconstruction.

For Professor Luntley, the good, like the truth, has an objective existence. This does not mean that we, or anybody else, have already discovered it. It only means a certain faith in the possibility of continually approximating it. Within the traditional community, there is a continuing dialogue on norms of the good life and it is a common enough experience that most of the time people move towards a consensus. Within the reference group, there is a convergence on the idea of the good, which in a way is what holds the group together. But when we make reference groups the grounds of our moral traditions, we are faced with a problem—the moral traditions of different reference groups are not identical, they may even be conflicting. But the large society, and finally the world community, must find space for all the local reference groups to coexist and, even if in a limited way, to cooperate. Conflicts in local ideas of the good life may then appear as rents in the moral fabric of the larger global association. The requirement of the idea that there is such a thing as *the* good life, says Luntley, demands that we find some way to repair such rents. How is that to be done? Perhaps the best way to do that is through a process, a reflective practice, of criticism from within. Conflicting ideas of the good life arise on account of erroneous or distorted moral intuitions. Such distortions, Luntley believes, are caused by economic interests. The best way of confronting a biased intuition of the good is to challenge it to defend itself on grounds other than those of economic interests.

By such a process of critical reexamination and reconstruction of local and proximate traditions, it should be possible to approach higher levels of apprehension of the idea of the good life and its practical requirements. This is not some work to be entrusted to and performed by a philosopher king. Rather what is required is an unending dialogue in which as many people as possible actively participate. It is in the basic reference groups and local communities, workers' committees and village councils, that direct participation of all or most members can materialise. A special characteristic of the dialogue at those levels is that the ethos of the community encourages decisions to be reached by consensus. It is this model of direct democracy along with the striving for consensus rather than division which assorts best with the spirit of Luntley's contemplated socialist society. To be sure, it cannot be made to work in assemblies representing larger territories and constituencies. But it still remains important as an ideal. It provides a standard by which the deficiencies and limitations of other democratic institutions can be judged and it hopefully sets a direction in which the practice and ethos of democracy can be developed and improved in future.

It is tempting to stop at this point and draw attention to the striking affinity, though not identity, between the ideas presented in *The Meaning of Socialism* and an important line of thought developed in India by people like M.K. Gandhi, Vinoba Bhave and Jayaprakash Narayan. Narayan, a Marxist in his younger days, was a kind of 'left-wing' Gandhian in his maturer years. A socialist who preferred to swear by *Sarvodaya* in his Gandhian phase, the idea of the face-to-face community occupied such an important place in his political philosophy that, to stress the point, he occasionally called himself communitarian. The affiliation of Narayan's line of thought with Gandhi's is beyond question. I can best indicate its affinity with Professor Luntley's ideas with the help of a short extract from one of my earlier writings:

> Gandhi had a step-by-step method of thinking, the steps leading from bottom upwards... One must begin with one's immediate neighbourhood, which is a face-to-face community, a village, let us say. It is here that human problems, whether of poverty or sickness or lack of education, appear not as an abstraction but as something immediately felt and seen, and it is here that love of one's neighbour and the good life begin. (Datta 1986)

I shall not proceed to describe the political structure, complete with direct democracy at the base and the principle of consensus, recommended by Gandhians, but it has obvious similarities with Luntley's model. This is a notable example of that convergence of ideas, however incomplete, which I am sure Professor Luntley will find welcome.

Gandhi had a special place for woman in his social philosophy. He once wrote, 'It is sad to think that the Smritis contain texts which can command no respect from men who cherish the liberty of woman as their own'. And he went onto add, 'the future is with women'. It is interesting to note that Luntley's book has a special place for woman; the word 'her' is consistently used where other writers would habitually write 'his'. Note, for instance, the following: 'The ideal socialist has a fire in her belly and a moral hymn in her heart.'

But there are differences too in style and substance. In the Gandhian philosophy, the emphasis on society is carefully balanced by an explicit recognition of the pivotal importance of the individual. 'If the individual ceases to count', wrote Gandhi (1942), 'what is left of society? Individual freedom alone can make a man voluntarily surrender himself completely to the service of society. If it is wrested from him, he becomes an automaton and society is ruined.' It is not apparent from Luntley's book that he is convinced of the need for such an emphatic recognition of the value of individual freedom.

Socialism, Gandhi once said, is a beautiful word. But he did not make a creed out of it. He painted an appealing picture of an ideal village community, but he was honest enough to call it a village of his 'dream'. The tradition of a community may be at least in part unjust, oppressive, unenlightened, inhuman. Distortion of moral intuition may not be caused simply by economic interests; it may be derived from hardened superstitions or accumulated deposits of fear and jealousy. The methods of direct democracy and open debate proposed by Luntley are, indeed, commendable; but a narrow-minded, even cruel, tradition may yet continue for long despite such methods. The social consensus is so often against the creative and deviant individual. The presumption about the moral superiority of the authority of the community or the nation is not always friendly to the idea of the good. What, under the circumstances, is the conscientious objector to do? It will not do clearly to endorse his rights in a capitalist society and be half-hearted about them under a socialist dispensation.

The glorification of such collective entities as the nation and the class has been one of the most disturbing features of the century which is now drawing to a close. Individual freedom has been sacrificed at the altar of such glorified collectivities. The brands of socialism we have seen in this century, the brands that have proved influential, are national socialism and the Marxian variety which in practice gives primacy to the collectivity of the class.

Socialism is a beautiful word; but can the tendencies just noted be effectively countered under the banner of socialism? The disintegration of community life and the atomisation of the individual are surely things to be worried about. Amidst the wreckage of possessive and power-hungry societies and empty restless selves, the task is to promote a culture hospitable to creativity.

It is important to emphasise, as Luntley does, the value of the place of society in the life of the individual. In fact, man is not man without society. But it is dangerously one-sided to end on that note. As F.H. Bradley carefully remarked: 'Man is not man at all unless social; but he is not much above beasts unless more than social.' To be creatively social, one has to be more than social.

There is a cosmic energy in man, a 'soul-force', that impels him to seek communion not only with society but also with nature and the universe. Love expresses itself through our relationship with other men whom we then see as ourselves, but it also goes beyond and lights up whatever in the universe it touches. There is in man what Ocampo, trying to explain Tagore's religion, called 'the hunger of unity'. Less demonstrative than its twin and rival, the hunger for power, it is yet no less tenacious. The individual derives his idea of good and evil not only from that social consensus that exists outside of him even when he participates in it, but also from that insistent spiritual urge within. It is from there again that he gets an intimation of a third meaning of freedom, besides the two discussed by Luntley. In our moments of communion with the universe, passing beyond the bourns of fear, we feel free. Although we bring that feeling from a larger universe, we struggle through the stresses and strains of our too material existence and the seductions of misconceived ideals, to find a place in society, as wide and secure as possible, for that spirit of inner freedom, and we make it part of our idea of the good. In any philosophy of the good life, whatever the name by which it goes, this more-than-social dimension of the true human ideal should not be lost.

References

Datta, A. 1986. *The Gandhian Way,* pp. 12–13. Shillong: North-Eastern Hill University.

Gandhi, M.K. 1942. *Harijan,* 1 February.

34

The Liberal Approach

Any living philosophy has to perform a double duty. On the one hand, it has to be faithful to its basic principles. On the other, it has to take into account changing circumstances and strive all the while to adjust its basic principles to changing circumstances because that is the only way of keeping them alive. Otherwise they get frozen. So that is the way a living philosophy grows and stays alive, asking itself every now and then, what is living in its teachings and what is dead, what has to be preserved and what has to be modified and how.

Let us first try to consider some of the basic principles of liberalism and then take into account some contemporary challenges and meditate on how best we can face those challenges. What are the basic principles? It has been rightly stressed that Liberalism is about freedom. It is about breaking bondages. That is a basic principle of Liberalism. What are those bondages that Liberalism revolted against, if you look at it historically? In the first place, Liberalism was a revolt against authoritarianism, a revolt, so to speak, against the tyranny of a powerful authority. Liberalism believed that power corrupted, and absolute power corrupted absolutely; so it started as a revolt against absolutism, in the first place, of a political authority, of the state as an organised political authority. At the same time, Liberalism is also a revolt against tyranny of a different type — the tyranny of tradition. As we had an obscurantist tradition, Liberalism is a revolt against the tyranny of both the state and an obscurantist tradition. In so far as it is a revolt against an obscurantist tradition, Liberalism stands for rationalism, a rational outlook on life.

Rights of man

So these are some basic things that follow from the Liberal adherence to the idea of freedom. Revolting against tyranny, Liberals place their faith in the idea of the rights of man. We talk of democracy. Now democracy is certainly one of the things that a Liberal believes in. But even more basic than democracy is the concept of the rights of man. In popular conception, democracy means the right of the people to rule themselves, which in practice means the right of the majority of the representatives of the people to enact laws and implement them. But what if the majority turns tyrannical? And a majority can turn tyrannical, as history shows. After all, Hitler came to power with the support of a majority. I suppose there was a time when Stalin enjoyed the support of the majority in his country. So there was a period in history when Hitler or Stalin was not functioning against the will of the majority. What were they functioning against then? They were functioning against the idea of the fundamental rights of man. If a majority decides to ignore the rights of man, then that majority is an illiberal majority. The idea of the rights of man is fundamental to the Liberal conception of a good society, and democracy itself must pay respect to the idea of the rights of man in order to be a proper instrument in the functioning of a good society.

Origins of the liberal faith

Let us consider now the particular historical circumstances in which the liberal faith arose because that might help us take into account later developments.

When we look at it in a historical context, what goes by the name of 'liberal philosophy' arose at a special historical juncture in a particular part of the world. Now, that historical juncture was marked by the unfolding of the market system. Liberalism, as it is known in modern history, was a child of a period of the unfolding of the market system.

How were the two things related? We can see the relationship very easily. In a traditional society, for example the Indian one, society is divided into different castes. In one form or another, such divisions have existed in all traditional societies, maybe from the time of Plato onwards. In what way does the situation change with the growth of a market system? It changes in a very simple way. The seller of a good does not consider the caste of the buyer. To the seller of a good, the buyer is simply a buyer, whether he comes from a higher caste or a lower one. If a seller makes a distinction between a higher caste and a lower caste, he is not a pure seller, and he has not embraced the very essence of a market economy; he is being influenced by some other factor. A seller as a seller can only take into account the ability of the buyer to offer the price for a given commodity. He can make no other distinction. And in that sense, the market system is a great equaliser, socially speaking, in not taking into account caste divisions or other stereotyped social divisions.

The evolution of the market economy

Also, in a growing economy, there is a new dynamism, a new mobility. So people can move up from one level of society to another. In that sense also, a market economy breaks down traditional social barriers, demonstrating that you can start from one station in life and move up to a higher station.

Furthermore, in a market economy, there is continuous innovation and technical progress. So there is a new feeling of mastery over the forces of nature because that is exactly what technology gives you.

So a market economy, as it evolved in history, in contemporary times, performed all these functions: of weakening social hierarchy, promoting mobility and enhancing man's mastery over nature. These are the historical circumstances that moulded the Liberal philosophy as it arose.

Problems of the market economy

What then were the problems? The problems too are well known. While on the one hand the market economy was no a respecter of traditional social divisions, as I said, treating all buyers equally so long as the buyers had the purchasing power, on the other hand, the market economy did permit and even promote economic inequality. And that created some problems. Also, as traditional communities disintegrated, there arose a situation when social security itself was threatened and something had to be done about that.

There were other problems to which I shall refer a little later, but let us consider the two problems that I just mentioned — of inequality and the breakdown of social security with the growth of the market economy. I am stating simple things, which are well known, and we also know the way in which, historically, society has responded to these challenges. Societies responded to these challenges by developing a new system of social security. That is what Western social democracy was about. Liberalism, confronted with economic inequality and the breakdown of social security, defended itself by creating a new society, where the state would guarantee a minimum security for people who were deprived. Social democracy was a logical outcome of the Liberal philosophy when confronted with certain very specific social problems.

Then there was also a deeper problem, deeper than what I have just mentioned. I talked of mobility, dynamism — dynamism, that is the positive side of economic development. But mobility also means in a certain way the dissolution of the old type of social solidarity, dissolution of the family and dissolution of social togetherness. There is something in human nature that desires human togetherness; it is needed for a person to remain sane and healthy. While it is necessary to have food and livelihood and while the state, to a certain extent, can guarantee a kind of social security, human beings also need something rather more intangible and yet very insistent and essential, and that is the capacity and the opportunity for positive, creative communion among different human beings.

Sociological problems facing liberalism

We sometimes fail to remember how important companionship is for a person to preserve his sanity. But if you want to convince yourself of its importance, consider seriously the plight of a person punished with solitary confinement. In his solitary cell, he has a roof above him, and he is supplied with food. What is he deprived of then? Just the companionship of other human beings. That can be enough for him to disintegrate psychologically and lose sanity. Companionship is very important. And if it so happens that a person is not in a solitary cell but in a crowd and is yet lonely, unable to fully communicate with others and with the feeling that social bonds are dissolving, what happens then? This is not an imaginary problem. This is a problem that human societies in contemporary history have faced time and again and for which they have come up with dangerous solutions, solutions we are all acquainted with. How does a human being, an individual, escape the stress of his loneliness? By drug addiction, by drowning himself in some kind of intoxication or by embracing some variety of collective excitement — collective excitement of the kind that fundamentalism provides. It is not an accident that in our time in societies, both rich and poor, drug addiction is growing, the rate of suicides is high and militant solidarity, with excitement and a strange attraction for violence and terrorism, is on the rise. The cause must perforce lie in something that is inherent in the social situation of our times is the so-called 'progress' notwithstanding. It is not an atmosphere in which the Liberal spirit can thrive, in which the Liberal dream of a good life can be realised. And they realised it. So what do we do about that?

I can add to that a simple, very material problem — the problem of unemployment. The Western solution in the developed countries to the problem of unemployment is to provide unemployment doles. Now, that is to assume that all that an unemployed person is deprived of is his livelihood; you give him a dole so that he can buy food and live. But there is something more that an unemployed person is deprived of. He is deprived of dignity, of an opportunity for doing service to society and to gain his livelihood. If you get your livelihood and at the same time you are deprived of the opportunity to make a contribution to society, you lose your sense of dignity. It is only by receiving in exchange for doing, that we can retain our dignity. So the problem of unemployment is not solved by simply providing doles. It is a bigger problem.

Remember, in a country like India, the very character of unemployment is different from that you find in the industrially developed countries. In the latter, the main kind of unemployment is connected with what is called trade cycles, cyclical unemployment. In a country like India, there is chronic unemployment, not simply cyclical. If you consider the last 50 years, on the one hand one Five-Year Plan has followed another in a long sequence, while on the other, decade after decade, the volume of unemployment has been growing steadily. This is something quite different from cyclical unemployment. Also, in a country like India, you have underemployment and disguised unemployment. This is a very important form of unemployment that is prevalent both in towns and (more so) in rural areas. It is not a small problem, but a very basic one, a problem that is swelling the ranks of anti-socials. From the culture of sick cities, its influence spreads into the villages. So sick towns and sick cities make each other more and more sick. And this whole process is connected with the phenomenon of growing unemployment.

So, growing unemployment is not simply an economic problem. It creates a social and cultural problem and vitiates our politics. What do we do about that? In the West, the situation has been different. When the West got industrialised, it had the opportunity, so to speak, of exporting its unemployed or surplus labour free to the New World — America, Australia and other parts of the world. There is no new world to be conquered today for the countries that are getting industrialised now. The problem persists, but in a different historic setting.

Rebuilding rural society

So we have to adopt not simply a system of doles and social security. We have to do something more, and that is rebuilding rural society from the base. I suppose it is not recognised sufficiently that in our historic setting, in the position where we are now, although industrialisation is important and it will and should continue, in a country like ours, growing industries cannot provide sufficient employment for all our 'surplus' population. And if it cannot provide sufficient employment for all our surplus population, it is going to produce the kind of sickness that I just explained. You cannot get rid of that sickness without adopting a different programme of development from the rural base.

This is what some of our tallest thinkers realised long ago. Tagore spoke of rural reconstruction. He was not just a poet — he experimented in rural reconstruction. And Gandhiji spoke of *Gram Swaraj*. They realised that in a country like India, unless you had a different vision of rural reconstruction and *Gram Swaraj*, you would not be able to solve the problem of a sick society and you would not be able to create an atmosphere in which a generous, Liberal philosophy of life can prosper.

Facing new challenges

I have tried to explain the kind of challenge, the kind of danger that has arisen as a result — the kind of danger which now is most acutely demonstrated by terrorism and the growth of militant fundamentalism. This is what our leaders today must turn their thoughts to. This problem was not present to this extent in the 19th century when Liberalism arose in the West. Our situation in the beginning of the 21st century is not the same as the situation in the West in the 19th century. Our Liberalism therefore has to function and remodel itself in this new situation. We have to preserve the best that the cities have to offer. As I have pointed out, the new market economy in the cities did create certain values of great importance — a recognition of the importance of social equality, social democracy, a recognition of the value of the individual, the uniqueness of the individual, not frozen into tradition. These things have to be preserved. But at the same time, we have also to adopt a programme that pays attention to reconstructing society from the base. This, as I said, is what our best thinkers of the 20th century had recognised and tried to bring to our notice.

The influence of Tagore and Gandhi

Liberalism today cannot ignore the teachings of people like Tagore and Gandhi. Liberalism today must strive to accept the fruits of their meditation, integrated within a Liberal philosophy fit for the 21st century. As in the past, Liberal philosophy must continue to be faithful to its basic principles today — to the principle or the idea of human rights and indefinite potentialities — the richness, the grandeur, the value of the uniqueness of the individual and the importance of the basic idea of freedom. But all these ideas have also to be combined with the recognition of the importance of reconstructing society from the base; reconstructing the community so that the individual can find fulfilment in the warmth of community life and not be left out in the cold of loneliness from which he can seek relief only in collective excitement which is fatal to Liberalism. The Liberals today have an agenda quite different from what 19th century Liberals had. The Liberals today have to realise the importance of this agenda and be faithful to it. If that happens, Liberalism would indeed be the most important faith that the 21st century can offer mankind.

The practice of liberalism

Liberal philosophy is rooted in a certain conception of social progress and human development. So first we have to try and understand this approach to social development. I will try to present the matter as simply as I possibly can.

Aristotle pointed out long ago that men had to cooperate, man had to become a social animal, because no one person was really self-sufficient. So, people have to cooperate even for self-development. The first step is taken from natural instincts. A man and woman come together, have children, start a family. With the creation of family, which is the first unit of social togetherness, the first step is taken towards mutual cooperation by natural instinct. Then a number of families come together and they form a tribe.

The tribal equation

After that, a problem arises which cannot be resolved by passions alone, but needs the guidance of reason and enlarged sympathies. What is that problem? When you have formed a tribe, others similarly have formed other tribes. So what should be the relationship between one tribe and another? At a more fundamental level, there is the question of what the relationship should be between one individual and another. To begin with, let us take up the question: what should be the relationship between one tribe and another?

Now, there are two alternatives. One tribe can try to prosper at the expense of the other. One tribe can try to plunder the wealth of the other. What happens in that case? Under the best of circumstances, what happens is that one tribe gains and the other loses. That is really the best situation when the tribal relationship is one of hostility. The other possibility is that both tribes lose. In the fight between themselves, it is possible that both the tribes get weakened or destroyed. So either both tribes lose or one tribe gains and the other tribe loses.

Through that experience, it is possible to arrive at a very important, you may say 'wise', conclusion, that if both tribes cooperate, then there is a better possibility. If both tribes cooperate, it is possible that both tribes gain. Through cooperation they are able to produce more wealth which they can share. So these are the possibilities.

Tribalism and nationalism

Obviously, the wisest course is for different tribes to cooperate. But what makes it difficult to adopt that wise course? What makes it difficult is tribalism itself, the blind passions attached to it. Tribalism presupposes that your ultimate allegiance is to your own tribe. As a matter of fact, militant nationalism is itself a form of tribalism. Your ultimate allegiance is to your nation. Just as tribalism leads to different tribes fighting among themselves, militant nationalism as a form of tribalism would mean that different nations will fight among themselves. And fighting among themselves, they will perhaps all lose. It has been said that in a war there is no real victory, that both sides ultimately lose. That is the most probable outcome. Even the best outcome under those circumstances would not really be good enough, considering that one side will gain and the other will lose. But that, as I explained, is only a probable outcome, it is not even the most probable.

Why is it not the most probable? Because whichever side loses will nurse within itself a certain vindictiveness, and at the next step, again, there will be a war because of that stored up vindictiveness. Finally, they have either to arrive at a decision that they must all unite, cooperate, or they will go on losing. For instance, Germany lost in the First World War. Germany nursed a certain vindictiveness, so there was the Second World War, and what was the outcome? The outcome was a frightful devastation of the continent of Europe. Somehow they became wiser through this experience and now they are moving towards European Union. France and Germany fought each other for so many years. That kind of warfare taught them that in the end, no side really gains, that the best option is to cooperate.

Cooperation, not conflict, is the key

So there is a certain approach to social development. You form a certain group and at every step there is not only a risk but a strong possibility that you will get so attached to that group that it will be difficult for you to go beyond the narrow attachment. So, whatever group you form, the best alternative is always to keep open the possibility of cooperating with other groups. Your loyalty to your own group should be such that it does not exclude the possibility of constructive cooperation with other groups.

If your outlook is such that your absolute allegiance is to your own group, cooperation becomes difficult. Then you develop a kind of militant philosophy which knows nothing better than trying to dominate the other side. Let us go deeper. Instead of talking of tribes, let us talk of the 'self' and 'the other'. What should be the relationship between the self and the other? You can easily see that from the standpoint of the self, there are two ways of looking at the other. Either the other is a rival, in which case your gain is a loss to the other and the other's gain is a loss to yourself. This is one outlook. Else, the other is really a creative opportunity for you to expand yourself. This is what happens in creative self-expression. In any creative self-expression, the self is joined to the other. There is an enlargement of the self, there is an enlargement of sympathy and the other is included in your perception of this enlarged self.

Conflict resolution: The liberal approach

The liberal approach would adopt this outlook of the relationship between the self and the other. The illiberal approach would always consider the other as hostile, the other as somebody who is potentially an enemy. The other can always be considered as potentially a friend or an enemy. This difference of outlook does matter because if you start with the idea that the other person is potentially an enemy, he will become an enemy. And if you start with the idea that the other person is potentially a friend, it is very likely that he will be a friend. This is not simply a question of philosophy, it is a very practical question in matters concerning human relations. So the liberal approach is to give, so to speak, the benefit of doubt to the other person that he can be a friend. The illiberal approach is that you do not give him the benefit of doubt, you take it that he is an enemy. That is, in the simplest terms, the basic difference between the liberal and generous approach and the illiberal or narrow-minded approach.

Now let us consider the matter like this. You are part of a particular community and there are other communities you do not belong to. You adopt an approach that enables you to cooperate with them, that is, you adopt a liberal approach. If you have a liberal frame of mind in relation to other communities, you have also to adopt the same in re-'lation to members of your own community. You cannot be liberal in your approach towards other communities while being illiberal in your approach to members of your own community. But, all individuals do not think alike within your own community. There are individual differences, preferences, tastes and views. Thus, there is the same question within your own community — the question of the choice of alternative approaches. What then does the liberal approach amount to, when it is applied to members of your own community? It would amount to a certain tolerance of plurality, within your own community, accepting that different people will have different views and tastes, and just as you would like to be allowed to follow your own taste and view, so too you need to permit others to follow their tastes and views.

The understanding of truth

Behind this, there is a certain conception of truth. What is that conception? It is that we never quite know the ultimate truth. We all try to understand truth from our own points of view, so we each have, so to speak, a partial view of the truth. Since nobody has a complete and ultimate understanding of truth, our partial understandings are bound to differ. This is how we approach truth. We start with our personal, partial perceptions and move forward through a process of dialogue, where we exchange our partial perceptions, our partial understanding, of truth. If I am to put it in the language of a well-known philosopher, one can never know what is the ultimate truth, but it is possible to know what is false. It is possible to know what is false, it is difficult to know all that truth is. What is false can be disproved but in a sense ultimate truth can never be proved. So what we do is try to find out what is false and we move forward like that, getting rid of what is false, peeling it away, moving hopefully nearer to truth. And we all do it from our own standpoint, moving in that direction.

Now, this can only be achieved through a process of cooperation. Remember that scientists all over the world, in so far as they are trying to discover the truth, are really cooperating. A physicist, whether he is Japanese or French, American or British, is all the time cooperating by communicating his views through journals and conferences. It is not that there is a British physics, a Japanese physics or a French physics. But they, all over the world, are cooperating in the search in their own ways. This is the essence of a liberal and cooperative approach to truth; we recognise that we have only a partial understanding; we cooperate through friendly dialogue; we criticise one another but it is friendly in the sense that even then we are, in a way, bound by a common goal. The common goal is to try to move towards the truth as best as we can, as best as fallible human beings can move towards a complete understanding of truth.

So one basic faith of the liberal is that we move towards truth through a dialogue in which people with different ideas exchange their own perceptions. This is the liberal process of moving towards the truth together. It is not a process where an authority announces the truth and the rest accept it because of that authority.

The liberal faith: Evolving through experience

You can also put it in a different way, when it comes to the practice of living. What I was saying in the name of scientists is one thing, but the practice of living is a different thing. The practice of living in freedom means that you are free to live according to your own conscience. Freedom of conscience is a basic faith of the liberal. Remember that conscience always belongs to the individual. Taking dictation from some other person is not an act of the conscience. Conscience belongs to the individual and it is a part of the liberal faith to permit every person to act according to his conscience in so far as this is consistent with similar freedom of other persons.

Now you may say that when it comes to the question of living and you are free to act according to your conscience, what happens when there is a conflict? That may be a serious problem. What does the liberal do there? Again when there is a conflict in the practical sphere of life, then the liberal conception is that you do not decide it by fighting; you decide it by taking recourse to a 'just process', let us say, the judiciary. If there is a conflict, then you can solve it either through dialogue, as I said before, or, as a last resort, by taking it to a court of law. But that means that there is a rule of law because a court of law must operate within the framework of the rule of law. So there is the idea of the rule of law which is a fundamental article of faith with the liberal. There is the rule of law, there is the judiciary and there is a possibility of individuals taking their disputes, as a last resort, to the court. This should really be as a last resort because it is always better to solve these problems through mutual dialogue.

These are some very simple things about the liberal faith. The liberal believes in certain rights of the individual and among these rights we count the right to freedom of conscience, the right to freedom of self-expression, also the possibility of resolving disputes under the rule of law by taking recourse to the judiciary. These are very simple but fundamental things about the liberal faith and if you come to think of it, you find that the world, the human society did not arrive at these ideas simply by philosophising. They arrived at these ideas through very important historical experience. What kind of experience?

Let me give you an example from European history. In the 17th century, the Protestants and the Catholics started fighting fiercely and there was in Germany the so-called

Thirty Years' War. The Thirty Years' War devastated Germany. The war spread to other countries too — France and Sweden. Through this devastation, through the experience of the religious war and also its aftermath, Europe learnt the lesson that the best way for a people to advance is not through the kind of intolerant war like that the Protestants and the Roman Catholics fought in the 17th century. The best way is through tolerance. So this was learnt not simply by philosophising, but through very important historical experience, the importance of tolerance as an essential factor for healthy social development. This was a lesson which became part and parcel of the liberal faith.

This is true not only for one particular society in Europe. In some form or other, it must be true for all mankind, for humans in every part of the world. It is obvious that this is something quite fundamental. It is quite fundamental that human beings will start by forming groups of their own, based on religion, language and other cultural differences, and it is elementary that among these different groups we have to evolve some way of tolerating diversity and cooperating for achieving some kind of common good.

Liberal democracy

Democracy has been considered to be a part of the basic faith of the liberal and there is no doubt that it is so. I have not mentioned the word 'democracy' so far. I have talked of the liberal philosophy and only now am I mentioning the word 'democracy'. Why is it so? Because in the 20th century, again through our experience, we found that democracy has become a very slippery word. It becomes unreliable for one very simple reason. As soon as you say that democracy means rule of the majority, the word 'democracy' becomes a very slippery word. If you say that democracy means rule of the majority, then what happens? In order to find out whether a country or a people are practising democracy, then you have only to find out whether it is the will of the majority which is being enforced. But that is a very poor test of democracy.

It is possible that in Hitler's time, a majority of Germans did support Hitler. But that does not mean that the Hitlerite regime was democratic. It is possible that during Stalin's time, Stalin had the support of the majority. But that does not mean that Stalin's regime was democratic. Why is it that Hitler's or Stalin's regimes should not be called democratic even if Hitler or Stalin enjoyed the support of the majority? Whether the Hitlerite regime or the Stalinist regime was democratic cannot be settled by counting the heads of Hitler's supporters during his lifetime or counting the heads of Stalin's supporters in his lifetime. Why so? It is so because what is basic to democracy is respect for fundamental human rights.

That is why I started by talking about fundamental human rights. When I started talking about liberalism, instead of discussing democracy, I started by discussing freedom of con-science, the right to freedom of self-expression, rule of law, judiciary and so on. All these things are connected with the concept of human rights.

Democracy does acknowledge the importance of the views of the majority, but the views of the majority can be considered democratic only in so far as this majority is respectful of fundamental human rights. A majority which is not respectful of fundamental human rights is acting against the basic spirit of democracy. You can have a kind of majoritarian dictatorship, which is not consistent with the liberal approach, the liberal philosophy of society. So what is basic is fundamental human rights, respect for fundamental human rights and, subject to that, the democratic procedure of taking decisions.

A philosophy most appropriate for India

All these things, I believe, are important when we come to consider our problems in India and the whole of the Indian subcontinent. India has so many groups that India is a whole world in miniature. Just as there are so many languages, religions, and cultures in the world, so also in India there are many languages, religions and cultures. As a matter of fact, all the major religions of the world are represented in India. Therefore, the great experiment in India is for this 'little world' to learn to live together in peace. If India can do that, then India will be showing how the world can live at peace with itself. We cannot live in peace unless we evolve some way in which these different cultures and the different groups and communities learn to cooperate and coexist. And we will not learn this if we go by the simple rule of majority supremacy. If we go by the route of majority rule, then the majority community would try to impose its own will on other communities and that would not really be consistent with the liberal approach. This is what I have been trying to explain by saying that the liberal philosophy stands for a certain approach concerning development — social as well as human. In the liberal conception, the basic thing about social and human development is the process of learning how diverse cultures can freely cooperate.

When we face democratic elections, this is what we have to keep in mind. An election is a way of finding out the opinion of the majority. This is necessary, but not enough. It is necessary to find out the opinion of the majority, but all this has to happen in a certain, shall I call it, 'cultural climate' which is informed with the liberal faith of tolerance. An election has to be conducted in that climate of tolerance or it is not really democratic. I said that Europe learnt this lesson through its own historical experience and I made a reference to the Thirty Years' War. I hope, we can only hope that India will move towards a deeper and deeper acknowledgement of the same lesson of world history and its own history.

In India, there are conflicts of different kinds—conflicts between high and low castes, as well as between different religious communities. I guess it does not really take great wisdom to realise that unless we find out a method of friendly resolution of these conflicts, our society will be in peril. There is no other way out. The only way for our society to prosper is to find out the way to peaceful cooperation among different religions, castes, language groups and so on, because in that way we can reap the benefits of cooperation. If we do not move in that way, then we will move towards civil war and that will be a situation in which all parties lose. I had said that when there is a war, under the best of circumstances, one party gains and the other party loses, but the most probable outcome is that all the parties lose. I put it to you that if we move towards civil war in India, all the parties will lose and everything with be lost.

For example, if Hindus and Muslims cannot resolve their problems amicably in a friendly way, it is not that Hindus will gain and the Muslims will lose, but both Hindus and Muslims will lose. In a situation like that, what will first happen is a coronation of fanaticism, and ultimately this will be a loss for India as a whole. I am not using this phrase simply as a piece of rhetoric. I mean it. Consider the question materially. Consider the consequences of a war, real war, between India and Pakistan, where both have nuclear arms. If war cannot be avoided, the entire subcontinent will be devastated.

We have to learn to live together. How can we live together? I gave you the example of Europe, where France and Germany found it very difficult to live together for long, long years. Now they are moving towards a union—the European Union. I guess that the Indian subcontinent will also have to move towards some kind of a union, a loose federation or a confederation embracing the Indian subcontinent as a whole. We cannot arrive at such a union in one big leap. We have to move gradually, and we have to keep in view that distant goal as the only goal worth moving towards as an alternative to common ruin for the subcontinent as a whole. On the communal question in particular, we have to judge every proposal by relating it to the basic requirement—liberal and humanist requirement—asking if it will help the peoples of the Indian subcontinent move towards larger cooperation in a spirit of tolerance and goodwill. This is the only alternative to total disaster.

35

A Finer Humanism

What are the fundamental characteristics of humanism? I believe that there are a number of ideas that go together to constitute the humanist approach. I will only mention those ideas, which appear to me to be the most important and particularly relevant in the contemporary context.

One fundamental conviction of a humanist is that mankind has a common destiny. What does that mean? And why is that so important today? I believe in the idea that in the final analysis, men all over the world have a common and indivisible interest. This idea, although perhaps philosophically existing before, has been further strengthened by developments, which show that man has in his power the capacity to destroy the whole of human civilisation. It was not a power within his reach in earlier centuries. Human civilisation in the next century will either survive or be destroyed as a whole. The same point has also been strongly emphasised, clearly brought out by our understanding, deeper than ever before, of the possibility of an ecological disaster. These are some of the developments of our time, which strengthen our conviction that mankind has a common destiny and that mankind will either perish or live as a whole. I suggest that this concept of inclusiveness is, or ought to be, one of the fundamental convictions of a humanist.

It is important to stress this because *our time* has certainly known other ideologies which have stressed something quite different. Among the dominant ideologies of our century, nationalism is one; Marxism is another; and there are also a number of other ideologies like fascism. In militant nationalism, it is the conflict of national interests that receives attention. In Marxist theory, it is the conflict of class interest that receives primacy. Not that such conflicts do not exist. Such conflicts do exist, but we now know more than ever before that they have to be viewed within the framework of this larger idea of a common destiny for mankind, of an indivisible link between men and women all over the world. In a nuclear holocaust, it is not that one class will prosper and the other will suffer. It will be a total disaster. Similarly, if there is an ecological disaster no one will be exempt. The suffering will be universal. This totality is what we need to keep in mind.

The theories of conflict of the past were not all wrong, but they were wrong in stressing conflict exclusively. A humanist would put these theories of conflict within the framework of a larger and deeper perception of the unity of human interests. In society as we know today there are not only conflicts of interest, but also other things which re-quire serious attention. The humanist believes in the value of the individual. He is painfully aware that there are social structures and attitudes that are deeply divisive and do not believe in the value of the individual. Untouchability would of course be the most obvious example of the denial of the value of the human person. As a matter of fact, something of that kind is ingrained in all kinds of racism, and racism is not something that characterises exclusively one particular country. When we look at the Indian subcontinent, we see that it is a world in miniature—there is hardly any problem of the world that does not find a reflection on the Indian subcontinent. It so happens that even on this subcontinent where we have some of the poorest countries of the world, there is a competition going on among rival states for the production of destructive weapons. It is obvious that this cannot go on indefinitely in the future without disastrous results for the whole subcontinent. So what is true about the world as a whole is also true of our subcontinent.

We must face resolutely the question of the poison that racism spreads in society and the need for protecting the dignity of the individual in the face of these racist tendencies. Racism is by no means dead with Nazism. It is still alive. And the battle against it, the struggle for emancipating mankind must continue for decades ahead.

Gautam Buddha and Socrates lived some 2,500 years ago. And what we learn from them has an important message for our times. The Socratic spirit was a spirit of critical rational scrutiny. The Buddha also believed in reason, but he knew that reason has to be combined with compassion. If humanism is to have a liberating influence on human society, then it has to combine reason with the spirit of compassion. It is unnecessary to go into the question whether reason by itself can produce compassion or whether compassion can purify reason. What can be said is that wherever the spirit of compassion leads us, true reason also catches up with that. Up to a certain point, the argument for reason is very simple. For example, when you talk about justice, that punishment should be proportional to the crime committed, it is very easy to argue in rational terms. But when you come to a proposition about turning the other cheek when somebody slaps you on one cheek, that is not something to which reason by itself leads you. But once you are led there, reason accepts that position and discovers a deeper value in it. It is not without significance that Bertrand Russell always talked of love and knowledge together, necessary for the freedom of society and men. The critical spirit makes men free because it helps men to get rid of superstitions. The compassionate

275

spirit makes men free because it frees men from the prison of egotism. And freedom in the deeper sense is the great objective of humanism.

Let me sum up. If we believe in humanism, it means that we believe in human solidarity. Along with that we believe in the dignity of the individual, in the value of the individual and in combining reason with compassion. We have to take humanism in that large and generous spirit. If we do not do that, then humanism will fail to achieve the mission which truly belongs to it. It is not simply a question of theism and atheism. A theist can be a fanatic, torturing heretics, but he can also be a very kindly person. An atheist like Stalin can be a fanatic but there are also atheists I know who are very kindly. Mankind will not be saved by these 'isms' alone, but will be saved by the spirit which condemns fanaticism, which believes that our final allegiance is not to any limited group but to all mankind.

When we add compassion to reason, the Buddhistic spirit to the Socratic, and deem it a humanist requirement, it becomes simpler to distinguish true humanists from false.

That I suggest to you is the finer spirit of humanism.

Index

Index

Schumpeter, Joseph, 51
science policy, in India, 115–17
scientific discovery and industrial
  development, relationship
  between, 113–14
scientific knowledge and research,
  in India
  need of creative teamwork,
    111–12
  research facilities for students,
    111
  science policy, need of, 115–
    17
  scientific research climate,
    creation of, 110–11
  scientists, migration of, 110
  system for passing scientific
    knowledge from top to
    bottom, 114–15
scientific literature, 115
'scientific rigging', 87
Second World War, experience
  after, 62
Sen, Amartya, 55
sensual pleasures, 77
Sevagram, 96
sex and corruption, 174
sex education, 129–30
Short-term problems
  commonsense solution to, 48
  idealistic approach for, 48–49
Singur project, by Tatas
  and unemployment, 25–26
Small Is Beautiful, 63
small neighbourhood sector, in
  market economy, 45–46
Smith, Adam, 26, 104, 176, 189
socialism, 59, 242
  Gandhian philosophy and
    Luntley's ideas, 247–49
  Luntley model of socialism,
    245–47
'socialist fatherland', 4

social organisation, forms of,
  226–27
social security, 205–06
Socrates, 275
'soul-force', 250
sovereignty of the Truth, 228, 231
Soviet educational system, 107–08
Soviet 'great leap forward,' 23–24
Soviet Union, 71–72
  collapse of, 61
  lack of freedom, in society, 62
Sphere of Common Prosperity, 16
Spratt, 141
Sriniketan, 96, 103, 120, 122
Stalinism, in Russia
  building Russia as military
    power, 183
  Hitler defeat, 184
  industrialisation under, 182–
    83
  Marxists on, 181–82
  role in World War II, 183
  Russian economy afterwards,
    184
  Tukhachevsky case, 183–84
States Reorganisation Commission,
  210
Studies in Gandhism, 146
'Swadeshi Samaj', 122

Tagore, Rabindranath, 103, 132–33,
  177, 205, 239, 259
Tagore's philosophy of education,
  118, 123–24
  atmiyata, concept of, 121, 122
  festivals and traditional fair,
    role of, 121
  freedom of the mind, and na-
    ture's laws, 120
  man's relation with his neigh-
    bours, 120–22

285

Index

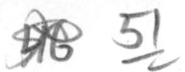

About the Author

Amlan Datta, an octogenarian scholar, is a well-known economist and educationist, and has held various positions such as Head of the Department of Economics and Pro-Vice Chancellor of University of Calcutta, Vice Chancellor of University of North Bengal, Director of Gandhian Institute of Studies and thereafter Vice Chancellor of Vishwa Bharati University, Shantiniketan. Possessing a sharp incisive mind that belies his age, he is a prolific writer on economic, social, political and philosophical issues both in English and Bengali. He received the Vidyasagar Award in 1999. His articles in newspapers discuss current issues and are widely popular. Some of his books are: *For Democracy; Perspective of Economic Development; An Introduction to India's Economic Development since the 19th Century; Socialism, Democracy and Industrialization; Beyond Socialism* and *In Defence of Freedom: Exciting Times and Quiet Meditations.*